REGICIDE AND
REPUBLICANISM

REGICIDE AND REPUBLICANISM

POLITICS AND ETHICS IN THE
ENGLISH REVOLUTION, 1646–1659

Sarah Barber

Edinburgh University Press

To AC, JWC, and NSS
musis constantiaeque

© Sarah Barber, 1998

Edinburgh University Press
22 George Square, Edinburgh

Typeset in Edinburgh by Hewer Text Ltd, Edinburgh,
and printed and bound in Great Britain by
the University Press, Cambridge

A CIP record for this book is available from the British Library

ISBN 1 85331 211 8

Contents

Preface

And what is faith, love, virtue unassayed
Alone, without exterior help sustained?
Milton, *Paradise Lost* (1667)

It is your own assent to yourself, and the constant voice of your own reason,
and not of others, that should make you believe.
Pascal, *Pensées* (1670)

Henry Marten, republican firebrand and man about town, believed that a dedicatory Epistle was as a porch to a house, a place where authors gather friends and supporters around themselves to protect them from the storms of potential critics. It pains me to say it, but I do not believe he is right. Others have likened writing a book to giving birth. I do not believe that either, but the imagery may be more appropriate. Producing the bulk of a book is the time when you gather to yourself the thoughts, contributions and criticisms of your friends. The preface marks the symbolic cutting of the umbilical cord and you and your precious thoughts are propelled into the world alone. In the hackneyed phrase of preface-writing, one is grateful to friends and colleagues for their help and contributions, but what goes to press is entirely the author's responsibility.

One of my lecturers at university (not, perhaps significantly, an historian) held that a human being does not have an original thought after the age of twenty-six, but continually refines, builds on and analyses thoughts sown much earlier. This volume certainly bears out that statement, since the simple idea at the heart of this book, which seemed so obvious at the time, came to me as part of my Ph.D. research, and that in itself was a continuation of several years of thought about the nature of republicanism and the British people's love affair with monarchy. When I began I was a lone voice. Only in the USA had Bill Everdell produced his *End of Kings*, and he too had to wait some time to see it in print. My thanks therefore go to Gavin Wigginton for saying, in 1983, 'they'll never give you a grant to study *that!*' and to the grant-awarding bodies which did not. Ten years later I am proud to say that I am a university lecturer, and my thanks for that are due to the late Alec Horsley and the Board of Northern Foods, whose sense of outrage, notions of equity and sheer bloody-mindedness matched my own and whose vision and choice injections of cash exceeded mine.

The universities which demonstrated a similar flexibility and constancy of support are to be commended for making the rules work in favour of people and not as a means to restrict them. The staff in the postgraduate office of Trinity College, Dublin, my supervisor, Professor Aidan Clarke, and my colleagues in the History Department of Lancaster University have fought tirelessly for the means whereby I could make my own mistakes.

Over the years that this book has formed, scholars have relaunched the checkered career of the Rump parliament, analysed the views of individual republicans and credited the interregnum period with being a time of serious political thought. Politicians and the general public have since had the courage to emerge from the closet and utter the political theory which dared not speak its name. In the late 1990s, republicanism is newly fashionable. As other scholars seemed to streak past, my thoughts coalesced, intermittently fired by individuals' comments, some of which remain anonymous. To those who have offered their opinion, I am grateful for their inspirational critiques. Those who have chosen to comment in person or whose friendship and support have cushioned the rocky moments include Stephen Pumfrey, Steven Constantine, Anneke Van Wersch, Lynn Abrams, David Norbrook, Steven Pincus, Jim Holstun and Bill Everdell. A note of admiration is addressed to Austin Woolrych, John Morrill and John Marshall for patient and constructive comment in the face of exasperating stubbornness. There are friends, both academic and otherwise, who have played a part in keeping me sane. They know who they are and they know how I feel, so I shall spare them the Oscar-night performance. To Nicola Carr and Richard Purslow, my thanks are due for providing the vehicle of print.

The biggest debt is to my parents who showed the greatest faith of all, and to the three muses, for having the faith to repeatedly pick me up and dust me off, and kindle enough of my own.

List of Abbreviations

Abbott, *Writings and Speeches*	William Cortez Abbott, *Writings and Speeches of Oliver Cromwell* (4 vols) (Harvard, 1939)
Aubrey, *Brief Lives*	Oliver Lawson Dick (ed.), *Aubrey's Brief Lives* (Harmondsworth, Penguin, 1987 edn)
BIHR	*Bulletin of the Institute of Historical Research*, now *Historical Research*
Burton, *Diary*	John Towill Rutt (ed.), *Diary of Thomas Burton, Esq.* (4 vols) (London, 1828)
CJ	*Journal of the House of Commons*
Clarke Papers	*The Clarke Papers: Selections from the Papers of William Clarke*, ed. C. H. Firth (4 vols) (Camden Society, London: vol. I, 1891; vol. II, 1894; vol. III, 1899; vol. IV, 1901), with vols I and II reissued by the Royal Historical Society (Woodbridge, Suffolk, 1992)
CSPD	*Calendar of State Papers, Domestic*
DNB	*The Dictionary of National Biography* (22 vols) (Oxford, 1921–2)
EHR	*English Historical Review*
Fortescue	G. K. Fortescue, *Catalogue of the Pamphlets, Books, Newspapers, and Manuscripts relating to the Civil War, the Commonwealth, and Restoration, collected by George Thomason, 1640–1661* (2 vols) (London, 1903)
Gardiner, *History*	S. R. Gardiner, *History of the Great Civil War* (4 vols) (Windrush Press reprint, London, 1987)
Gardiner, *Commonwealth and Protectorate*	S. R. Gardiner, *History of the Commonwealth and Protectorate* (4 vols) (Windrush Press reprint, London, 1989)

GCD	Samuel Rawson Gardiner, *The Constitutional Documents of The Puritan Revolution, 1625–1660* (Oxford, 1979 edn)
HJ	*Historical Journal*
HPT	*History of Political Thought*
HR	*Historical Research*, formerly *Bulletin of the Institute of Historical Research*
Hutchinson, *Memoirs*	Julius Hutchinson (ed.), *Lucy Hutchinson: Memoirs of Colonel Hutchinson* (London, 1908)
JBS	*Journal of British Studies*
JHI	*Journal of the History of Ideas*
LJ	*Journal of the House of Lords*
Ludlow, *Memoirs*	C. H. Firth (ed.), *The Memoirs of Edmund Ludlow* (2 vols) (Oxford, 1894)
Machiavelli, *Discourses*	Niccolò Machiavelli, *The Discourses of Niccolò Machiavelli*, ed. Bernard Crick (Harmondsworth, Penguin, 1970)
Maseres, *Select Tracts*	Francis Maseres (ed.), *Select Tracts Relating to the Civil Wars in England in the Reign of King Charles the First* (2 vols) (London, 1815)
P&P	*Past and Present*
Thurloe State Papers	John Thurloe, *A Collection of State Papers of John Thurloe Esq.* (7 vols) (London, 1742)
Underdown, *Pride's Purge*	David Underdown, *Pride's Purge: Politics in the Puritan Revolution* (London, 1971)
Whitelocke, *Memorials*	Bulstrode Whitelocke, *Memorials of the English Affairs* (2 vols)
Worden, *Rump Parliament*	Blair Worden, *The Rump Parliament* (Cambridge, 1974)

NOTE

Unless otherwise stated, all contemporary tracts were consulted from the Thomason Tracts collection of the British Library, London (BL). The class mark which is given for these tracts, usually prefixed by E or 669.f in the case of broadsheets, refers to the BL classification. Should the pamphlet carry a date, this is the date given. Should the date appear in square brackets, e.g. [24 Apr.] 1647, the printer registered that it was printed during 1647 but the bracketed date refers to that on which George Thomason noted that he received his copy.

Introduction
Regicide and Republicanism

This book describes regicide and republicanism as they are examples of political practice, taking as its particular context the regicide of Charles Stuart and the subsequent republican government known as the Commonwealth. The execution of Charles I and the establishment of the Commonwealth government by the Rump parliament were consequential in a chronological sense: Charles was executed on 30 January 1649, and between 1649 and 1653 England was a republic. In the specific context of England in 1649, republicanism was also a political consequence of regicide: one led to the other. I shall argue, however, that although regicide and republicanism were, to a certain extent, dependent on each other, their intellectual parentage was different. In order to demonstrate this, the practice of regicide and republican government is analysed within two more general interpretations of political philosophy which underpinned them: an ethical critique of magistracy, and the distinction between the magistrate as a person and magistracy as an office.

Authority relies on a general acceptance of political agency, both in terms of the medium through which the polity disseminates authority – statute and law – and the agents who are entrusted with making political decisions. Placing one's trust in the magistracy – at every level, from village constable to king – is a political action, the performance of which contains two distinguishable elements: a decision to abide by the laws and obedience (and obeisance?) to the individuals who implement them. The ability or desire to distinguish between the two gives rise to a fundamental difference of political view. Was authority conveyed by the laws or was it owed to the people who constituted the authorities?[1] Law might be absolute, abstract and binding on all, or a construct, implemented by the good and trustworthy. Was government necessary because all people were equal, either equally wise or equally foolish, or was government required because some were more wise than others? Were all people liable to be corrupted by the temptations of office, and

1

did the nature of some offices offer more temptations than others?[2] A theory of contract lies beneath these questions.[3] Contract, in turn, is underpinned by an ethical evaluation of people in general and magistrates in particular, informed by voluntarism. Did the centrality of contract lay in willing oneself under a government because the governors were good, or because the act of voluntary consent defined good government?[4] Politicians and commentators could be rearranged into those who believed good laws made good men and those who held that good men made good laws. This makes for a different analysis of political positioning in the mid-seventeenth century, which relies as much on moral philosophy as political theory. Perhaps we should look to Aristotle's *Ethics* as much as to his *Politics*.[5]

Regicide is the most dramatic example of a kingly magistrate having lost the trust of those he governs. For the loss of trust, Charles Stuart lost his life. A regicide is one who participates in the act of killing a king, and 'the regicides' is a term which has come to mean the specific witnesses of Charles I's death warrant.[6] It was also, however, an action which marked the climax to a process of thought. If one believed that the ills which had befallen the English people, culminating in civil war, were the primary or sole responsibility of Charles Stuart, the act of regicide was an end. Charles was the person with the 'wicked design' to rule tyrannically, who 'traitorously and maliciously' made war on the people he had sworn to protect, 'caused and procured' his people to die and 'maintained . . . carried on . . . [and] renewed' the war for personal ends.[7] The regicide was therefore the closing act in the process of regicidal thinking. One can trace the events by which individuals so spectacularly lost their trust in their king that they were prepared to countenance his judicial execution and the writings through which they expressed their increasing mistrust. Fifty-nine people signed Charles' death warrant. The regicides were few in number. Beyond the signatories lay a corpus of writing by individuals who sought to lobby for, explain or justify the regicide, because they thought it a proper end to nearly a decade of civil unrest. They argued for regicide: they thought regicidally.

The regicide was the end of a person, but the beginning of a political experiment. As soon as a receptive parliament had been secured, by purging it of those members who were willing to continue to negotiate peace with Charles, the king's trial ran parallel to a series of measures to secure a constitutional settlement which excluded his family. The resultant Commonwealth of the Parliament of England was a republic, and historians can study its founding legislation in order to demonstrate the nature of its republicanism. However, there was no necessary connection between regicide and republicanism. If one believed that the guilt for the war lay with the person of Charles Stuart, the end of the war and the end of its perpetrator might have enabled a return to the old system. Instead, an unknown and alien form of politics was introduced to the English people. Separation of the king's person from his office provides the reason that it proves possible to sever the connection between the regicide and the subsequent governmental structure.

This account studies two sets of practice and two strands of thought which emerged during the late 1640s, as notions of person and office were tested by a series of political crises. Regicide and republicanism are used as terms which define both specific political practices and bodies of rhetoric from which were drawn political theories. The repository of potentially regicidal or republican statements is made deliberately wide-ranging. Richard Ashcraft has recently reminded historians of the variety of sources from which political ideas and inferences could be drawn: 'political parties or movements express themselves not only through the highly formalized medium of books, but also through newspapers, pamphlets, sermons, broadsides, and various literary forms (plays, novels, poetry). Political theory as a social language flows through all these media.'[8] The purpose of this book is to marshal the evidence for regicide and for republicanism within the widest context for political belief.

The individuals which emerge here are politicians, polemicists, writers, poets, soldiers, clerics, even the occasional lowly citizen. They are often branded with the generic term 'radicalism' – they are accused of saying or doing something radical. 'Radicalism' has proved a treacherous word for historians of the seventeenth century but Colin Davis has outlined a schema which is one of the best attempts at definition so far.[9] Davis argues that radical political action possesses three parts: the delegitimisation of the incumbent authority; the construction of a model or models for its replacement; and devising a 'transfer mechanism' by which the former polity could be overthrown and the new polity established. Within this framework, this is a study of radical change. Chapters 1 to 3 outline the ways in which a small group of individuals delegitimated monarchy. Chapters 6 to 8 describe the political models which they put in its place. And Chapters 4 and 5, the regicide, provide the political means by which they went from one to the other by delegitimating Charles Stuart.

During 1643, most English MPs had sworn to uphold the reformed religion and the person of the king, in return for military and financial assistance from a Scottish army by taking the Solemn League and

Covenant. As soon as it was mooted, Edmund Ludlow and Henry Marten publicly, and presumably others privately, objected to the oath, because they could foresee a situation in which the prerogatives of the king would not be consistent with the privileges of parliament.[10] It was not until the war had been won, in 1645/6, that internal inconsistencies in the Covenant were thrown into stark relief by the debates over the peace proposals known as the *Propositions of Newcastle*.[11] Individuals felt compromised by having taken an oath to protect the person of the king, whom they no longer (if they had ever) felt could be trusted to safeguard the liberties of the people. The focus of this study on the person/office distinction dictates that the end of the first civil war should be its starting point. Chapter 1, therefore, examines the debate about peace in 1646, during which we can start to build up a personnel for whom the balance between Charles' trustworthiness and the liberties of the people was the most important issue. They ranged from known extremists in the Commons – Marten, Thomas Chaloner, Thomas Scot, Alexander Rigby – to more minor figures in the localities, such as John Musgrave and Thomas Westropp. They constituted a small but vocal and organised group which mobilised the person/office distinction to direct a particular response against the dominant parliamentary line. They were an irritant, constantly vexing those of more mainstream opinions.

They also tended to have close links with the Levellers. Chapter 2 therefore analyses contemporaneous Leveller statements for their republican (or, indeed, regicidal) import. This is achieved through a textual analysis of Leveller writings during 1646 and 1647 which married with the practical political action being pursued by Chaloner, Marten, Rigby and others in the Commons. It also carries Leveller thinking on to the Putney debates and discusses the implications of the Levellers' complete omission of monarchy from consideration in the *Agreement of the People*.[12] If we take contemporary comments seriously, that there was a separate and separable faction, more well-disposed to Independency than Presbyterianism but nevertheless wary of the Independents' willingness to make peace terms with the king, we have a small, identifiable third faction.[13] It was not synonymous with the Levellers or with their agitator allies in the New Model Army, but there were significant areas of overlap. This is also true of the parliamentarians identified in Chapter 1.

Chapter 3 examines this group from the point of view of a shared cultural background. In doing so, we encounter several notions which, individually or collectively, might have applied to the anti-Presbyterian 'Independent' grouping as a whole. This faction might even be said to have emerged out of Independency.[14] However, more general cultural attitudes which had recognisable Independent roots were turned to the political crises of the years 1646–8 in a way which produced both a practical political response and a way of thinking which would ultimately inform the type of republican polity which they constructed in 1649/50. They shared a gentry background and an ideological dynamic behind seemingly materialistic demands to recover the losses which they had incurred during the war. They were direct heirs of a county–community attitude which determined that their response to the English constitutional crisis was insular and parochial. They were nationalists and notably anti-Scottish. In 1648, they argued that their approach gave them warrant to raise private regiments. These allowed them to continue to pressure for ultimate martial victory over the king and his forces, even while their putative allies were still prepared to offer peace terms.

The crux came in December 1648. In response to another attempt to continue negotiations with Charles, a group within the army and the Commons, led by some members of the third faction such as Marten, Ludlow and Grey of Groby, purged parliament and set up a High Court of Justice to try Charles as the 'man of blood'. Chapter 4 examines the background of the language which called for regicide. Although the practical step of purge and trial was implemented for civil, political reasons, the rhetoric of justification was drawn from a different source. The justification for regicide came primarily from the Law of the Old Testament. The result was a personalised attack on Charles; his blood-guilt gave rise to his new status as sacrifice and the purification which would result from the vengeance to be taken against him. The prosecution at Charles' trial claimed that England had been at war because Charles' actions revealed him to be an ungodly, even an evil man.[15] Remove Charles, and England could return to godly magistracy.

The texts of the trial of Charles I, with which Chapter 5 is concerned, reveal the fact that the (regicidal) attack on Charles Stuart and the (republican) attack on monarchy grew from different intellectual roots. Within the language of the prosecution, even within statements made by the same individual, were two different indictments which it proved difficult to reconcile. One charged Charles with bad stewardship of an otherwise legitimate office. Regicide would end this imbalance because it was caused by Charles himself. This differed significantly from a potentially republican response: Stuart rule demonstrated that any individual, invested with powers of potential absolutism, would be tempted to abuse his (or her) office. Therefore, only a thorough-going reform of the executive office would produce stable government. It proved possible, in practical political terms, for certain individuals within the potential republicans identified in Chapters 1 to 3, to reconcile regicide and republicanism. For others, the regicide split them from their allies. Many fellow travellers, who had agreed with the moral critique of monarchy, could not countenance a particular man's execution, particularly at the hands of what they saw as an unrepresentative junta.

The last part of this book examines that tension in practice, starting with the regicide and concluding with the death of Oliver Cromwell in 1658. It begins by demonstrating that the tensions lay at the very centre of the government. Among the small group of people whose engagement with the arguments previously outlined had led them to power in 1649, there were a variety of opinions. What to some was a positive example of a Commonwealth was to others a negative image of the Rump of legitimate authority. In the earliest months of the Commonwealth there were a number of ways in which these tensions were expressed. There were difficulties in defining the form of the government, the forms of election, the distribution of power, and the symbols by which the government represented itself to its citizens.[16] Chapter 6 analyses the legislation by which England was converted into a republic and the statements of those who commented on this process to reveal the rather shaky ideological basis on which the Commonwealth rested.

Chapter 7 carries these tensions away from the centre of government and out into the localities. The Commonwealth government needed to encourage allegiance to the new political form. It offered a far from novel means – swearing an oath of loyalty, known as the Engagement – to achieve an unprecedented end – unity under a republican polity.[17] As such, while offering a way to achieve unity, it revealed dissent. English people could use the Engagement as a means to accommodate themselves to republican government or as a target to aim their arguments against it. Some were prepared to accept both regicide and republicanism, some one, but not the other. The practicalities of government during the 1650s exacerbated the divisions between those at the heart of the republican government and highlighted the fact that there was not one republican theory but several. Individuals came to recognise the virtues of a republican polity for different reasons, at different rates and with subsequently different consequences for their definition of republicanism.

The collapse of republican government and the rise of Oliver Cromwell revived the debate about the ethical status of the magistracy, the nature of executive office and the person of the incumbent. In the speech with which he dismissed the Rump parliament, Cromwell made much of the personal vices of its members and their consequent unacceptability for rule. The Rumpers were dismissed as corrupt time-servers and licentious individuals, who would be replaced by men 'fearing God and of good conversation'.[18] Government by the saints proved equally inadequate and when Cromwell assumed the Protectorate, his rule was justified because he was a pious, godly, virtuous individual who had thereby earned the privilege of being an exemplar. To those excluded from power in 1653, Cromwell represented the betrayal of the republican experiment. The Protectorate therefore offered them a fresh opportunity to rehearse arguments for republicanism, which they attempted to bring together in lobbying for the return of republican rule. The Good Old Cause, however, highlighted that there was still no consensus about what constituted a republican state.

The later 1640s and 1650s revealed a number of interesting political alignments based on the ethical suitability of the magistrate. Cromwell judged king Charles I and arch republican, Henry Marten, equally unsuitable as law makers.[19] Royalists, for whom Charles was a man whose virtue was saluted by the Lord[20], achieved a propaganda victory with *Eikon Basilike*, by presenting Charles as a man of patience, honour and stoicism. They, as much as the regicides who attacked Charles for promoting 'wicked designs, wars, and evil practices', were celebrating the importance of the person of the magistrate.[21] The Rumpers who replaced him were detracted as libertines and self-seekers.[22] Henry Robinson, Henry Ireton and James Harrington all called – in different ways – for the aristocratic (in the Aristotelian sense) rule of the few, because the world contained elite individuals, worthy as a consequence of character, interest or 'nobility' to govern those who were lacking.[23] The rule of the saints, a modern-day sanhedrin or magistracy exercised by those who feared God, implied similar judgements. John Hall, on the other hand, believed a government should be based on accommodating the individual talents of all of its varied citizens, while pessimists who believed the consequence of universal sin was individual weakness, were loathe to pick out one or a few as better than the rest.[24] The Leveller *Agreements of the People* and the Commonwealth's Engagement of loyalty, represented attempts to erect a 'fundamental law of freedom', allegiance to which could not be withdrawn, above the flawed individuals who carried the burden of administering it.[25]

These arguments, applied to Charles' ministers, to the king himself, to the Commonwealth and then to Cromwell's Protectorate, provide a continuity of thought which bridges the 1640s and the 1650s[26], but does not downplay the sense in which the regicide was the revolutionary action of the period. The arguments used to promote and justify it emphasised the degree to which Charles I had failed at a personal level. He had been a bad magistrate, an evil man. Removing the single individual who had caused the war – the 'man of blood' – could be the enabling factor in establishing a future godly magistracy. For others, in the main supporters of the republican experiment of 1649, the regicide was not the answer (or a sufficient answer) because they were not asking the same question. When several denied any personal malice towards Charles at their own trials in 1660, they were not trying to save their skins.[27] They were not denying their 'guilt'. They had been trying to implement a form of government which did not rely on the virtue of an individual, but on the virtue of all.

NOTES TO THE INTRODUCTION

1. This analysis presupposes that those studied accepted that mankind was a social animal whose existence needed to be regulated by laws and for whom government was a necessary evil.

2. James Harrington, *The Commonwealth of Oceana and A System of Politics*, ed. J. G. A. Pocock (Cambridge, 1992) p. 41; Charles Blitzer, *An Immortal Commonwealth: The Political Thought of James Harrington* (Yale, 1960) p. 161, an idea also propounded by Grotius and Machiavelli.

3. Harro Höpfl and Martyn Thompson outline the many possible sources of contract theory – Old Testament, Medieval biblical exegesis, feudal relations, the Church Fathers, the Conciliar movement, Luther and Calvin, civil law, the ancient city states and the Roman Republic, the German Empire, Aragon, Switzerland, Poland, Holland, the breakdown of the extended family, capitalism, individualism, rationalism and the scientific revolution. Harro Höpfl and Martyn P. Thompson, 'The history of contract as a motif in political thought', *Am Hist Rev*, 84.4 (1979) 919–44, p. 920.

4. Patrick Riley, *Will and Political Legitimacy: A Critical Exposition of Social Contract Theory in Hobbes, Locke, Rousseau, Kant, and Hegel* (London, 1982).

5. Hinted at in Pocock, *Machiavellian Moment*, pp. 384–5; Aristotle, *Nicomachean Ethics* (Penguin, London); Cary J. Nederman, 'Bracton on kingship revisited', *HPT* V.1 (1984) 61–77; Eugene Garver, 'After Virtù: rhetoric, prudence and moral pluralism in Machiavelli', *HPT* XVII.2 (1996) 195–223.

6. A. W. McIntosh, 'The number of the English Regicides', *History* 67 (1982) 195–216.

7. The sentence against Charles I: *GCD*, pp. 377–80.

8. Richard Ashcraft, *Revolutionary Politics and Locke's Two Treatises of Government* (Princeton, 1986), pp. 6–7; Richard Ashcraft, 'Political theory and the problem of ideology', *Journal of Politics* 42 (1980) 687–705; Alan Craig Houston, "A way of settlement': the Levellers, monopolies and the public interest', *HPT*, XIV.3 (1993) 381–420.

9. J. C. Davis, 'Radicalism in a traditional society: the evaluation of radical thought in the English Commonwealth, 1649–1660', *HPT*, III.2 (1982) 193–213, p. 202.

10. A. B. Worden (ed.), *A Voyce from the Watch Tower* (Camden Society, 4th ser. 21, 1978), p. 141 (774), written, of course, in retrospect.

11. The Propositions sent to the king at Newcastle: *GCD*, pp. 290–306.

12. *An agreement of the People for a firm and present peace*, 28 Oct. 1647, E412(21).

13. Ludlow, *Memoirs*, I, pp. 151, 168; Clement Walker, *The Compleat History of Independency upon the Parliament begun 1640* (London 1661); Lucy Hutchinson, *Memoirs of Colonel Hutchinson* (London, 1965), p. 251; Thomas May, *A Breviary of the History of the Parliament of England*, in Francis Maseres (ed.), *Select Tracts Relating to the Civil Wars in England* (2 vols) (London 1815), I, p. 108.

14. Take, for example, the route travelled by John Cook, who, at the end of 1648 was chosen prosecuting counsel at the trial of Charles Stuart, but whose 1647 tract, *What the Independents would Have* [1 Sep.], 1647, E405(7), is an unremarkable account of Independent demands.

15. John Morrill, 'Charles I, tyranny and the English Civil War', in his collected essays, *The Nature of the English Revolution* (London, 1993), pp. 285–306.

16. M. J. Seymour, 'Aspects of Pro-government Propaganda during the Interregnum', PhD, Cambridge (1986); Sean Kelsey, *Inventing a Republic: The Political Culture of the English Commonwealth, 1649–1653* (Manchester, 1997).

17. The Engagement to be taken by all over the age of eighteen: *GCD*, p. 391; Thomason Tracts E1060(77); see especially Chapter 7 below.

18. *Declaration by the Lord General and the Council on the Dissolution of the Long Parliament, GCD* pp. 400–4; *Summons to be a member of Barebone's Parliament, GCD*, p. 405.

19. *Mercurius Elenticus*, 21–28 Feb. 1649; Whitelocke, *Memorials*, IV, p. 5.

20. *Mercurius Elenticus*, pp. 2–3; *The Monument of Charles the First*, [5 Jun.] 1649, 669.f.14(36).

21. Charge against Charles in *GCD*, pp. 371–4, p. 373. *Eikon Basilike. The Pourtraicture of his Sacred Majestie in his Solitudes and Sufferings*, 9 Feb. 1649, Thomason Tracts C.59.a.24, was the most famous of the propaganda pieces issued by royalists shortly after Charles' death, though the presses were flooded. It professed to be an account of the war years, written by Charles himself, though it is generally thought to have been written by someone close to him, probably Gurdon.

22. *Declaration by the Lord General and the Council on the Dissolution of the Long Parliament,* cited from *GCD,* p. 401; Whitelocke, *Memorials,* IV, p. 5; Ludlow, *Memoirs,* I, pp. 352–3; see below, Chapter 8.

23. [Henry Robinson], *A Short Discourse between Monarchical and Aristocratical Government, Or a sober perswasive of all true hearted Englishmen, to a willing conjunction with the Parliament of England in setting up the Government of a Common-wealth,* 24 Oct. 1649, E575(31), p. 14; Ireton's speeches at Putney in C. H. Firth (ed.), *The Clarke Papers* (2 vols) (Royal Historical Society reprint, 1992), I pp. 226–410; James Harrington, *Oceana,* p. 75ff.; Gary Remer, 'James Harrington's new deliberative rhetoric: reflection of an anticlassical republican', *HPT,* XVI.4 (1995) 532–57.

24. John Hall, *The Grounds and Reasons of Monarchy,* 1651, pp. 14, 31, 39, 42–3.

25. John Lilburne, *The Engagement vindicated and explained or the reasons upon which Lieut. Col. John Lilburne tooke the Engagement,* 23 Jan. 1650, E590(4), p. 5; Blair Worden, *Rump Parliament, 1648–1653* (Cambridge, 1974), pp. 215, 227 and *passim;* Pocock, *Machiavellian Moment,* p. 380.

26. And it may be possible to argue, although there is not room for such a controversial claim to be explored here, that both arguments were attempts to stem the increasing tide of interest theory which would characterise republicanism later in the century. Interest theory calculated outcomes rather than motivation: Slingsby Bethel, *The World's Mistake in Oliver Cromwell* (London, 1668), pp. 20–1; Jonathan Scott, *Algernon Sidney and the English Republic, 1623–1677* (Cambridge, 1988), pp. 125–6; Steven C. A. Pincus, *Protestantism and Patriotism: Ideologies and the Making of English Foreign Policy, 1650–1668* (Cambridge, 1996), pp. 18–19.

27. Ludlow, *Memoirs,* II, pp. 303–25.

Unparliamentary Language and the Dignity of the Crown

The defeat of the royalist forces at the battle of Naseby in June 1645 was the last set-piece battle on English soil of the first civil war. Following the battle, the parliamentarians seized a casket of letters, written by the king to his wife, Henrietta Maria, in which he solicited the military help of foreign Catholic powers. It was too late. The following September, the Earl of Montrose, leading the king's Scottish troops, was defeated at Philiphaugh. As the war had seemed to drag on, the end when it came seemed swift and relatively bloodless. By April of 1646, the 'vanquished' king raced to join the Scottish forces camped at Newark, where he surrendered two months later. The Scots were supposed to hold the king at Southwell,[1] but instead took him north to their garrison in Newcastle, where news came of the collapse of the royalist stronghold of Oxford. The king was in the hands of the Scottish army, camped around Newcastle-upon-Tyne, when terms for a settlement were presented. They called upon Charles to sign the Solemn League and Covenant, suppress Catholicism and confirm ordinances made by the English Houses since the outbreak of war. The Houses would control the militia for the space of twenty years,[2] after which time, the situation would be reviewed.[3] A year later the Newcastle Propositions still formed the basis of the parliamentary overtures for peace.

Much has been made of the variety of views within the parliamentarian camp during the mid-1640s. The main division between those who were anxious to create terms for a treaty and those who wanted to push the conflict to a military solution – the peace and war parties – had given way to Presbyterians and Independents. The differences of opinion which grew out of the war were exacerbated rather than healed by the cessation of 1646. This chapter traces those from within the parliamentarian side who were most hostile to the prospect of making peace with the king and anxious to press for the maximum possible concessions from the defeated. We could call them the war party ultraists. They were nominally part of the Independent faction but hovered on its most extreme fringe. It is hardly surprising that the figures with whom they clashed most often and with considerable venom were the controversialists of Presbyterianism such as William Prynne, Clement Walker and Sir John Maynard. The ultraists emerged willing to discuss and dismiss monarchical prerogative, in terms most shocking to Presbyterians, whose concern for the royal person had been encapsulated in the Solemn League and Covenant. Some of our evidence for the attitudes and activities of the extremists come from these hostile sources because both were discussing the same issue from opposite sides of the fence.

The civilian personnel among the ultraists emerged through three political crises: the so-called speech without doors against the Scottish Commissioners' reply to the Newcastle Propositions; the campaign against renewed addresses for peace to Charles; and the change of sides brought about by the alliance of *Engagement*[4] between Charles and the Hamiltonian Scots. These three issues threw attitudes towards Charles and subsequently (and consequently) towards monarchy into relief. The presence of the king and the Scots in Newcastle-upon-Tyne and Charles' answers to the Newcastle Propositions prompted a very small but well-organised and vocal lobby against the readmittance of the person of the king to the peace negotiations or the presence of the Scottish Commissioners. They countered the role in English politics played by the Scottish Covenanting army and its Commissioners, and the concern for Charles' person expressed by both. Unlike both Presbyterians and the majority of Independents, this small group were wary of any moves to bring the war to a conclusion by treaty. They did not trust the figure of Charles Stuart and the ending of hostilities was 'a day of discovery'[5] that began a process of rethinking about the causes, course and ending of the war which, by the end of three years' campaigning, would introduce the revolutionary aspect into English politics. The fact that the ultraists were so few leads one to question how they managed to project themselves to the centre of power in a mere two years. One of their opponents, Denzil Holles, attributed their rise entirely to tactics:

> Who but they drew all business into the Parliament, especially when themselves, of their friends, were any thing concerned? And had they not an art of delaying men, and making them attend, when they could not mischief them by dispatching the business? were any more violent in an arbitrary way of proceeding then they? . . . could a Mayor, or Officer, or a Burgess for Parliament be chosen almost in any town of *England*, but with their leaves, and according to their likings?[6]

While opponents like Holles were clearly overstating their case for effect, there is plenty of evidence to show that shrewd parliamentary and extra-parliamentary manipulation was the chief way in which a vocal minority projected its voice.

When Charles was offered terms, the Propositions of Newcastle, his reply revealed that he did not intend to engage in negotiation. His first answer, dated 1 August 1646, was a flat rejection, because he believed that the conditions amounted to a fundamental reassessment of church and state. In order to discuss issues of the magnitude he believed were being propounded, he would need to return to London, 'with freedom, honour and safety', and this would 'raise a mutual confidence between him and his people' and 'have these doubts cleared, and these difficulties explained unto him'.[7] While his absence from London undermined his personal authority, the conditions offered to him were 'destructive to his just regal power'. The royalist position stressed the necessary and inviolable unity between the king's human, mortal capacities and his exercise of authority: the distinction between person and office. His attendance in his capital would provide a visual demonstration that the corporeal presence of the king and the executive office which he held should necessarily be united. '*Salus Regis*, & *salus Republicae* are not onely Twins,' confirmed a royalist pamphleteer, 'but *Gemini*, Inseperable, and individuall; Cursed be those that have hitherto divided them'.[8]

The assault on the royal person was deemed to lay in his opponents' willingness to debate the nature of dignity, which was intended to refer to the natural rather than the politic body of the king – the physical presence of the monarch.[9] Charles' readmittance into London would be the final, clinching stage of the peace process. English (and Scottish) forces were wary of having Charles in their respective capitals, lest he act as a destabilising influence before the peace terms could be secured to the point at which his erstwhile opponents felt safe. Nevertheless, as far as royalists and the moderate, Presbyterian promoters of the Newcastle Propositions were concerned, Charles' return to London as king would cement the final peace, being received with pomp and ceremony into the capital from which he had fled in January 1642. The attendance of the king added the gravitas and solemnity which were an integral part of government which contained a single-person element. Thus, for the supporters of Charles, the separation of physical and authorative power was sufficient reason to oppose the peace offer as totally unacceptable. At the other end of the spectrum, the radical MP, Henry Marten, demolished the link when he mocked those with scrofula who rushed to the presence of the surrendered king to receive the laying on of hands. Since parliament had taken over the executive functions of monarchy, he jibed that maybe the Great Seal would be as effective.[10]

In terms of an attack on the executive powers of his office, the major sticking point was the parliament's demand to control the militia for twenty years following the treaty. The removal of Charles' personal control of an army was a huge diminution of sovereignty, as Charles outlined in his third answer.[11] Losing this prerogative power, even for twenty years, would be 'divesting himself, and disinheriting his posterity of that right and prerogative of the Crown which is absolutely necessary to the Kingly office, and so weakening monarchy in this kingdom that little more than the name and shadow of it will remain'.[12] The parliamentarian pamphleteer, Henry Parker, confirmed the king's view. 'The king would not understand', Parker despaired, 'that the setling the Militia at this time in confiding hands, to prevent civill war, was any other, then the taking the Crowne from his head'.[13] There was evidence from some quarters that Charles' stock of public esteem had dropped below a point at which he would be entrusted with control of the militia and therefore with the physical safety of the people. *Salus populi*, the safety of the people, was in danger.[14]

Despite Charles, and the royalists' protestations that the royal person and office could not be separated, it was the particular example of Charles' own actions and statements which enabled them to be distinguished. Conservatives and radicals flung texts from Proverbs at each other: from the one, referring to the parliament, 'for the transgression of a Land, many are the princes thereof';[15] from the other 'if they be Princes, it was never the transgression of the Land, but the transgression of the Prince of the Land, which made them Princes'.[16] Another cited Proverbs 15: 22: 'without counsell, purposes are disappointed: but in the multitude of counsellors they are established'[17]. In a practical and material sense, Charles' flight from London and declaration of war had divided the person of the king from the office which he held, and in his absence, the two Houses had assumed his executive functions. The ability to prise apart the concepts of person and office could facilitate a radical review of other notions for which their remaining inseparable had been the foundation of their legitimacy. In particular, Charles' physical separation from the office opened the door to a personal examination of his character, and he was then careless in revealing evidence by which some could paint it black. The king's letters, captured at Naseby, revealed his attempts to solicit foreign powers to his aid, in what would be, effectively, an invasion of England. The letters were subsequently published, most famously as *The Kings Cabinet Opened*.[18] The king's intentions were submitted to public scrutiny, diminishing the trust in which he was held by casting doubt on his personal qualities. The king was seen to be a duplicitous man.[19]

The release of the letters showed, in Parker's words, that the king 'sat in the *Chair of the scornfull; &* . . . *walked in the counsels of the ungodly*'.[20] It was a moment which made it possible to polarise politics: 'thou art either a friend or enemy to our cause'.[21] Charles agreed that any delay on his part and 'the rebels will go to all extremities'.[22]

With a wave of publications throughout October 1646 broadcasting Charles' untrustworthiness, the Commons debated the peace process.[23] It was within a tense atmosphere that on 26 October,[24] Thomas Chaloner, recently recruited MP for Richmond, North Yorkshire, rose to address the House. His speech was a response to the reading of the 'Scotch papers', the name given to the Scottish Commissioners' reply to the English parliament's votes on the so called 'disposal' of the king's person.[25] One paper concerned the disposal of the person of the king in the hands of the Scots, and the other was 'touching the distractions of the North; by reason as they say of the now [*recte* non] payment of their Army'.[26] Chaloner spoke to the first, since he knew others who would speak on the troubles of the north. According to his most scandalised critic, he called the king a dog not worth whistling after, and joked that the royalist parliament in Oxford had found it so difficult to decide where to erect Charles' throne that some onlookers had concluded it would be better not to erect it at all.[27] It was coined 'the Speech without Doors' and 'many hard invective writings were published, on both sides, for the space of divers months'.[28]

'A great dissention happened between the two Kingdoms', was how Chaloner's friend, Thomas May, was to describe the period in his retrospective history of the Long Parliament.[29] Chaloner's speech argued that the war had been fought by two kingdoms: the peace should be settled by one, or more precisely the respective settlements of England and Scotland should be negotiated separately. The fact that the physical presence of the king was not deemed necessary to executive authority would enable a peace to be settled without reference to the king's appearance in either of his capitals.[30] It was a radical twist on a standard element of English constitutionalism. Although the height of the constitution was the king-in-parliament, the king, having separated himself from his parliament, '[n]o man can be sayd to be *Rex* but in *Regno*'.[31] When Charles was removed from parliament, he was an ordinary man whose character and actions could be judged as any other. He was guarded by the Scots, but according to Chaloner, Charles had been defeated by an English army and his feet were still on English soil.[32] Both Charles and the army of the Scots, camped in the north, were therefore subject to the law determined by the English parliament.

This speech, and the pamphlets which followed it, gleefully exploited a Scottish theorist to attack his fellow countrymen. Samuel Rutherford, the man credited with the authorship of the 1644 tract *Lex Rex*, had made great play of the difference between the person of the king, *in concreto*, and his office, *in abstracto*, in order to demonstrate that obedience to the civil magistrate did not extend to the point at which the ruler acted tyrannically.[33] Chaloner also claimed that the Scottish Commissioners' report on the peace proposals used the word 'king' in two different senses. Chaloner defined the power of kingship *in abstracto* as 'the Royall power, Function, and office of a king',[34] an argument which relied for its coherence on an absolute, physical distinction between the person and the office. Chaloner dared to state, openly, that the physical separation of the king in Newcastle from the two English Houses at Westminster reflected a real separation of authority. Powers which prior to 1642 had been in the hands of a monarch were now in the trust of the parliament of England. This imbued it with the authority, within the traditional definition of sovereignty, of the prerogative power to declare war and, of particular import in 1646, to conclude peace. The English parliament's executive obligation was to secure the law for its constituents before it turned its attention to the safety of the king's person. In Chaloner's words:

> I pray (Sir) first settle the honour safety and freedome of the Commonwealth, and then the freedome of the King, so far as the latter may stand with the former, and not otherwise. Wherefore I shall conclude with my humble desire that you would adhere to your former vote that is, that the King be disposed of as both Houses of Parliament shall thinke fitting; and that you enter into no Treaty either with the King or your brethren in Scotland, least otherwise thereby you retard the going home of their army out of England.[35]

Because Charles was physically separating himself from the parliament by remaining in Newcastle and by being in the hands of the Scots, English ultraists claimed that Charles was in a position equivalent to the king's power being in demise.[36] This was normally the term reserved for kingship when it was compromised by wardship, mental infirmity or old age. It was pointed out, however, that parliaments had continued to sit, on these occasions, because '[a]ll Parliaments are called by the Kings power, and the summons goe out in the Kings name, as an absolute Prerogative incident to his Crowne and Dignity, *21 Rich.2.c.12*. yet not alwaies personally by the King himselfe'.[37] The royalists countered by attempting to reinsert the inseparability of moral virtue and physical presence in a monarch:

> It is a bold Assertion between you both (Scottish and English Commissioners), to enter into a saucy dispute about the disposing of the Sacred person of the

King, as if he were a Child, a Ward, or an Ideot; when God can beare him
witnesse, Hee hath more Wit, more Judgement, and more Honestie in Him,
then any of you all or all of you together. Here let me interpose with my short,
and true definition of him, both as He is a Man, and as He is our King. As he is a
Man, me thinks I heare my Saviour saluting him, . . . Now as He is our King,
how can both Houses, as M. Challener saith; or how can both Kingdoms, as my
Lord Chancellor of Scotland would have it? dare to take upon them to dispose
of him, who hath under God the sole disposall of us all, with this limitation;
with the joynt consent, and wholesome advise of the honest and great Councell
of each Kingdome, and this is both Law and Gospell.[38]

The conclusion warned that the Scottish and English Commissioners
were out to destroy the person of the king, though, since the author
considered person and office indivisible, the proposals would presumably destroy them both.[39] Royalist commentaries erected both the
person and the office-holder to a capacity beyond that of normal
humanity, in response to attacks which sought to reduce Charles to
someone who was less than a king but also flawed as a human being.[40]

In most modern accounts of the 1640s, the Speech without Doors
controversy is overlooked, possibly because it was important to only a
few people. Those who supported Chaloner are regarded as unrepresentative and extreme, their views so outrageous as to be marginalised in
parliament.[41] Presentation and tactics was therefore vital in order to
disseminate these ideas to a wider audience, create the impression of a
far more representative viewpoint and put pressure on more dominant,
numerically greater factions. One of the main tactics was the manipulation of the presses.

One of the printers who cast the words of the Scottish Commissioners to a wider English audience was Francis Leech. Leech was the
printer of a regular bulletin called *A Continuation of Papers from the Scots
Quarters*, claimed, wrongly, to have been ordered by the English
Parliament.[42] Leech was also keen to publicise the Irish rebels' support
for Charles, which invariably had a negative effect.[43] He was also the
publisher of a list, arranged by county, of *The great Champions of England*
which, although it was compiled before the splits between Presbyterian
and Independent resulted in purges of the New Model Army, still
contained some surprisingly radical and unrepresentative figures.[44]
Leech printed Chaloner's Speech, dubbed the Speech without Doors
because it used parliamentary privilege to attack the person of the king,
and because by being printed up, it opened up the debate to all manner
of petty scribblers. Two other pro-Chaloner tracts came from Leech's
press.[45] Of all the contibutions to the Speech without Doors controversy, Leech's version of Chaloner's speech was the only one to be
registered with the stationers' company.[46]

A second tactic involved claiming a false publisher. The most obvious example of this is the number of tracts which appeared to be printed by Charles' Edinburgh printer, Evan Tyler. An appearance of a tract printed by him would seem to be an expresion of royalism, and only after the tract had been read would it manifest itself as the opposite. This was the tactic employed by Chaloner's chief supporter within the House, Henry Marten. Marten had only recently been readmitted to the Commons benches, having been excluded for declaring it was better the king perish than the whole nation.[47] His concern with the Speech without Doors controversy is clear, however, for his style is recognisable. Marten played with the authorities who sought to suppress his scurrilous writings, and his well-turned phrases place Marten as the author of *A Corrector to the Answerer to the Speech without Doores* and *An Vnhappie Game at Scotch and English*.[48] A further four drafts, including one in which Marten claimed to be Chaloner's groom, were drawn up but did not reach the press.[49] Evan Tyler was employed again when *Some Papers given in by the Commissioners of the Parliament of Scotland*, were printed and published.[50] Thomason believed that these Scottish papers had been printed by Robert Bostock, who had appeared before John Lisle's committee of privileges six months' previously, having confessed to printing '(s)ome papers of the commissioners of Scotland'.[51]

Supposedly anodyne proposals for the new modelling of the forces of the Western Association, 'printed' by Evan Tyler, were, as Thomason corrected on the frontispiece, 'Independant' proposals.[52] Thomason also queried a report of the sufferings of the people of Cleveland under the Scots forces, 'said to be written but made at Lond[on] by ye Ind[ependents]'.[53] *Mercurius Civicus* reported large extracts from Chaloner's speech (and no others) concerning *abstracto* and *concreto* and the assumption of executive powers by the parliament, while promising more of the debate in *The Kingdomes Weekly Intelligencer*, 'if the Stationer and Printer will not interpose, but let the writer alone to himself, and give him but faire play, which is the known desire of every honest man'.[54] Stationers and printers passed on information about their treasonous colleagues and Henry Walker thought it his duty to publish *A Reply to a Letter printed at Newcastle*, because it laid claim to have been written by the Geneva divine, Giovanni Deodati, but must rather have been the product of 'some profane Atheist'.[55] Edward Bowles asserted authority from parliament in order to defend the 'Independents' from the charge that they

serve themselves into imployments, engage the Pamphleteers to set forth lyes and tales for them, confes of disturbances, blasphemies, heresies, violations of the Covenant, undermines, factious, guilty of malicious plots, bringers of confusion into the Church, and consequently Anarchy into the State, men that doe all for by-ends, that joyne with others, as the Papists with Malignants for their own ends.[56]

False imprimaturs and anonymity allowed for unparliamentary language. Marten played unambiguously with the person/office distinction, asking 'what the proper difference is *between a King and Tyrant*, and finding the latter character upon him, how then ought they to dispose of his Person', so that Charles, who had 'infinitely transcended' Strafford and Laud 'in Treasons against the Commonwealth' should not escape 'scot-free'.[57] He subsequently chose to express it in terms of voluntarism:

in our answer to the Will of the King, we must consider that Will, as the Will of Charles Steuart, contrary to whose Will, you will not have him disposed; so that in deed and in truth, you place the whole power of the disposall of Charles Steuart, in the Will of Charles Steuart, and make that his personall Will, the Essence of that Disposall; for the Will of Charles Steuart . . . may contradict null, and make voide whatever gainesaies.[58]

This second pamphlet was deemed fit to be burnt by the common hangman, but no one seemed to realise who was the author.[59] He had clearly crossed a line. It was one thing to say that the king was never more in majesty than when he sat with his parliament, even that his physical separation made him liable to be regarded as a 'private man'.[60] It was quite another to judge that private man a malignant worthy of condign punishment: '[f]or if he were here (England) in the Capacity of a King of *Scotland* he were a Subject, and then you might know well enough what should become of a King of *Scotland* as you (the Scots) have formerly done of some of them, who yet have plotted less then others have acted'.[61] The author of *The Justification* sought to deny that there had been any 'acrimonious' statements about the king, but wished that some which had been made to the effect that the 'disposing may be deposing or worse' could have been toned down, out of respect for the degree of indulgence which the English had traditionally and historically displayed towards their monarchs in comparison with continental states.[62]

The Speech without Doors pushed another traditional argument further than many wished to take it. While *The Justification* blamed Charles for the war itself, it hinted at discontents with his rule with a longer history.[63] Henry Marten more explicitly charged Charles with malignant behaviour which went back much further than the declaration of civil war. He had

for sixteene yeares without intermission *brake the Law, turned the government upside downe; Null'd Parlements*, and when craft and cruelty would not suffice, *rais'd*

a most unnaturall Warre against this Parliament, intermixing the most devillish plots that
ever were to destroy the most religious and peaceable People in all places and never by all
intreaties, Treatyes, Covenants [and indulgence in all these] could be drawne to give
over his violent and inhumane courses, till necessity enforc'd, and then by a
most unparaleld contrivance to intangle this Nation more than ever.[64]

By abdicating control over the executive functions of government, Charles had turned against those he was sworn to protect. The argument about prerogative was turned on its head. Prerogatives were reassessed as functions which kings had usurped, defining kingship by the way they had been abused in order to set the monarch apart, rather than as integral powers originally invested in kingship which Charles had failed to fulfil. This enabled some parliamentarians to claim that they had always been part of parliament's authority. A *de facto* separation of powers was giving birth to a *de jure* claim to the prerogative of peace-making.

Chaloner and his allies were engaged in an argument which ran parallel to ancient constitutionalism, by seeking to protect the executive functions of parliament by claiming that they were 'naturally' a component of parliamentary authority in the face of attempts by royalists to wrest them back. The English constitution demanded pre-existence. Because all claims to new powers were liable to the charge of innovation and usurpation, they were referred back to an origin beyond record.[65] It was therefore vital that these forms of authority should not be described as newly vested in the parliament, playing into the royalists' hands by allowing them to claim that it was in fact parliament which was usurping royal authority. Powers were described as newly recovered, rather than new in themselves, and natural law was drafted in to provide a justification. The pro-Chaloner author of *An Answer to severall Obiections* admitted that these functions had only recently been claimed, but they were immemorially legitimated by natural law and had been the real, at the time obscured reason behind the union with the Scots: 'the honour, or safety, and freedome of the whole people . . . was first considerable both in the Covenant, and the law of nature it selfe'.[66] Edmund Ludlow summed up the powers claimed by the English parliament as a result of its disagreements with the Scots: the exclusion of the king from matters concerning the militia, disbanding the armies and an act of oblivion, as well as the removal of Scottish influence in the government of England, and the provision of education for the king's children.[67] These were executive functions over which the English parliament intended to keep a tight rein.

The Speech without Doors highlighted a sentiment based on the defence of local patrimony from both the Scots and the king, now in Scottish hands and based in Newcastle-upon-Tyne. One exasperated

English commentator railed that the Scottish Commissioners deemed Newcastle to be in Scotland.[68] Chaloner had estates around Guisborough, Cleveland, and a grievance against the Stuarts for potentially arbitrary action in rescinding his family's alum mining patent, based in the area.[69] Chaloner's speech was sufficient to get himself named to the otherwise conservative committee which discussed the Scotch Papers.[70] He had only just appeared at its first session when the Scottish Commissioners brought a complaint of a pamphlet entitled 'A Declaration concerning the miserable sufferings of the Country under some of the Scotts Forces, that quarter in the North of England'. The petition came from Stainton and Cleveland and was accompanied by similar representations by Thomas Westropp[71] and Chaloner's younger brother, James. Two days later, a further petition arrived from the same small geographical area.[72] Westropp based himself in London in order to lobby on behalf of the Yorkshire gentry and in November, six members of the Yorkshire committee for sequestrations forwarded their complaints about the excesses of the Scottish soldiery.[73]

On the other side of the Pennines a similar camapaign was under way. Cumberland men, John Musgrave, Richard Crackenthorpe and John Osmotherley, sent information up to London that the parliamentary affairs of their region were in the hands of malignants, particularly complaining about Richard Barwis, MP for Carlisle and one of the commissioners negotiating with the Scots.[74] Musgrave was called to give evidence, refused to speak, and was imprisoned for contempt.[75] He was also, therefore, employing the tactic of challenging parliamentary privilege and then claiming anonymity when pushed to reveal the form of his lobbying.[76] Musgrave manipulated the role of the Scots in several ways. He claimed malignants had taken against him from the start, because he had been 'chief instrument in bringing in the Scots to take away the Service-book'.[77] But he was no Presbyterian. In fact, he was an Independent, so the Scots were happy to support his petitions because 'Master Musgrave is of a different judgement from the Church of Scotland in matters of Church Government, and stands for the Independency of particular congregations, and therefore his Information is the lesse to be suspected of partiality towards the Scottish Army'.[78] He could then also cast doubt on the Scots' loyalty. Crackenthorpe warned Musgrave that the Scots' army deliberately stayed on the eastern side of England so that the royalist forces could move freely through the west.[79] Like Marten, whose *Vnhappie Game* stepped far enough out of line to merit strict censorship, when the House was informed of what was in fact Musgrave's pamphlet, called *Yet another Word to the Wise*, 'tending to the Breach of the Privilege, and the great Scandal and Contempt, of this House', it seemed not to realise who had written it and went on to recommend that this same petition by Musgrave and Crackenthorpe be referred to the committee for Northumberland and Durham.[80] As Westropp used Chaloner, so Musgrave and his party lobbied through Alexander Rigby, MP for Wigan.[81] In June 1646, Musgrave wrote from the Fleet to Rigby, with copies of the 'Scottish papers' and his reasons for not answering them, which he had sent to Lisle for consideration by the committee for privileges.[82]

Nevertheless, the negotiations with the king continued and the next time the ultraists had an opportunity to express astonishment that so much effort was being put into making peace with Charles, they had two rival peace proposals to counter. An alternative way to marginalise the Scots was to strengthen alliances within those parties in England which could repudiate the religious clauses of the Covenant on the grounds that they promoted Calvinism. Oliver St. John, Sir Henry Vane the younger, Sir John Evelyn, Oliver Cromwell, Henry Ireton and others prepared alternative peace proposals during the summer of 1647, known as the *Heads of the Proposals*.[83] Its sponsors were parliamentarians alarmed that the link between the promoters of the Newcastle Propositions and the Calvinist Scots would lead to a Presbyterian church settlement. The *Heads* were predicated on religious toleration. Ultra-independents were more liable to express a slight preference for the *Heads* since one of the liberties which they sought to secure before the prerogatives of the monarch was the right to freedom of conscience. That said, the army grandees were dangerous, for their support for religious toleration met half-way the wish that the people's rights should be primary, leaving the potential both to work with the army and to be held to ransom by it.[84] Those who spoke from a minority position and sought the power to alter the direction of policy could not afford to alienate the soldiery. But, if the *Heads* were accepted, the ultraists would be isolated.

When the king's latest answer to the Propositions, as well as a copy of the *Heads* – 'agreed on by the General and the Council of the army'[85] – was presented to the Commons on 21 September 1647, it was noted that Charles rejected the Propositions and expressed a preference for the *Heads*.[86] In order to stymie Presbyterianism, the *Heads* generally took a less hardline approach to matters of the royal prerogative. Although it called for biennial parliaments, the *Heads* offered to reduce the period during which parliament would control the militia to only ten years, after which the king and his family would be restored 'to a condition of safety, honour and freedom in this nation, without diminution to their personal rights, or further limitation to the exercise of the regal power.'[87] While the difference between the Propositions and the *Heads* was primarily about religion, there was also a debate between the two about the role of the monarch.

The day after the receipt of the king's answer, the House accepted a motion from the Cromwell-Ireton-Evelyn group, that the House turn itself into a Grand Committee to 'take into Consideration the whole Matter concerning the King'. A clear majority in the Commons agreed that it was of paramount importance to keep open the lines of communication with Charles, either on the basis of the Propositions or the *Heads*. Those telling for the negative on this occasion, spear-heading those who opposed debating the position of the king, were Sir Peter Wentworth, MP for Tamworth, and Colonel Thomas Rainsborough, the recruiter member for Droitwich, Worcestershire. They could muster only thirty-four votes against the accommodationists' eighty-four, and the House proceeded to debate the clauses of the Propositions, agreeing first to return to the king those which dealt with the militia.[88] Because 23 September 1647 was a Thursday, Cromwell and Rainsborough left the House to return to the army, either to attend the weekly sessions of the full General Council, which Fairfax had called to meet that day, or the sub committee consisting of Cromwell, Rainsborough, Ireton and Hammond, which Fairfax had established on 30 August to deal with business 'of publique and common concernment to the Army or Kingdome'.[89] In the House, Cromwell and Rainsborough were replaced by Sir Arthur Haselrig and Henry Marten respectively.[90] When the Commons voted whether 'the House will once more make Application to the King, for those Things which the House shall judge necessary for the Welfare and safety of the Kingdome'[91], Marten and Wentworth again tried and failed to block this move. Now they could muster only twenty-three votes, the numbers on both sides reduced by the vagaries of Commons' attendance and some members' return to military service.[92] The House sent back the clauses on titles, the Great Seal, bishops' lands and indemnity.[93]

We can therefore add Wentworth and Rainsborough to a list of those within the Commons prepared to oppose attempts to include the king in the peace negotiations. In the language of the day they were countering the design to 'send addresses' to the king. The vote of 23 September was a negative reaction to the move by a numerically significant faction to continue talks. At this stage, Marten, Chaloner, Wentworth and Rainsborough were in such a minority that they reacted to the actions of others and could not direct matters themselves. The majority in parliament were prepared to go to considerable lengths to continue talking, even when the king escaped from the Scots, sailed to the Isle of Wight and placed himself in the hands of Cromwell's friend, Robert Hammond, at Carisbroke Castle. Charles offered a conciliatory hand to the army, while the Lords codified the Newcastle Propositions and prepared to submit them as four bills.[94] They were sent down to the Commons on 26 November and accepted by nine votes. In this instance, Algernon Sidney and Sir John Evelyn were telling for the ayes. The representative for the borough of Lewes, Herbert Morley, joined Marten in opposing the bills.[95] Relatively little is known about the indisputably hardline Morley, but he was a man whom Thomas May regarded with some respect.[96]

The king eventually broke with his tactic of playing all sides against the middle. The Independents had warned against the Scots switching their allegiance, and in December 1647 the Hamiltonian faction signed an engagement by which Charles exchanged a promise to abide by the Covenant for Scottish military intervention. Charles rejected the Four Bills and tried to escape from Carisbroke. Blatant armed intervention by the Scots, represented by the *Engagement*, confirmed the Independents' most negative feelings about the northern kingdom and, anxious to secure a degree of toleration, they were alarmed at the comprehensiveness of the Scots' catalogue of ungodly agents against whom both parties would seek to engage. The king and the Scots vowed to strike out 'Anti-Trinitarians, Anabaptists, Antinomians, Arminians, Familists, Brownists, Separatists, Independents, Libertines, and Seekers'.[97]

Charles' obvious tactical shift provided a far wider cross-section of Independents with a view of the king as an untrustworthy man. Those who had been the minority in the September vote on addresses could now attempt to seize the initiative. On 3 January 1648, they introduced their own resolution of no further addresses to the king. Their motives were described by Clement Walker, a Presbyterian in both its religious and political senses and fierce upholder of monarchical prerogative. He stood at the opposite end of the spectrum from those who campaigned for no addresses, but the extremes of the debate were arguing reverse sides of the same coin, both seeking to define royal prerogative.[98] Walker's account of the politics of the period therefore attached considerable importance to the moves to exclude Charles from a peace settlement, and particularly the Vote of No Addresses. He gave a flavour of events, which also introduces two of the firebrand MPs of the south-west, Edmund Prideaux who sat for Lyme Regis, and Sir Thomas Wroth – 'Jack Pudding to Prideaux the Post-master'[99] – part of John Pyne's alternative clientage network and recruiter member for Bridgwater.[100] Wroth was chosen to open the debate, testing the mood of the House through the use of deliberately overblown rhetoric. The analogy he chose was '(t)hat Bedlam was appointed for mad men, and Tophet for Kings: that our Kings of late had carried themselves as if they were fit for no place but Bedlam.'[101] He did not much care what form the government of the country took, so long as it was not by 'Kings or Devils'. Wroth was inverting the person/office distinction. Madness, which would have consigned Charles to bedlam – 'as if he were . . . an Ideot'[102] – was one of the conditions whereby the person of the monarch was said to be in demise. Now kings were mad. According to Walker, constitution breakdown was the direct result of the Independents' assessment of Charles' character. The whole debate was

> sharp, vehement, and high, about the State and Government of the Commonwealth; and many plain speeches made of the King's obstinate averseness, and the people's too long patience; it was there affirmed, that the King, by this denial, had denied his protection to the people of *England*, for which only subjection is due from them; that, one being taken away, the other falls to the ground. That it is very unjust and absurd, that the Parliament, (having so often tried the King's affections) should now betray to an implacable enemy, both themselves and all those friends, who, in a most just cause, had valiantly adventured their lives and fortunes: that nothing was now left for them to do, but to take care for the safety of themselves and their friends, and settle the Commonwealth (since otherwise it could not) without the King.[103]

The debate revealed a number of men for whom Charles' actions had provoked a shift of attitude. Ireton, who had promoted the *Heads*, now seconded the motion for no addresses and Cromwell summed up the debate. Haselrig and Evelyn, tellers for the affirmative side of the debate of further addresses, also now distrusted the king to the point at which they would not negotiate with him.[104]

Several scholars have described the tactical or rhetorical mechanism at work here. Glenn Burgess believes it derived from an expansion of the arenas of acceptable discourse, in which the language of one sphere – royal prerogative, for example – is set to analyse another in which the language was previously considered inappropriate or anachronistic. Terms of analysis 'jumped' from one realm into another.[105] Nigel Smith has described a similar process as one of 'invasion' and 'literary displacement'.[106] Annabel Patterson analyses the process by which something which is a cultural construct, defined by those in power, can be revealed to be ridiculous should it come into conflict with a competing set of social priorities.[107] Having started from a position in which parliamentarians could only snipe and jibe at the conventions of royal sovereignty using the cover of anonymity, false imprimatur and burlesque language, they could now openly use such inversions of royalist commonplaces within the House with radical political effect.

Charles' actions forced members of his parliament to assess their obligations and place them in competition.[108] The promise made to protect the king's person in the Covenant became diametrically opposed to an obligation on representatives to secure the liberty and safety of the people. When Charles signed the Scottish *Engagement*, he placed it in opposition to the obligation to secure peace in England. The result of the clash brought the whole basis of his kingship into question.

A nine-strong committee – Henry Marten, Thomas Chaloner, John Lisle, Richard Salway, Herbert Morley, Thomas, Lord Grey of Groby, Edmund Prideaux, Nathaniel Fiennes and Henry Pierrepont – was appointed to compose a justification for the vote. Fiennes was a member of the so-called middle party and Pierrepont the only moderate, but the declaration printed in the name of the two Houses on 17 January[109] prefixed a conservative preamble from the Lords. The Four Bills 'did contain onely matter of Safety and Security to the Parliament and Kingdom', while all other matters would be referred to a Personal Treaty, and the Vote of No Addresses was only necessary so that 'the Houses may receive no Delays nor Interruptions'. The declaration then repeated the votes taken on 3 January, calling on Members to distribute news of them throughout the country. A statement alluding to the continuing possibility of a personal treaty was an unlikely child of such a radical committee: most had already rejected the idea. Ludlow described

> a declaration, prepared by Colonel Nathanael Fiennes, shewing the reasons of their sad resolutions; wherein, amongst other miscarriages of the King's reign, was represented his breaking of Parliaments, the betraying of Rochel, his refusal to suffer any inquiry to be made into the death of his father, his levying war against the people of England, and his rejecting all reasonable offers of accommodation after several applications to him on their part.[110]

A correspondent to Lord Lanark believed the declaration to have been brought to the House by Fiennes, but 'penned' by the jurist, John Sadler.[111] There may have been two declarations; Ludlow's version was noted, but rejected in favour of a more conciliatory variant.

Nevertheless, the Vote of No Addresses marked a turning point, with men like John Milton pinpointing the 'change of Government' to early 1648.[112] It demonstrates another series of jumps. A specific action on Charles' part provoked a specific response within the confines of parliamentary action. A series of these actions led to mistrust of Charles which undermined his role in the peace process. Charles' actions were then used as a means to describe unchanging traits. Ludlow's justification of the Vote of No Addresses did not fix on one 'crime', misdemeanour or mistake – a specific action – but chronicled a series of misjudgements, crimes and evil intentions taken from the whole of Charles' life, which were the result of flaws of character. While moderates stressed the patience with which they had dealt with Charles and the length of time during which they had indulged him, the radical response was to delve even further back to collect evidence of the king's behaviour. Chaloner and Marten had set the tone of exasperation in the Speech without Doors campaign, when the people ought to 'consider *what the King hath done both before and since the Warre?*'[113] Offered peace proposals, indulged and mollified, Charles was still intent on behaving like a tyrant, so why had people not become 'discontented with the King's Actions long agoe' when 'so many Oathes, Protestations, Declarations and Covenants, (were) made by the Parliament for the safety of the Kings person, but never any mention at all of the safety of the Common-wealth'.[114] Charles' inadequacies were taken beyond the point at which he had broken his trust with the people by leaving the capital or by declaring war on the parliament. He was held up as someone who had consistently ruled tyrannically by showing evil intent towards parliament and people.[115]

A peace treaty was a form of contract and any contract demanded two parties. The personal treaty, however, demanded that one party be the single figure of Charles Stuart. The person who had sworn to protect the liberties of the people had proved himself to be untrustworthy, so his actions had destroyed the prospect of contracting with him. The treaty would be inequitable. One person's security was balanced against the security of everybody else. It would be unjust. The victors were being dictated to by the defeated commander.[116] Thus,

> no Treaty can be indeed altogether equal betwixt the King, and the peoples Parliament, for he deals but for himself, and perhaps for some of his own Family and Posterity; they for two whole Nations. Again, the matters to be Treated on, concern him in the extent, or the Retrenchment of his power to do hurt: They concern us in our wel being, if not in our being.[117]

Those who had fought against their king were uneasy that he might be allowed back into power without their own indemnity having been secured and that an untrustworthy man was being readmitted to government without having demonstrated that he would act differently in the future.[118]

Henry Marten was able, following the Vote of No Addresses, to state his view openly. He continued the attack on the Scottish Commissioners in defence of the 'rights, laws and liberties' of the English and their parliament, and counselled the English people to secure their rights by conquest: Charles would prove a 'broken reed' if any group

depended on him for peace.[119] To the Scots he declared, '[y]ou are
come to a degree beyond being friends with him (Charles), to be
advocates for him, not in mediating that his submission might be
accepted, his crimes obliterated, and their salary remitted, but in
asserting the same cause which we have been all this while confuting
with our swords.'[120] This bombast was published as *The Independency of
England*, another Commons' speech which was subsequently broadcast
to a wider public in print. Sir John Maynard followed Marten in debate
and also circulated his traditional, Presbyterian contribution.[121] Still not
prepared to distinguish the powers of the office from those of the
person, he charged that Marten '[c]ontrary to the oath of Allegiance,
Protestation Vow and Covenant, . . . hath spoken against ye Kings
person . . . Against the fundamentall Laws of the Realme, . . . against
the Royall power which you have acknowledged to be the ffountaine
of Justice'.[122] Maynard also felt free to be able to impute another jump
to Marten. Because the person and office were inseparable, striking at a
particular king was an attack on any king and all kings. Where the
radicals had praised non-monarchical regimes, Maynard criticised them:
'Consider the state of Venice, Switzerland, Holland and the Hans
Townes. Are not the Gentlemen of Venice, and Burghemasters of
Switzerland and the Hans Towns tyrants? And what was Holland? was
not the prince of Orange almost absolute.'

The English system was a series of bodies of administration –
legislative and judicial, but now, crucially, the executive as well –
on one side of an equation, with the single figure of Charles on the
other.[123] He had, by his own actions and the course of the war, been
frozen out of the political equation. If the ideal polity was one which
was in balance, the *de facto* postwar situation was one in which the peace
proposals posited a set of scales in which executive, legislative and
judiciary sat on one side and the lone representative of kingship on the
other. Charles' actions had pricked the bubble of monarchical preten-
tions, represented by the unity of person and office. Once he was out in
the cold, he could be judged as an ordinary man might be judged. The
safety and the rights of the people were to be settled before those of the
king because the security of the commonweal was more important than
that of one man. This was a question of private versus public good.

The debate about a balanced constitution was all about a straight
choice; either the treaty restored the king's rights or guarded the
people's rights. Glenn Burgess has noted the 'duplex theory' of
prerogative in which the language of constitutions already consisted
of a series of dichotomous relationships. These could be expressed as
absolute *versus* ordinary prerogative, legal and extra-legal powers, regal

or politic capacities or, the version most relevant for this radicalisation of the theory, natural body and body politic.[124] In turning down the opportunities provided by the Newcastle Propositions, the *Heads of the Proposals* and the Four Bills, Charles had missed the chance to recement the traditional relationship between the kingly office and the kingly person, in which the person was honoured for his or her legitimate exercise of the authority of office. By denying the treaty, Charles set up a dichotomy which presented parliament with a direct choice between capitulation or deposition: Charles was 'to this day set in his heart, upon being either an absolute Tyrant over us, or no King'.[125] Through a series of debates and political decisions, people had begun to question the ability of the person to carry out the office and the degree to which he should therefore be allowed to speak for – to represent in its widest sense – a much larger section of the population which had demonstrated qualities which the king lacked. The greater the number of people who regarded Charles as an unworthy holder of the office, the easier it was to claim it to be absurd to give him equal weight with the people. A set of scales in which one pan was reserved for the king's throne was becoming easier to knock over.

NOTES

1. T[homas] M[ay], *Historiae Parliamenti Angliae Breviarium tribus partibus explicitum,* [29 Mar.] 1650, E1354(3), translated as *A Breviary of the History of the Parliament of England,* [29 Jun.] 1650, E1317(1), and reprinted in Francis Maseres, *Select Tracts relating to the Civil Wars in England* (2 vols) (London, 1815), I, pp. 1–128, pp. 86–7; S. R. Gardiner, *The History of the great Civil War* (4 vols) (Windrush Press reprint, 1987), III, pp. 103–5.
2. For the role of the militia issue, see Chapter 3.
3. The text of the Newcastle Propositions is reproduced in *GCD,* pp. 290–306.
4. There is the possibility of confusion within this study between the engagement made between Charles and the Scots, and the oath of loyalty to the Commonwealth which acquired the same name. In order to minimise this, italics will be used when describing the alliance between Charles and the Scots of 1647, and non-italics when discussing the Engagement of loyalty to the Commonwealth.
5. *Three Speeches spoken at a Common-Hall, Thursday the 3. of July, 1645, by Mr. [John] Lisle, Mr. [Zouche] Tate, Mr. Brown, Members of the House of Commons,* published according to order (London, 1645), Thurs., 14 Jul. 1645, E292(29), p. 9. The most likely Mr Brown MP is John Brown, MP for Dorset since 1641.

6. Denzil Holles, *Memoirs of Denzil, Lord Holles* in Masares, *Select Tracts*, I, p. 266.

7. The king's first answer to the Newcastle Propositions, 1 Aug. 1646, reproduced in GCD, pp. 306–8, p. 307.

8. *Lex Talionis: or. a declamation against Mr Challener, the Crimes of the Times, and the Manners of You Know Whom*, [5 Jul.], 1647, E396(20), p. 9.

9. Ernst Kantorowicz, *The King's Two Bodies: A Study in Medieval Political Theology* (Princeton, 1957). The Kantorowiczian contribution, a distinction between the mystical and mortal persons of the king, has recently been challenged by David Norbrook, but the person/office distinction remains sound.

10. Bodleian Library, Oxford, Clarendon MSS II App XXXVII, 26 Apr. 1647.

11. Issued on 12 May 1647.

12. GCD, p. 314.

13. [Henry Parker], *The Kings Cabinet Opened: or, certain packets of secret Letters & Papers, written with the Kings own Hand, and taken in his Cabinet at Naseby Field*, 14 Jun. 1645. Published by special order of Parliament (London, 1645), [14 Jul.] 1645, E292(27), p. 52. The attribution to Parker was made by Thomason.

14. *Argvments, proving that we ought not to part with the militia to the King, nor indeed to any other, but the Honourable House of Commons*, London, Jun. 1646, [23 Jun.] 669.f.10(60), point 10 (of 11); see below, Chapter 3, p. 71. This is the first time in the course of this study that we have had cause to encounter the phrase *Salus populi, suprema lex*. The phrase, tucked away towards the end of Cicero's *De Legibus Libri Tres* (BK. III, iii.8) is believed to have originally meant little more than that the safety (welfare) of the people should be the ultimate guiding principle for the Roman militia in the field. It developed in the seventeenth century into a major statement of the paramount nature of the people's sovereignty. The original reads 'Regio imperio duo sunto, iique preaundo, iudicando, consulendo, praetores, iudices, consules appellamino: ollis salus populi suprema lex esto': W. D. Pearman (ed.), *Cicero: De Legibus Libri Tres* (Cambridge, 1881), pp. 112–13.

15. Prov. 28:2; *An Answer to a Speech without Doores, or Animadversions*, [16 Nov.] 1646, E362(9), p. 1. A full discussion of the 'Speech without Doors' follows below.

16. *The Justification of a safe and wel-grounded Answer to the Scottish Papers*, 23 Nov. 1646, E363(11), p. 1.

17. *An Answer to severall Obiections made against some things in Mr. Thomas Chaloners Speech*, [23 Nov.] 1646, E362(27), p. 1.

18. There is the possibility that there was a play on the word 'cabinet' involved, intending to emphasise the private and secluded nature of both the king's letters, kept in a cabinet, and the counsellors to whom he turned, hand-picked and meeting in private.

19. See below, Chapter 5, n. 38; Hutchinson, *Memoirs*, p. 224, which refers to Charles' 'falsehood'; John Cook, *King Charls his Case* [9 Feb.] 1649, E542(3), pp. 7–8, 35. Blair Worden has challenged the references to Naseby in Ludlow's *Memoirs* I, pp. 145–6), as those which show stylistic evidence of Toland's later editorship. This is a vital point, and I should like to hear more of the evidence; A. B. Worden, *A Voyce from the Watch Tower* (Camden Society, 4th ser. 21, 1978), p. 66.

20. Ps. 1: 1–2: 'Blessed is the man that walketh not in the counsel of the ungodly, nor standeth in the way of sinners, nor sitteth in the seat of the scornful. But his delight is the law of the Lord; and in his law doth he meditate day and night.'

21. *The Kings Cabinet*, A3; May, *Breviary*, I, pp. 93–8.

22. J. Bruce (ed.), *Charles I in 1646. Letters of King Charles the First to Queen Henrietta Maria* (Camden Society, old ser. LXIII, London, 1856), p. 153; Robert Ashton, *Counter-revolution: The Second Civil War and its Origins* (London, 1994), pp. 8–9, who agrees that the king delayed a response for a considerable time; Denzil Holles, *Memoirs of Denzil, lord Holles*, in Masares, *Select Tracts*, I, pp. 183–310, p. 225.

23. *The Kings Packet of Letters taken by Colonel Rossiter as they were carrying from Newark to Belvoyr*, 6 Oct. 1645, E304(22); *Two remarkable Letters concerning the Kings Correspondence with the Irish Rebels*, 9 Oct. 1645, E300(8); *The Irish Cabinet: or His Majesties secret Papers for establishing the Papall Clergy in Ireland*, 17 Oct. 1645, E316(29).

24. *CJ*, V, 125.

25. Thomas Chaloner, *An Answer to the Scotch Papers delivered in the House of Commons in Reply to the Votes of both Houses of the Parliament of England, Concerning the disposall of the Kings Person, as it was spoken when the said Papers were read in the House*, [10 Nov.] 1646, E361(7).

26. Chaloner, *Answer to the Scotch Papers*, pp. 1, 3.

27. *An Answer to a Speech without Doores: or, Animadversions upon an Unsafe and dangerous Answer to the Scotch-Papers*, [16 Nov.] 1646, E362(9), p. 2. These words, or anything like them, did not appear in Chaloner's printed speech, but the jibe about the throne in Oxford was referred to by Marten in *A Corrector of the Answerer to the Speech out of Doores*, [Nov.] 1646, E364(9), p. 2. The Animadvertor's follow-up was titled *The Speech without doores defended without reason*, [5 Dec.] 1646, E364(5).

28. May, *Breviary*, p. 91. There may well have been more tracts than this. This was the number recorded in the collection of George Thomason. For the term 'Speech without Doors', see George Wither, *The Speech without Doore, delivered July 9 1644 in the absence of the Speaker and in the hearing of above 0000003 persons then present; who . . . voted the same fit to be divulged, as very pertinent to the publike welfare*, [10 Aug.] 1644, E4(30); *The Justification of a safe and wel-grounded Answer to the Scottish Papers*, 23 Nov. 1646, E363(11), p. 2. Thomas Scot's own defence in 1660 claimed that

as a member of parliament he had the right to free speech within the confines of the Chamber; Ludlow, *Memoirs*, II, p. 307.

29. May, *Breviary*, p. 91. May is used as a source of events for three reasons. Firstly, as a historian of the civil wars he is frequently overlooked in favour of Clarendon or Whitelocke. Secondly, as the historian favoured by the republicans in the Rump parliament, the material which he chose to include in his history provides us with a valuable insight into the events and characters which the republicans thought were important. Finally, he was a close friend and political ally of many of the characters highlighted in this study, especially Thomas Chaloner; N. Yorks Record Office, ZFM Alum Deeds, No. 5.

30. The Anglo–Scottish aspects of this question were first examined in the *ante- and post-nati* debate about the Union of the Crowns. If Scots had common law rights in England as a result of the accession of James VI as James I of England, would it be the case that if Philip and Mary had succeeded in producing an heir, all Spaniards would be entitled to the rights held by the English? In 1646 this argument was reworked to show that Scotland was just as foreign a country as Spain. For the test case of Anglo–Scottish citizenship, see Calvin's Case: J. R. Tanner, *Constitutional Documents of the Reign of James I* (Cambridge, 1930), pp. 23–4.

31. G.G., *A Reply to a Namelesse Pamphlet, Intituled, An Answer to a Speech without doors, &c*, [23 Nov.] 1646, E362(26), p. 5.

32. Although some supporters of Chaloner wailed that the Scots were claiming Newcastle upon Tyne to be in Scotland; *The Justification of a safe and wel-grounded Answer to the Scottish Papers, printed under the name of Master Chaloner his speech*, a direct reply to the Animadvertor, 23 Nov. 1646, E363(11), p. 10.

33. [Samuel Rutherford], *Lex Rex: the Law and the Prince*, 7 Oct. 1644, E11(5), p. 265. Rutherford was replying to Bishop John Maxwell, *Sacrosancta regum majestas* (1644). Rutherford wrote the classic piece of Calvinist resistance theory in the 1640s, arguing that 'truth to Christ, cannot be treason to Caesar', and asked the rhetorical question 'whether, in the case of Defensive Warre, the distinction of the person of the King, as a man, who can commit acts of hostile Tyrannie against his Subjects, and the Office and Royall power that he hath from God, and the People, as a King, can have place?' Ian Michael Smart, 'The political ideas of the Scottish Covenanters, 1638–88', *HPT*, I.2 (1980) 167–93, especially pp. 175–80; *The Justification of a safe and wel-gounded answer*, pp. 3–4; Noel Henning Mayfield, 'Puritans and regicide: Presbyterian-Independent differences over the trial and execution of Charles I', PhD, Mississippi (1984), pp. 156–62.

34. Chaloner, *An Answer*, p. 4; *An Answer to severall Obiections made against some things in Mr. Thomas Chaloners Speech*, [29 Nov.] 1646, E362(27), p. 7.

35. Chaloner, *Answer*, p. 15; G.G., *A reply to a Namelesse Pamphlet*, p. 3.

36. Edmund Plowden, *Commentaries or Reports* (London, 1816), 233a; Kantorowicz, *King's Two Bodies*, p. 13 n. 13.

37. *The Moderator: in reply to M' Thomas Chaloners Speech and the Scots Papers, concerning the disposall of the King's person,* [19 Nov.] 1646, E363(12) [miscatalogued as E362(11)], pp. 3, 6.

38. *Lex Talionis,* pp. 2–3; Luke Harruney (pseud.) [Henry Walker], *A Reply to a Letter printed at Newcastle . . . about matters concerning the King and the Government of the Church,* 15 Dec. 1646, E367(7) n.p.

39. This notion predated the propaganda exercise practised by *Eikon Basilike,* which presented Charles Stuart as a martyr king. *Lex Talionis,* or the 'Law of Retribution', is noteworthy for another reason. It is a royalist use of the idea of inevitable divine vengeance on those who disobeyed God's word. Though this is an isolated pamphlet, it comes several months before the idea of vengeance became the driving force behind the actions of the New Model Army. God's vengeance on the evil committed by the New Model, rather than on the wrongdoers among the royalists, was an argument which was to gain considerable force with the execution of the king. After Charles' death there was a very obvious act which the royalists considered to be against God's law to which to attach their concept of divine retribution.

40. Compare this superhuman view with the images chosen by Sir Thomas Wroth to introduce the debate on the vote of no addresses – see below, p. 25.

41. The two historians, from different traditions, who in recent years have drawn readers' attention to the person/office distinction made in 1646 have both done so from the point of view of the English attitude towards the Scots, once Charles was in Scottish hands but still present in England. Robert Ashton used the 'two bodies' argument in *The English Civil War* (London, 1978; reissued 1989) and in a Scottish context in *Counter-revolution,* p. 312. The other person to mention Chaloner's speech in this context is Richard Tuck, *Philosophy and Government, 1572–1651* (Cambridge, 1993), p. 259, who makes an interesting connection between the Scots' broken alliegance to Charles as a result of his defeat and the arguments concerning alliegance to the Rump during the Engagement crisis – see Chapter 8 below. Ashton refers to Chaloner as a 'radical Independent', Tuck as a 'republican'.

42. For example, the edition of 12 Nov. 1646, E362(4). Leech also published *The Copies of the Kings Letter and Generall Order for the Surrender of all his Garrisons,* 10 Jun. 1646, E341(6).

43. *The Irish Papers, containing Lord Digbyes Letter and the Lord Inchiquins answer,* 2 Sep. 1646, E355(26); see also *The Moderator,* listed twice in Fortescue, *Thomason Tracts,* once relating Chaloner's speech to the Irish papers and the second time to the Scotch Papers. Both listings are wrongly catalogued as E362(11). In fact it is at E362(12).

44. *The great Champions of England: being a perfect List of the Lords and Commons that have stood right to this Parliament; and the general Officers, and Colonels of the Army,* [30 Jul.] 1646, 669.f.10(69).

45. Thomas Chaloner, *An Answer to the Scotch Papers*, 26 Oct. 1646, E361(3); *The Moderator in reply to Mr. Thomas Chaloners Speech*, 26 Oct. 1646, E362(12); *An Answer to severall Obiections made against Mr Thomas Chaloners Speech*, 26 Oct. 1646, E362(27).

46. Eyre, Rivington and Plomer, *A Transcript of the Registers of the Worshipful Company of Stationers, from 1640–1708 AD* (3 vols) (London, 1917), I, p. 252, 9 Nov. 1646, 'Entred under the hand of Master Mabbott, *An Answer to the Scotch Papers made in the house of Commons &c* by Tho: Challoner – vi[d].

47. Edward Hyde, Earl of Clarendon, *Clarendon: Selections from the History of the Rebellion* and *The Life by Himself*, ed. G. Huehns (Oxford, 1978 edn), p. 27.

48. [Henry Marten], *A Corrector of the Answerer of the Speech without Doores*, E364(9), also published with Tyler's imprimatur, as *A Resolve of the Person of the King*, Wing STC M824A; in reply to *An Answer to the Speech without Doores; or, Animadversions upon an unsafe Answer to the Scotch-papers*, E362(9); [Henry Marten], *An Vnhappy Game at Scotch and English*, [30 Nov.] 1646, E364(3), pp. 23–4; H. N. Brailsford, *The Levellers and the English Revolution* (Nottingham, 1976 edn) p. 131, suggests it is by the Leveller, Richard Overton, and the attribution was carried on by D. M. Wolfe, *Leveller Manifestos of the Puritan Revolution* (London, 1967), pp. 14–15. If so, Chaloner, Marten and Overton must all have been sitting around the same table as they jointly composed their contributions.

49. BL Add MSS 71532/ff.11–11[v].

50. To which Marten referred in *An Vnhappie Game*.

51. *CJ*, IV, p. 508, 14 Apr.1646; *CJ*, IV p. 731, 30 Nov. 1646; *Some Papers given in by the Commissioners of the Parliament of Scotland*, 29 Oct. 1646, E360(12); *An Vnhappie Game*, p. 5.

52. *Propositions for the Westerne Association, with the Westerne Intentions for their owne Preservation*, [19 Nov.] 1646, E362(8). The importance of these proposals is discussed in Chapter 3 below.

53. *A Declaration concerning the miserable sufferings of the Countrie under the Scots forces that quarter in the north of England certified by several letters from the inhabitants of Stainton*, [24 Oct.] 1646, London, by E.E., E358(18).

54. *Mercurius Civicus*, no. 179, 22–9 Oct. 1646, pp. 2447–8.

55. *The Petition and information of Joseph Hunscot, Stationer, to Parliament*, 10 Jun. 1646, E340(15); Luke Harruney, *A Reply to a Letter*, Animadvertor's Epistle; Joad Raymond (ed.), *Making the News: An Anthology of the Newsbooks of Revolutionary England, 1641–1660* (Windrush, Glouc., 1993).

56. [Edward Bowles] (attribution Thomason), *Manifest Truths, or an inversion of Truths Manifest, containing a Narration of the Proceedings of the Scottish Army*, [4 Jul.] 1646, E343(1), p. 71, quoting p. 128 of *Truths Manifest*.

57. [Marten], *A Corrector*, pp. 5, 7.

58. [Marten], *Vnhappie Game*, p. 5.

59. *CJ*, IV, p. 731, 30 Nov. 1646.

60. There was a considerable difference between a prince and a *'private man'*; or the holder of an office 'ruling in peace and justice' and 'one who hath beene long in actuall Warre against the *representative Bodies* of his two Kingdomes'.

61. *The Justification of a safe and wel-grounded Answer to the Scottish papers*, 23 Nov. 1646, E363(11), p. 11.

62. *The Justification*, p. 13. Continental states included Scotland, which had favoured the young James VI over his mother, Mary Stewart.

63. *The Justification*, pp. 11–12.

64. *The Justification*. pp. 5–6. See also [Marten], *Vnhappie game*.

65. For the debate on ancient constitutionalism, see J. P. Sommerville, *Politics and Ideology in England, 1603–1640* (London, 1986), pp. 89ff; J. G. A. Pocock, *The Ancient Constitution and the Feudal Law* (Cambridge, 1957; reissued 1987); Glenn Burgess, *The Politics of the Ancient Constitution: An Introduction to English Political Thought, 1603–1642* (London, 1992), pp. 156–67.

66. *An Answer to severall Obiectons*, p. 3, which also made reference to *Lex Rex* (p. 4).

67. Ludlow, *Memoirs*, I, p. 137.

68. *The Justification*, p. 10.

69. Thomas Chaloner and his brother, James, later MP for neighbouring Aldborough (Richmond, N. Yorks), were convinced that the crown's dealings with their father over the patent to manufacture alum around Guisborough, had deprived them of a considerable inheritance. The historian of the republic, Thomas May, was one friend who took part in the campaign to recover the mines: N. Yorks. Record Office, ZFM Alum Deeds Nos 1–5; William Page (ed.), *Victoria History of the County of York: North Riding* (2 vols) (London, 1968), II, p. 355; *The Justification*, p. 11.

70. The other members were William Pierrepont, Nathaniel Fiennes and Sir John Evelyn.

71. Thomas Westropp was a gentleman of Newham Hall, Cleveland, and was certainly, by 1650, a great friend (and creditor) of Henry Marten. Westropp and Marten knew each other as early as 1642; University of Leeds, Brotherton Collection, Marten Loder MSS (ML) 40/32^v; 43/unfol; 64/137; 64/145–7; 64/149; First series 1/unfol, articles of agreement 25 May 1664 between John Wildman and John Loder; George Marten Letters/2 and 9; *Victoria County History*, North Yorks, II, p. 266.

72. *CJ*, IV, p. 711. All the examples come from an area of about six square miles at the northern extremity of the North Yorkshire moors – Guisborough, Hemlington, Hutton Lowcross and Great Ayton. See also *Mercurius Civicus*, no. 180, 29 Oct.–5 Nov. 1646, E360(11), pp. 2433–4; *A Declaration concerning the miserable sufferings*, dated 13 Sep. 1646, published 24 Oct.; *A Continuation of Papers from the Scots Quarters*, printed by Leech, including a letter from M.R. in York, 3 Nov. 1646, pp. 2–4.

73. *A Remonstrance concerning the Misdemeanours of some of the Scots Souldiers in*

the County of Yorke, dated 20 Nov. 1646, printed 6 Dec. 1646, E365(9), presented to his worship Thomas Westropp of Newham, Yorks.

74. CJ, IV, p. 311, 25 Oct. 1645.

75. CJ, IV, p. 311, 25 Oct. 1645; CJ, IV, p. 508, 14 Apr. 1646.

76. The Kingdomes Weekly Intelligencer, no. 173, 3–10 Nov. 1646, E361(8), p. 295.

77. [John Musgrave], Yet another Word to the Wise: shewing that the lamentable grievances of the Parliaments friends in Cumberland and Westmerland, [1 Oct.] 1646, E355(25).

78. [Musgrave], Yet another Word, pp. 12–13.

79. David Stevenson, Revolution and Counter-revolution in Scotland, 1644–1651 (London, 1977), p. 44.

80. CJ, IV, p. 682, 3 Oct. 1646.

81. [Musgrave], Yet another Word, p. 27.

82. [Musgrave], Yet another Word, p. 36.

83. It is John Adamson's assertion that the impetus for this proposal came from peers such as Saye, Wharton and Northumberland, who employed MPs in a client relationship. Despite impressive research, this author remains to be convinced: J. S. A. Adamson, 'The Peerage in Politics', PhD (Cantab), 1986. For just a flavour of the furore which followed, the argument is extended in 'The baronial context of the English Civil War', Royal Historical Society Transactions, 5th ser. 40 (1990), 121–51, and in the debate with Mark Kishlansky, chiefly carried out in the pages of the Historical Journal. For Vane and the Heads, see Violet A. Rowe, Sir Henry Vane the Younger: A Study in Political and Administrative History (London, 1970), pp. 97–100.

84. Holles, Memoirs, in Maseres, Select Tracts, I, p. 285.

85. CJ, V, p. 311.

86. GCD, p. 326; Ian Gentles, The New Model Army in England, Scotland and Ireland, 1645–1653 (Oxford, 1992), pp. 181–4, discusses both religious and constitutional provisions, but the lead is usually taken from Gardiner's concern with the divisions between Presbyterians and Independents; Gardiner, History, III, p. 330 passim.

87. GCD, pp. 21–2.

88. CJ, V, p. 312, 22 Sep. 1647.

89. Clarke MSS 1XVI; Clarke Papers, I, p. 224; A cal to all the souldiers of the Armie, by the free peple of England, [29 Oct.] 1647, E412(10).

90. Historians remain unclear how tellers were chosen, and therefore whether the fact that they were telling for or against a motion constituted an accurate judgement of their political position. In view of the words of Rainsborough at the Army Council's debates, while Marten was acting as his replacement teller in the Commons, there can be little doubt that both men had a strong commitment to the defeat of the resolutions in the House. See the following chapter for a discussion of the Putney debates.

91. *CJ*, V, p. 314.
92. Those in favour of these clauses numbered seventy.
93. *CJ*, V, p. 315.
94. *LJ*, IX, p. 541. The militia was to be in parliament's control for twenty years. Charles' declarations against the parliament were to be revoked, as were the honours he had bestowed since the outbreak of war. Finally, the parliament was to have the right to adjourn itself, including to a place of safety outside Westminster. The emergence of four bills meant that they were first ratified by the English parliament alone, before being negotiated with the Scottish Commissioners. Asking the king to assent to the bills also meant that he had ratified the clauses before receiving them again as part of a personal treaty.
95. May, *Breviary*, in Maseres, *Select Tracts*, I, pp. 107–8.
96. For his parliamentary management during the Rump, see Blair Worden, *The Rump Parliament* (Cambridge, 1974), pp. 29–30, and his strong presence on the Council of State in 1651, pp. 280–1.
97. The *Engagement*, 26 Dec. 1647, reproduced in *GCD*, pp. 347–52. The king was prepared to sign the *Engagement* having been assured 'that their intentions are real for preservation of His Majesty's person and authority according to their allegiance, and no ways to diminish his just power and greatness'. As soon as Charles was free to attend the parliament in person, he would confirm the Solemn League and Covenant.
98. Hence the feuds between, in particular, Henry Marten and William Ball on the one side and David Jenkins, Sir John Maynard and William Prynne on the other: *Vindication of Judge Jenkins*, [29 Apr.] 1647, E386(6); H[enry] P[arker], *An Answer to the poysonous sedicious Paper of Mr. David Jenkins*, [12 May] 1647, E386(14); *Salus Populi, solus Rex*, [17 Oct.] 1648, E467(39); William Ball, *The Power of Kings discussed*, [30 Jan.] 1649, E540(21); [John Lilburne], *A Plea, or Protest*, 16 Mar. 1649, E432(18); [Henry Marten], *Prynne against Prynne* [26 Jan.] 1649, E540(6); Sir John Maynard, *Speech in answer to Mr Martyn*, Jan. 1648, E422(32), and many others.
99. Edmund Prideaux, MP for Lyme Regis, provides an interesting potential geographical link with Wroth, recruiter MP for neighbouring Bridgwater. Almost half way between the two boroughs was Curry Mallet, home of John Pyne, extremist MP for Dorset and another of those who incurred the wrath of a Presbyterian polemicist, in this case, Walker. See below, Chapter 3, and Sarah Barber, ' "A bastard kind of militia": localism and tactics in the second civil war', in Ian Gentles, J. S. Morrill and Blair Worden (eds), *Soldiers, Writers and Statesmen of the English Revolution* (Cambridge, forthcoming 1998).
100. David Underdown, *Pride's Purge: Politics in the Puritan Revolution* (London, 1971), pp. 31–2, 64, 69, 74; Thomas G. Barnes, *Somerset, 1625–1640* (Cambridge, Mass., 1961), pp. 15–16; David Underdown, *Somerset in the Civil War and Interregnum* (Newton Abbot, Devon, 1973).

Prideaux was a Presbyterian in religious practice, but a war-party stalwart in political terms, and had skilfully managed the electoral politics of the south-west until the political Presbyterians managed to remove him as Commissioner for the Great Seal in 1646.

101. Clement Walker, *Relations and Observations, Historical and Politick, upon the Parliament, begun Anno. Dom. 1640* (The History of Independency) (London, 1648), pp. 69–70. Tophet was the place of burning in Jerusalem, where the filth of the city was incinerated. It was also the dumping ground for the ashes of false images and idols which had been destroyed by the righteous – Isaiah 30: 33: 'For Tophet is ordained of old; yea, for the king it is prepared; he hath made it deep and large: the pile thereof is fire and much wood; the breath of the lord, like a stream of brimstone, doth kindle it.'

102. See *Lex Talionis*, p. 9; see above p. 17.

103. May, *Breviary*, p. 108.

104. *CJ*, V, pp. 415–16.

105. Glenn Burgess, *The Politics of the Ancient Constitution: An Introduction to English Political Thought, 1603–1642* (London, 1992); Glenn Burgess, 'The divine right of kings reconsidered', *EHR* CVII (1992) 837–61.

106. Nigel Smith, *Literature and Revolution in England, 1640–1660* (Yale, 1994), pp. 9–10.

107. Annabel Patterson, 'The egalitarian giant, representations of justice in history/literature', *JBS*, 31 (1992) 97–132.

108. Harro Höpfl and Martyn P. Thompson, 'The history of contract as a motif in political thought', *Am Hist Rev*, 84.4 (1979) 919–44, pp. 941–3.

109. *GCD*, p. 356.

110. Ludlow, *Memoirs*, I, p. 182. May's description of the declaration sounds more like that of Ludlow: *Breviary*, p. 112.

111. This was John Sadler, a lawyer whose fidelity to the Commonwealth was rewarded after 1649 with an offer of the post of Chief Justice of Munster, which he declined. He preferred his place at Chancery; Ludlow, *Memoirs*, I, p. 182n.

112. Austin Woolrych debates the point which Milton regarded as a turnaround in English politics. He concedes that this Vote of No Addresses was one such, though Milton could have been referring to the period after Pride's Purge: Austin Woolrych, 'The date of the digression in Milton's *History of Britain*', in Richard Ollard and Pamela Tudor Craig (eds), *For Veronica Wedgwood these: Studies in Seventeenth-Century History* (London, 1986), pp. 217–46, pp. 228–9, and 'Dating Milton's *History of Britain*', *HJ*, 36.4 (1993) 929–43; W. R. Parker, *Milton: A Biography* (2 vol) (Oxford, 1968); D. M. Wolfe, *Complete Prose Works of John Milton* (8 vols.) (New Haven, Conn., 1953–82), V, pp. 129–30.

113. [Marten], *A Corrector*, p. 5.

114. *The Justification*, pp. 11, 12.

115. J. S. Morrill, 'Charles I, tyranny and the English Civil War', in *The Nature of the English Revolution* (London, 1993), pp. 285–306, who notes

that the charges of tyranny laid at Charles' door at his trial in 1649 were a reflection of statements made as far back as 1642. I would argue that, from the vantage point of 1648, the charges went even further than this, charging Charles with a tyrannous character, evident even before he acceded.

116. Höpfl and Thompson, 'History of contract', pp. 921–6.

117. Marten, *Parliaments Proceedings*, p. 10.

118. See Marten's comments on the Newcastle Propositions in the House, reported by Ludlow, *Memoirs*, I, pp. 142–3.

119. Machiavelli counselled that although one had to learn both pacifist and belligerent ways to achieve one's aims, war was the more honourable, because winning another's friendship often involved fraud: Machiavelli, *Discourses*, III.2; Garver, 'After Virtù', p. 196.

120. Marten, *Independency*, p. 17.

121. The copy which exists in the Thomason collection is a manuscript copy which Thomason has transcribed in his own hand: 'said to be Sr John Maynard's for wych he was turned out of the House'.

122. [Sir John Maynard], 'A Speech in Answer to Mr Martyn', [Jan.] 1648, E422(32).

123. John Lisle MP in his speech on the letters captured at Naseby, *Three Speeches spoken at a Common-Hall*, p. 6.

124. Burgess, *Politics of the Ancient Constitution*; Marten, *Independency*, p. 27 – 'reall and judisdictive (boundaries), not personal and titulary'.

125. Marten, *Independency*, p. 14. The intervention of the Scots gave Marten's interpretation of the balance between the one and the many a new twist: '[a] King is but one Master and therefore likely to sit lighter upon our shoulders then a whole Kingdom, and if he should grow so heavy as cannot wel be born, he may be sooner gotten off then they' (p. 17). Although ostensibly his target was the Scots and his purpose was to show that they were even worse than the king, he had nevertheless set up the position in which the single person of the king was balanced against the interests of the whole nation. Chaloner, *An Answer*. 'For either wee must take him as a King or a Subject, since betwixt them two there is no medium, as a King wee cannot take him, unlesse wee should commit Treason against our naturall Prince, and subject ourselves to any but to him' (p. 7).

2

'A Mere Man': Charles Levelled

In Chapter 1 we followed the political action taken by a small number of radical MPs in the Commons which developed into a critique of monarchy. Each leap by which one point was established and the next developed was not always logically consequent, but could be made to sound like a rational progression, and at each point an element in its justification was that the next step was made necessary by the oppressive, arbitrary and tyrannical actions of opponents. A parallel process was discernable within extra-parliamentary political agitation, and the progress of these arguments is here traced within the texts of Leveller writings and the practical agency of Levellers within the New Model Army.

The chapter describes the activities of a group which Austin Woolrych called the 'populist faction' – a term full of resonance, since it describes both an agenda and the means of securing it.[1] Several themes, both tactical and ideological, recur. Within the Commons, the army and outside, a small minority harried, embarrassed and chided the majority, leaping over the majority position by claiming to represent the people as a whole. They presented themselves as the champions of the people, whose voice the establishment tried to stifle. The parliamentary campaign was about freedom to speak out in response to particular political issues: the Leveller campaign concentrated on the freedom to disseminate ideas using the vehicle of pamphlet and broadsheet literature.[2] Individuals expressed ideas which the majority censored because it believed them to be extreme. The attempt to silence them was used by the radicals as further evidence that court, church, parliament or army was muffling the voice of the people. At first, the Levellers used the presses to circulate ideas and publicise their campaigns. Later, civilians discovered issues of common cause with rank-and-file soldiers and channelled their grievances through the command structure of the New Model Army. The officers, or grandees, denounced the populists 'as a form'd and setled partie distinct and divided from others'.[3]

That the construction of the critique of monarchy followed a similar path is illustrated in the Leveller tract, *Vox Plebis*. Writing at the end of 1646, the author of *Vox Plebis* took advantage of parliament being in session – 'during which time the Presse ought to be free and open' – to express an opinion about the structure of revolution. The argument outlined in the text mirrored the practical campaigns of the ultra-Independents.[4] The premise was that a strong polity depended on the virtue of its magistrates. There was 'no better way to make the Subjects of a State good, and to incline them to virtue, then that those that sit at the Helm of that State . . . should hold forth cleare examples of piety and justice, in their own lives and actions'.[5] Should the magistrate prove immoral, the example outlined in I Samuel 15:33 justified inquisition after blood on behalf of the oppressed people.[6] Thirdly, it posited a contractual relationship, in which the laws relating to the liberties of the people as a whole were balanced against those which concerned the life of one individual. In the final stage of the argument, should a ruler commit an action which broke the law:

> at that very instant they begin to lose their State. For by so doing, the Governours draw the *Odium* of the people upon them, and incite the people to find out and invent wayes unusuall, and of innovation, to free themselves from their oppressors . . . all the Lawes that are made in favour of liberty, spring first from the disagreement of the people with their Governours . . . For the people bite more fiercely after they have recovered their liberty, then while they have continually maintained it: And having once gotten possession of their ancient rights, they will watch them so carefully, and with such strength and vigour, as that they will hardly be surprized again, or their rights any more wrested from them.[7]

Vox Plebis does not shy away from using the term republic, citing with approbation historical examples of republican structures, nor of warning arbitrary rulers of the tenacity with which an oppressed people would cling to the freedom which those structures held out to them.[8]

Vox Plebis is clearly part of the Leveller canon of tracts, though it has received less attention from scholars than other pamphlets and there is some debate about the author. It was most likely composed by John Lilburne and Marchamont Nedham, imprisoned together during 1646.[9] Having refused to take the Covenant and having been excluded from the New Model Army, Lilburne's time was freed for a considerable career as a pamphleteering self-publicist.[10] An attack on the lukewarm prosecution of the war by the Earl of Manchester in June 1646 resulted in arraignment at the bar of the Lords and imprisonment for contempt.[11] Captivity could be turned to advantage, providing both time to write and a focus for outrage. It encouraged others to campaign on the prisoners' behalf and offered a practical example of the way in which, it was argued, wider English liberties were being suppressed.

Vox Plebis was one of a considerable number of tracts in which a discursive history of English liberties in a general sense was incorporated into an account of Lilburne's personal struggle for the liberty to be free of imprisonment. Lilburne's chief ally during 1646 was Richard Overton, also subsequently imprisoned in Newgate, who complained at Lilburne's imprisonment in July in *A Remonstrance of Many Thousand Citizens*.[12] While Henry Marten warned his English audience to question more scrupulously the activities of the Scots, he chose to remind them of the fate of 'Lieutenant Col. *John Lilburne* and Mr. *Overton* the two prerogative *Archers* of *England*' who had already landed in jail for having done so.[13] He probably referred to *An Arrow against all Tyrants*, in which Overton had addressed a specific admonition to Marten. Marten chaired a committee which examined the Levellers' claims of illegal imprisonment, because they had been accused and judged by the Lords, and not by a jury of their peers, according to common law.[14]

Press censorship, imprisonment, and infringements of common law were abuses of the liberties of the Leveller leaders in particular, and represented the means by which England's liberties had been more generally debased. It is easy to avoid an attempt at a definition of 'English liberties', and its cousin, '*our Birthrights*, (that is the power of our lives, estates and liberties'.[15] Both phrases could assume all the qualities of a slogan, and lack precise articulation.[16] Birthrights or liberties were portrayed as entitlements which, although intrinsically due to every English man,[17] had become so debased by the 1640s that they had to be 'recovered'.[18] Hence, there was always a form of authority against which to kick, which could be admonished and pilloried for having usurped the rights due to the ordinary person. It was the usurpation of birthrights which explained the roots of hierarchy and status. The definition of the institutions of oppression could vary. It depended on the nature and circumstances of the attack, and the particular instance in which people or institutions demonstrated that their power was the result of privilege or prerogative and not moral worth or representativeness. Although the force of the evidence here will be directed at kings, there was a whole gamut of potentially oppressive institutions, and it was possible to envisage situations in which kings had to be tolerated in order to counterbalance a more immediate threat to liberty.

When a king (or other institutions) presumed upon the people's rights, he placed monarchy outside the naturally mutual, trusting relationship which ideally existed between government and governed. Institutions which operated outside this representative relationship of mutual trust were part of an arbitrary imposition. The system which functioned in the 1640s was denounced by the Levellers because 'if We want a *Law*, Wee must awaite till the *King* and *Lords* assent; if an Ordinance, then Wee must waite till the *Lords* assent', while 'knowing their assent to be meerly formall, (*as having no root in the choice of the People, from whom the Power that is just must be derived*'.[19] 'Meerly formall', in this context, meant formalistic, externally constructed and not fundamental – neither necessary nor sufficient. King, lords and clergy were alien cankers on a sound English rootstock, which sought to seize power for themselves by imposing their will on the people. As such, they needed to be shut out of the system for daring to breach the fundamental freedoms of the sovereign people. Because the power of institutions such as kingship was formalistic, exercised over the people without their consent, it was by definition alien, tyrannous and must be maintained by coercion.[20]

The possession of, and recourse to, a formal element in the constitutional process was denounced as irrational. The system in the 1640s relied on faulty logic. Having established that a law could not be passed without the consent of king and lords, and yet that those institutions were not fundamental, the people were nevertheless required to 'importune their assent, which implies a most grosse absurditie'. The English people, taken as a whole, could not delegate their power to any institution or individual of equal or greater power than themselves. To talk as if it were possible to abrogate authority to a superior was illogical and absurd. In order to reverse the process in which alien accretions onto the English constitutional system were made sovereign, sovereignty had to be returned to the people. The traditional hierarchical pyramid had to be demolished, and replaced by a constitutional system which was harmonious, balanced and strong because it was a self-contained, circular construction. Alien bodies would be frozen out. All that was necessary to government was the people, who directly elected their representatives – '[w]ee are your Principalls, and you our Agents'[21] – and representatives who were directly accountable to the people. Indeed, they were part of the people. Overton's reference to the English people's 'owne' House of Commons implied that they both owned it and it was a part of them.

The process by which the English constitution became bastardised by hierarchy, coercion, and formalism was demonstrated by historical example, which, with its appeal to patriotism, invested attempts to explain the Englishman's loss of his birthrights with a popular and emotive edge. 'Native' rights had been stolen away by William of Normandy's usurpation in 1066. Since the Conquest, the people who governed the English and the laws by which they did so were deemed to be alien French imports. The English people were bowed under the Norman Yoke.[22] Six centuries later, the alien character of the magistracy was little diminished, sometimes even further corrupted by the passage of time, because '(t)he History of our Fore-fathers since they were Conquered by the Normans, doth manifest that this Nation hath been held in bondage all along ever since by the policies and force of the Officers of Trust in the Common-wealth, amongst whom, wee always esteemed Kings the chiefest'.[23] The single, unlawful action represented by the Conquest set in motion a chain of oppressions, which Lilburne believed ought to reveal

> from how *wicked, bloudy, triviall, base, and tyrannicall a Fountain our gratious Soveraignes, and most excellent Majesties of England* have sprung; namely, from the Spring of a *Bastard, of poore condition*, by the *Mothers side*, and from the pernitious springs of Robbery, Pyracie, violence, and Murder, &c. Howsoever, fabulous Writers, strive . . . to abuse the credulity of after Ages, with Heroicall, or miraculous beginnings, that surely if it be rightly considered, there will none dote upon those kind of *Monsters, Kings;* but *Knaves, Fools, Tyrants, or Monopolizers,* or *unjust wretched persons,* that must of necessity have their *Prerogative* to rule over all their *wickednesses.*[24]

We are in the midst of a repeating historical pattern. A king of dubious moral virtue, by committing a single illegal act, set consequences in train which illuminated the immoral behaviour of subsequent rulers.

Such emphasis on native English rights gave rise to a tendency for Leveller demands to be parochial rather than universalist. What constituted foreign influence was interpreted with latitude but was invariably to be resisted. Something un-English could be direct and obvious, such as the call for a simplified law code, easily comprehended by those who were expected to abide by it rather than those who implemented it, and written in the vernacular.[25] In a broader interpretation, the recovery of institutions, laws and feelings of Englishness provided a rallying cry, by which the 'true' cause was that followed by a patriot. Those who disagreed with a position were revealed to be unpatriotic and therefore not truly concerned with the interests of the people. John Hare, who published, towards the end of 1647, *Plaine English to our wilfull bearers with Normanisme*, attacked those who would continue to negotiate with Charles, because they would leave England under 'the slavery of an unjust, disgraceful, pretended, Conquest'.[26] When the soldiers of the New Model Army failed to comply with the Presbyterian-dominated Houses in their demand that they disband, Lilburne commended the forces for 'refusing to serve the Arbitrary power of the State and agreeing together as English men, to stand upon Principles of Right and Freedome'.[27]

The problem with Norman Yoke theory was that, as well as demonstrating a continuous line of bastardy and arbitrary government, it could also be used to show that although William of Normandy was a conqueror, his rule was subsequently ratified by the people. It was this act of ratification which was the demarcation of the contractual nature of government. The people could choose to withdraw their approval from a monarch should the monarch act in a way which destroyed the bond of trust which the ratification implied. The people had given their voluntary consent to the government, and could therefore exercise dissent. A series of orations, which the Elizabethan Jesuit, Robert Parsons, had published in 1594 to justify 'the power of Parliament, to proceed against their king for misgovernment', seemed appropriate to be reissued in January 1648, because Parsons had shown that after William's victory

> God prospered his pretence, and hath confirmed his of-fspring [sic] in the Crown of England more than 500 yeares together so as now acc[o]unting from the death of King Edmond I consider unto this man, we shall find . . . in lesse than 50. yeares, that 5. or 6 Kings were made in England one after another, by only authority and approbation of the Commonwealth contrary to the ordinary course of [l]ineall sucession by propiquity of blood.[28]

Overton's *Remonstrance* rationalised the historical rule of kings, however unsavoury, because they had been accepted by the people's consent. Original kingship was an office of trust, albeit an alien one. John Lilburne agreed. The king had been historically entrusted with the protection of people's lives and property, a privilege which the people could withdraw from an individual king, just as they had granted it.[29] In history, the revocation of consent had resulted in the deposition of English monarchs.[30] John Lilburne employed the person/office distinction, '*Charles Stewart* as *Charles Stewart* [was] different from the King as King'. Charles Stuart was a 'meer man'.[31] As a man, he had acted illegally and should suffer the appropriate punishment, but his actions were exercised under the prerogative and privileges of a king. When he issued commissions under the power of array, to counter the Militia Ordinance, he had upset the principle that '[the militia] were for (the people's) preservation' – and thus 'C.R. ought to be executed'.[32]

The events of 1066 demonstrated both that all kings after William were usurpers and illegitimate in themselves, or that they were legitimate, but limited by the continuing approbation of the people. The Norman Yoke theory was employed as evidence that William's rule was both agreed and not agreed. It therefore demonstrated both a line of continuous tyranny, which could only be ended by cutting off the Norman line, or a conditional relationship between people and governor which could be rescinded in the light of a particular action which broke their contract. One interpretation of Norman Yoke theory could justify the deposition of a particular ruler: another could

be used to cast doubt on an entire dynasty, though both the agreement
and disagreement arguments could be employed to argue for Charles'
deposition. This absurdity was highlighted by Leveller petitioners in
August 1648, who noted that the 'moderated sovereignty that springs
from and is the exercise of a Conquest' was an impossibility. Better to
erase traces of the conquest at the roots so the 'Bands of this our
Nationall Captivity' had to be 'dissolved'.[33]

As Machiavelli had noted, the passage of time revealed the previously
disguised wickedness of one's rulers.[34] Overton's explanation of the
crisis of the 1640s was that it was the result of a process of degeneration,
in which the corruption of notions of governmental trust were finally
revealed. The people had placed their trust in a chimera, because kings
corrupted their understanding by 'infusing false Principles'.[35] To take
the peace negotiations of 1646 as an example, the veil which obscured
people's genuine perception of their interests was Charles' association
with the Scottish Commissioners. Marten published *An Vnhappie game*
to dispel 'Scotch Mists and their Fogs; their sayings and gaine-sayings
. . . their King-craft present design'.[36] The Scots would find 'that *wilfull
murthers* must have another reckoning; maugre all *King craft, Clergy craft,
and Court-craft* in the world'.[37] *A Remonstrance* was concerned with the
way in which monarchs had disguised their oppressions with 'their
Policies and Court Arts . . . King-waste and delusion'.[38] This was
kingship as a devious ruse by which the honest people were cozened,
entranced or dazzled. Monarchy was 'but the gilded name for
Tyranny'.[39] By casting doubt on the statements of king, Presbyterians
or Scottish Commissioners, the populists portrayed themselves as the
real patriots with a mission to reveal the truth.[40]

On the other hand, although kingship was an anachronism in that it
carried a false, formalistic image, in fact behind the veil lay real and
oppressive powers capable of further corrupting the genuine trust
which should exist between the people and their officers. While
kingship contrived to keep the people in ignorance and delusion, it
simultaneously oppressed them in a brutally obvious way. Overton
drew attention to the '16. Yeeres reigne' which was 'one continued act
of the breach of the Law'[41] and Marten to the Newcastle Propositions
which enabled Charles to escape 'scot-free that for sixteene yeares
without intermission brake the Law'. Charles combined obvious acts of
tyranny with disguise and underhandedness. He was 'craft and
cruelty'.[42] The history of the Norman Conquest provided an explanation for the paradox in which kings were both of a pair of seemingly
incompatible characteristics. The fact that two accounts of the consequences of the Conquest appeared to be in tension could, ironically,

reconcile the confusion caused by the people's *post hoc* rationalisation of the usurper. According to Lucy Hutchinson, wife of John, the recruiter MP for Nottinghamshire, William the Bastard was able to transform his rule into the legitimate government of William I of Normandy, 'partly by violence, partly by falsehood'.[43]

Having explained Charles' character and the nature of his actions, the argument moved on to question kings in general. As the accounts of English history had shown, kings who made war, impoverished previously affluent people and turned them into 'slaves' had a long ancestry and 'none but a King could doe so great intollerable mischiefes'.[44] Within the rhetoric of Leveller writing, Charles was deployed as a representative of the universal nature of kingship. He was a particularly graphic example of its general corruption. The Commons should

> declare and set forth *King Charles* his wickednesse openly before the world, and withall, to shew the intollerable inconyeniences [*sic*] of having a *Kingly Government* . . . and so to declare *King Charles* an enemy, and to publish your resolution, never to have any more, but to acquite us of so great a charge and trouble forever . . . and untill this be done, wee shall not thinke our selves well dealt withall in this originall of all Oppressions, to wit *Kings*.[45]

Here was the last step of the argument outlined in *Vox Plebis*, in which the crime of Charles Stuart was transferred to all kings, and the people having wrested back their liberties would not relinquish them to kings again. '[O]ur Lawes, Lives and Liberties are more pretious, then to be prostitute to the exhorbitant boundlesse *will* of any mortall *Steuart* under the Sun,' said Marten; 'wee are neither such fools nor such cowards, or yet such Traitors to our selves or to our posterities, to our Lawes or to our Liberties, as after we by the blood of us and our children have gained a conquest over that Arbitrary faction so basely to returne like Sowes to the mire, or Dogges to the vomit againe.'[46]

In order for reconstructed rights to be protected from the mire they had to be safeguarded for the future. This could be achieved through a process of identification and codification, by which the people's rights would be laid out and enshrined within a universally binding constitutional statement. Rights would be recovered back to a point at which English liberties could be encapsulated in the 'foundations of freedom'.[47] The foundation point may always have been obscured, its origins beyond record or memory, but recourse to the language of foundation protected its users against the charge of innovation, in itself a form of constitutional usurpation. It also created the impression that these rights or liberties were not, in fact, privileges awarded by the authorities or graciously granted by kings. The foundations rested in natural law, the law of reason, on which all other laws were founded. Reason was a 'natural radical principle' and 'necessity is a law above all laws'.[48]

During 1646 to the summer of 1647, Leveller writings revealed arguments about kingship which moved from the specific failings of Charles Stuart to the historical malign agency of kings. The Levellers' statements outlined general principles. They made some very specific references to abuses which needed to be reformed. They used their own camapigns against imprisonment as a peg on which to hang more abstract arguments. It is striking, however, that they rarely mentioned the specific context in which Charles had triggered this situation. The almost total absence of references to England having so recently been at war is astonishing.[49] They railed against kings, lords the Scots and the failures of the House of Commons. The language of England's liberties was abstracted, generalised and of far greater import than the specific agents responsible for countering this latest, short-term threat.

At first, the soldiers of the parliamentarian army constituted an infringement of the people's liberty in themselves. Ordinary people were taken away from their livings and their families and pressed into armed service. After the cessation, the soldiers were still billeted on ordinary people, who were obligated to provide free quarter, food and fodder. The soldiers stole sheep and goods and their behaviour was coarse.[50] The New Model Army under Sir Thomas Fairfax and the numerous auxiliary and garrison regiments dotted around the country attracted widespread unpopularity, not because they expressed minority or extreme political views, but because they continued to drain over-exploited and wasted land. We have already noted the complaints from the northern border counties at the cost and behaviour of the Covenanting army. William Ball, a close friend of Henry Marten, who helped him to the Abingdon seat in 1646,[51] reported the hardships of the people of his native Berkshire at the mercy of the soldiers. The army required exactions 'w^{c}h under the most tirannicall tyme of the Enemy was nothing so badd'.[52] Ball worried that the actions of the soldiers would undermine support for the parliamentary cause. Many had made material commitments to secure their liberties and would find the presence of the army counter-productive. Andrew Pottinger of Woolhampton, Berkshire – 'a freeholder of 60^{li} p Ann a very cordiall Man for the Parliam^t' – was killed by soldiers as he tried to prevent them from stealing his sheep. Ball reminded the Commons that the unpopularity which continued billeting and free quarter heaped on the heads of the soldiers was easily transferred to those who kept them in service.

Criticism of the beleaguered parliament came from several angles, including the soldiers themselves. Short of money for pay and provisions, the parliament debated the army's future in terms of either disbandment or service in Ireland. Instead, the army's campaign to achieve redress of their material grievances became a means by which the soldiers were politicised. They directed their frustration towards their ultimate masters. In the spring of 1647 the soldiers and officers of the New Model Army addressed a petition to parliament, which they entitled *A Vindication of the Officers of the Army.*[53] Cromwell and Skippon also passed on to Speaker Lenthall *Apologie of the Common Soldiers of Sir Thomas Fairfaxes Army*, a document from the rank and file.[54] The latter was composed by sixteen agents, elected by the New Model cavalry, who described themselves as 'agitating in behalf of their several regiments'.[55] The agitators were grass-roots campaigners within the army itself, elected by the rank and file.

Agitation for the redress of the army's grievances – arrears, disbandment and indemnity – alarmed the Presbyterians in parliament and fuelled their rush to try to disband or disperse the New Model. It also caused unease within the army itself. An army which prided itself on godly discipline now seemed susceptible to mutiny. For most of 5 June 1647, Fairfax addressed a rendezvous at Kentford Heath, near Newmarket. As a result, he staved off a mutiny within the ranks, and encouraged acclaim of a united declaration of the army, its *Solemn Engagement*. Officers and soldiers alike declared their refusal to disband until their grievances had been met, although the statement was keen to distance the army from a factional political standpoint.[56] There was not necessarily going to be an army line, nor military intervention in civil affairs. This was essentially a compromise. It was also dissimulation after the fact. The New Model's claim to such consideration was that it was, in a phrase which was to become famous, not a 'mere mercenary army'.[57] As such, it assumed a position which potentially set it apart from common citizens, who were either pressed into armed service or who had soldiers billeted on them. The godly forces of the righteous army operated at a distance from the ordinary people from whom they had sprung and claimed for themselves an additional and special reason to be the recipients of rights.

The politicisation of the army provided a mechanism by and a political arena in which Leveller principles could be advanced. At a point at which the generality of the people could find a sense of common cause with the soldiers, it proved possible to unite the campaigns for civilian and military rights. A mutual recognition of their aims and targets fostered cooperation between London Levellers and the agents or agitators in the army. When army representatives were able to channel their material grievances with

the more ideological concerns of Leveller discourse, civil disturbance
became revolution, or at least it became possible to turn revolutionary
ideas into a plausible organised movement.[58]

Political organisation between army, Levellers and sympathisers was
relatively wide and well drilled. Henry Marten kept the key to the cipher
by which they communicated.[59] This period proved so formative for
Marten and his nephew-by-marriage, Wildman, that they continued to
use their cipher letters, O and A, throughout their lives, and described
their respective partners using the same letters in lower case.[60] As well as
specifically named individuals, there remained a faction referred to as
'ffreinds in generall', which corresponded on matters political, military
and possibly religious.[61] A list of allies reveals the following names:
William Walwyn and John Wildman, the Levellers, Colonel Thomas
Rainsborough, Colonel Robert Overton, brother of the Leveller,
Richard, Colonel William Eyres,[62] and 'Petter', who was most likely
the Oxfordshire gentleman, Maximilian Petty.[63] In addition, there were
cipher letters for the cavalry regiments of Fairfax, Cromwell, Fleetwood,
Harrison, Tomlinson, Rich, Scrope and Horton, and the artillery
regiments of Fairfax, Deane, Pride, Hewson, Barkstead, Constable,
Hammond, Lilburne, Skippon, Overton and Sir Hardress Waller.
There was also a list of hated institutions and enemies.[64]

The more generalised complaints of the commonalty and the horrors
and hardships of military life were channelled into a united rhetoric of
anger in the composite production, *The Case of the Armie truly Stated*.
The campaigns of the civilian Levellers and the New Model soldiers
began to dovetail because the behaviour of the Presbyterian faction in
parliament gave the soldiers a target for outrage which matched that of
the people at large.[65] The army signatories of the *Case* came from agents
of five regiments, who presented 'grievances, dissatisfactions, and
desires' of both 'Commoners and Soldiers'. The soldiers complained
of parliament's tardiness in settling their grievances: arrears of pay,
indemnity and provision for soldiers' families. Furthermore, the soldiers
felt the need to defend themselves against the charge of presumption
because they had entered the political arena in daring to petition at all.
They were a minority, which felt denied access to free speech and
representation by the attempts to stifle their just demands. The civilian
case was made by John Wildman.[66] In 1647, he was a fiery twenty-four
year old. He detailed grievances against 'arbitrary Committees, iniustice
in the Law, Tythes, Monopolies, and restraint of free trade, burthen-
some Oathes, inequalitie of Assessments, Excize', though the confusion
remained over whether the soldiers' case was separate and special,
parallel or identical with that of the people at large.[67]

One of the ways in which the rendezvous at Kentford Heath and the *Solemn Engagement* had staved off a possible mutiny, was by establishing a forum in which the army, broadly defined, could discuss the political settlement. This enlarged Council of War would welcome contributions from soldiers, officers and lay members, in itself a physical demonstration of the ways in which the army sought to re-establish itself as an integral component of the people and to speak on their behalf.[68] It was within this remarkably open arena that a meeting took place at Putney, in November 1647, to debate the peace process. Three documents were tabled at the start of the debate, attempts to pre-form the shape of the discussion. The agents arrived with *The Case of the Armie Truly Stated*, and its follow-up and rationalised cousin *An Agreement of the People*. Representatives of the army establishment – its senior officers or grandees – tabled their own peace formula, the *Heads of the Proposals*, which was being promoted through the ranks, most prominently by soldiers of Particular Baptist congregations.[69]

The *Agreement* was a short, punchy document, often described as England's first written constitution.[70] It called for the dissolution of the current parliament, to be succeeded by biennial, sovereign parliaments elected on a revised franchise. Parliament would implement the *Agreement* and thereby establish and codify the foundations of free-dom. These included both freedoms which emerged specifically out of the war – indemnity and an end to impressment – and broader freedoms, such as liberty of conscience and equality before the law. Its structure reveals a careful and deliberate intent to tie the interests of rank-and-file soldiers to those of common civilians. The following passage opened the justificatory statement attached to the *Agreement*:

> For your sakes, our friends, estates and lives, have been deare to us; for your safety and freedom we have cheerfully indured hard Labours and run most desperate hazards, and in comparison to your peace and freedome we neither doe nor ever shall value our dearest bloud and wee professe, our bowells are and have been troubled, and our hearts pained within us, in seeing & considering that you have been so long bereaved of these fruits and ends of all our labours and hazards, wee cannot but sympathize with you in your miseries and oppressions. It's grief and vexation of heart to us; to receive your meate or moneyes, whilst you have no advantage, nor yet the foundations of your peace and freedom surely layed.[71]

The descriptors – your, our, we, you – alert us to the clever and sophisticated use of language which incorporated the concerns of the soldiers with those of the civilian population.[72] The soldiers had shed their blood for the people's safety but their labours had not yet produced the desired result of the people's liberty. The need to make the fight of the rank-and-file soldier seem worthwhile, therefore, was intimately bound up with the ability of both groups to secure peace and liberty, by the process of universal subscription to the constitutional blueprint outlined in the *Agreement*.[73]

The *Agreement* was therefore a statement of the unity and sovereignty of the people as a whole and the equity between each individual member of the common weal.[74] The foundations of freedom which had been outlined in *The Case* would be 'setled unalterably' by the *Agreement*, through the mechanism of universal subscription.[75] This ensured that the people who constituted the electorate and those specifically elected to magistracy were one and the same, and despite election, remained of equal status. It bound together those who swore to the *Agreement* and those who implemented it, universalising the contract of trust represented by government. It made a constitutional statement sovereign in England, erecting a set of fundamental legal principles above all of the flawed individuals who comprised the common weal. It guaranteed the 'clearnes, certaintie, sufficiencie and freedom of your power in your representatives'[76] because 'the power of this, and all future Representatives of this Nation, is inferiour only to theirs who chuse them, and doth extend, without the consent or concurrence of any other person or persons; to the enacting, altering, and repealing of Lawes.'[77] The existence of a parliament to legislate on the people's rights was not sufficient in itself to secure them. How many times had a law been passed for annual parliaments and yet the people were still waiting for them?[78] Framing a document restating the inability of the people to create a body greater than themselves was a fundamental definition of the people's sovereignty. Any parliament could be corrupted by malign individuals, but the entirety of the people would always remain sovereign. Henry Marten noted that the people elected 500 delegates to parliament, but should these 500 try to corrupt the people's interest, the people could choose to make 1500 members.[79]

The Council delegates who came to defend the *Agreement* included the agents, Edward Sexby, William Allen and Robert Lockyear, two further representatives of the regiments of Colonel Whalley and Lieutenant General Cromwell,[80] and the civilian Levellers John Wildman and Maximilian Petty.[81] They were joined by their most articulate champion, Thomas Rainsborough. They arrived at Putney having already made clear their contempt for the principles behind the *Heads of the Proposals*, made worthless because ultimately they relied on Charles' approval, and thus the people's labours to recover their liberties were voided by the king's will.[82] According to Wildman, 'the degrees of oppression, in-justice, and cruelty, are the turning stairs, by which he ascends, to his absolute *stately Majesty*, and greatnesse; yet he must be depended upon, to remove

oppressions' and thereby 'cleannesse must come forth out of unclean-
nesse'.[83] At the meeting of the General Council, Sexby reiterated the
point. The outcome of past obligations on the army's part was that it had
become the prop for two rotten pillars of the old establishment. One, the
king, had vacillated, manipulated and dissembled; the other, the two
Houses, were dedicated to disbanding the army and compromising with
Charles. By continuing to maintain obligations to uphold either or both,
they were involved in a greater breach of faith, ethically compromising
their consciences and politically compromising the people.[84] The grandees
threw back the argument about trust and obligation, because the agitators
sought to overturn previous oaths and covenants and go back on the
promises they had made in the *Solemn Engagement*.

It was only a month since Cromwell and Rainsborough had been on
opposing sides of the House during the debate of further addresses. The
Thursday meetings of the General Council were denounced as the
creature of Cromwell and Ireton's wills, who sought to suppress the *Case
of the Armie* without giving it a reading.[85] Cromwell was accused of
presumption in claiming to speak for the whole army.[86] An irate Edward
Sexby denied that this was the case and employed the rhetoric of balance,
in which the interest of the king was weighed against that of the people:
'[w]e sought to satisfie all men, and it was well; but in going [about] to
doe it wee have dissatisfied all men. Wee have labour'd to please a Kinge,
and I thinke, except wee goe about to cutt all our throates, wee shall not
please him.'[87] The *Case* and the *Agreement* were reprimands to the
grandees, warnings that in declining from its first principles, they would
join the catalogue of institutions which oppressed the people, by
allowing the king to recover his former powers before the liberties of
the people had been secured. The rights demanded by the *Case* and the
constitutional structure outlined in the *Agreement* were not predicated on
a monarchical system.[88] Cromwell equated this with the existence of a
separate party which aimed at republican government. The *Agreement*
'does containe in itt very great alterations of the very Governement of
the Kingdome, alterations from the Governement that itt hath bin
under, I beleive I may almost say since itt was a Nation . . . Would itt
nott make England like the Switzerland Country, one Canton of the
Switz against another, and one County against another?'[89]

A second implication of the *Agreement* was a radical reworking of the
franchise. It was an axiom of a government which was delegated by those
who could not create a body with greater power than themselves that
'every man that is to live under a Governement ought first by his owne
consent to putt himself under that Governement'.[90] Electoral participation acted as confirmation that sovereign power lay with the people and

their directly elected representatives.[91] At Putney, the debate was shaped by disagreement over the degree to which previously unenfranchised members of the community had earned the right to choose a future government to which they would be willing and bound to owe their allegiance. It remained to determine just how far every man was possessed of an independent will in order to be in a position to enter into the contractual relationship which was implied by government.

The debate on the franchise revealed the Levellers' continued failure to reconcile the soldiers' special case with the universal cause of soldier and civilian acting together. At some points it appeared that adult suffrage was intended. Rainsborough argued that the 'poorest he that is in England' was possessed of a voice to place himself under the government as much as 'the greatest he'. He found support from Wildman's adoption of Norman Yoke theory to claim that all law before the present day, including that which settled the personnel and structure of landed proprietorship, was invalid, having been created by conquerors for the people's enslavement. Now, '[e]very person in England hath as cleere a right to Elect his Representative as the greatest person in England'.[92] Rainsborough, Sexby and Wildman demanded a much enlarged franchise as the price extracted by the soldiers' effort. If all did not have a right to choose the government then they really had been 'meere mercenarie souldiers'.[93] Pressed about the particular circumstances and consequnces of the war, however, Rainsborough admitted that the soldier had demonstrated an interest in the constitution above that of the ordinary citizen whose vote might be a birthright, because the soldier had risked his life and estate for its preservation. On this reading, the expansion of the franchise brought about by role of the soldier was a limited extension of the grandees' position. As Ireton outlined it, the vote was bestowed on those who could demonstrate that they possessed an active stake in the constitution, usually by holding land.[94] Voting was not by this a right, but a privilege granted to those who had displayed a particular type of commitment to the polity and by extending the type of commitment, to include risk of life and limb, the soldiers had earned an interest.

That the debate about the franchise could also be couched in terms of the exercise of will is a point which has been made before. Macpherson famously argued that the Levellers did not intend universal adult suffrage. Servants or beggars, because they relied on wages or alms, had been dispossessed of the autonomy of will required to place oneself under a government.[95] The exercise of will, voluntarism, more widely underpinned most of the debate on the constitution. If there was a form of equality amongst individuals, in which all were equally wise or equally foolish – Pocock has described this as 'a radically free natural capacity'[96] –

all people must be enabled to maximise their potential, which should include the right to choose a government which reflected their desires.[97] This was Overton's universal assumption of rationality, the 'natural radical principle'.[98] The act of willing involved two fundamentals: the act itself gave the government legitimacy, and would only guarantee freedom if everybody was prepared to submit because the government would then represent the interests of all.[99] The representation of all then ensured that consent, once given, could not be withdrawn.[100]

These demands received little satisfaction at Putney. With a note of desperation, agitators and Levellers addressed another petition to Parliament, taken to the Commons by Thomas Prince, Samuel Chidley, Captain Taylor, William Larner and Mr Ives.[101] They were all committed to Newgate. Their struggle, they deduced, had come down to a straight choice: whether the king or the Commons should exercise supreme power over the people. At the behest of the parliament, the ordinary citizen had turned soldier to 'preserve that your (parliament's) just authority, and therein their own freedoms'. Parliament had imprisoned them and burned their petitions and they had turned to the 'ruling part' of the army. Now the officers considered the army mutinous and the grandees had joined the ranks of the oppressors. The arrival of the grandees as a focus for complaints of arbitrary treatment was reiterated in *Englands Freedome, Souldiers Rights*.[102] The 'Nownsubstantive Soldiers' had been slandered 'with imputations of plottings and designing not only the Kings death, in a base murderous way; and of imbrueing the nation in blood, but of strange endeavours to levell all mens estates'.[103]

Ironically, the Leveller movement was further subdued after Charles signed the *Engagement* with the Scots. Army grandee members were sufficiently alarmed to vote with the MPs most sympathetic to Leveller demands, and on 3 January 1648 the argument against sending any further addresses to the king won a majority in the Commons. The cause previously championed by Marten and his small band now seemed persuasive to Cromwell and Ireton.[104] Political demands within the Leveller manifestos were toned down or abandoned in order to keep support on board, and most noticeable was the change in tone in Leveller inspired writings, away from secular political reformism. It was replaced by chiliastic anguish.[105] A petition which lobbied parliament two weeks after the Vote of No Addresses cried 'Woe (saith God) to the oppressing City'.[106] The people had brought their miseries and bloodshed upon themselves because they had set up false idols and presented the Lord with burnt offerings.[107] Instead of angry people demanding their rights, the oppressed people issued 'lamentations' on

their economic plight.[108] Frustration at the economic burdens produced by the first war, the slow progress towards a treaty and increasing
nostalgia for the stability remembered under the king sparked reactionary armed risings.[109] The country was plunged once more into war,
and the Levellers were given a new martyr when cavaliers attempted to
seize Colonel Rainsborough, intending to offer him for a prisoner
exchange. The colonel put up resistance and was run through with a
sword. Thousands of Londoners, wearing the sea-green ribbon of
levellerism, accompanied his funeral cortège.[110]

The second civil war was to have some radical consequences which led
directly to the regicide. It was also ushered in by a wave of reaction which
switched the emphasis away from the search for a workable new constitution, with or without a monarchical component, and highlighted again the
sole figure of Charles Stuart. As an ultimate irony, the renewal of war undid
all of the work which had culminated in the Vote of No Addresses. MPs
who had steered the vote through the Commons returned to active service,
leaving the Presbyterians once more in control of the Houses to return to the
task of constructing a peace treaty with would induce Charles to finally lay
down his arms. In response, the Levellers and soldiers tried to combine their
calls for a constitution which did not balance the single figure of the king
against the whole of the people with calls for justice on the mere man who
had once more embroiled the nation in blood. The Leveller petition of 11
September 1648 chided the Commons that God having granted them
victory, little had changed in the previous two years:

> according as ye have bin accustomed, passing by the ruine of a Nation, and all the
> bloud that hath bin spilt by the King and his Party, ye betake your selvs to a Treaty
> with him, thereby putting him that is but one single person, . . . in competition
> with the whole body of the people, whom ye represent; not considering that it is
> impossible for you to erect any authority equall to your selves.[111]

This competition, between the people's liberties and the king's person,
was restated in the language of biblical judgement, because 'mercy to
the wicked, is cruelty to the innocent: and that all your lenity doth but
make them the more insolent and presumptuous'.[112] The royalist
principles that the king could do no wrong or could not be brought
to justice by his subjects, were 'begot by the blasphemous arrogancy of
Tyrants upon servile Parasites, and foster'd onely by slavish and ignorant
people, and remain in our Law-Books, as Heir-looms onely of the
Conquest.'[113] Mercurius Pragmaticus noted that the Leveller petition was
a combination of secular calls for equality before the law and wrathful
cries for vengeance, which led junior officers to announce that 'they
knew no use of a king or lords any longer'.[114]

While the calls for justice to be executed on Charles grew increasingly insistent, Leveller leaders – in particular William Wetton, John Lilburne, John Wildman, Maximilian Petty and William Walwyn – still expressed hopes for discussions between the parliamentary Independents and the army grandees. Their primary concern remained to secure the liberties of the people before any other action was taken, and the soldiers' roar after Charles' blood accelerated the pressure to achieve it quickly. Thus, when it came to Charles' personal fate, some of the Leveller leaders appeared to perform a *volte face,* and stood in opposition to the army's stated aim of bringing him to justice. In 1646, Lilburne had launched one of the earliest and most vitriolic attacks on the institution of monarchy, declaring that 'C.R. ought to be executed'.[115] At the birth of England's republican government, established by military coup, Lilburne opposed the army because it wanted to 'cut off the King's head'.[116] Lilburne argued that if this were the first item on the agenda of reform, the resulting power vacuum would be filled by the army grandees, who would take their turn to tyrannise the people. The grandees also argued that time was short, but because a parliamentary treaty with Charles was imminent, necessity dictated first a purge of the parliament and disposal of the king.

Lilburne recalled that negotiations began in November 1648, with the aim of redrafting an *Agreement of the People.* Discussions were conducted between the Leveller leaders – himself and Wildman – the grandees and the 'civilian Independents'. Eventually, it was decided to instigate negotiations among a group of sixteen: four from each interest group – the grandees, Independents, MPs and Levellers. The parliamentarians were regarded as a separate 'interest' for this purpose, and the four chosen represented the radical, republican wing of the House: Henry Marten, Thomas Chaloner, Thomas Scot and Alexander Rigby. Of these, only Marten took an active part. We do not know the views of the other three. Chaloner and Scot may have pleaded that their role on the Commons' constitutional committee took up their time, but Marten was also named to that committee and took an active part in its deliberations. He may therefore have had a greater commitment to the consultative and conciliatory process which the *Agreement* represented.

Lilburne claimed that an agreed document did emerge from this process. It established the fundamental principle of representativeness and a protective mechanism to fix it in stone, for '[i]t cannot be imagined that so many of our Countrymen would have opposed us in this quarrel, if they had understood their own good.'[117] All adults of independent means would have the vote, provided they signed the *Agreement,* under an expanded franchise which would maximise the participation of the well-affected by adding representation for, by way of example, the Leveller stronghold of Southwark. It restated the sovereignty of the people and their representatives in parliament, the need for regular and 'representative' elections, the end of feudal privileges and, the foundation of freedom, a statement that the *Agreement* constituted the supreme law.

However, according to Lilburne, not all of the parties regarded this statement as the end point. For the grandees, this was merely a starting point for a continuing debate within the Council of Officers, which produced an amended, less straightforward, more legalistic document. This action provided the Levellers with further evidence that the grandees were part of the oppressors. They were devious, perfidious and only concerned with using force to corrupt the will of the people, purge parliament and create a 'mock' creature which would set up a High Court and execute the king.[118] This was, of course, the precise course of action taken by the grandees, but Lilburne was writing after the fact. The Levellers' could travel as far as the grandees in regarding 'the King as an evil man in his actions' but their experience had made them almost as wary of the parliament and the army, so they concluded it was best to retain all three potentially oppressive institutions for the time being in order to play one off against another until the people's rights and safety could be secured. This would ensure that the authority of the institutions depended on the will of the people, rather than allow the people to become subservient to the force of the institutions.[119]

NOTES

1. Austin Woolrych, *Soldiers and Statesmen: the General Council of the Army and its Debates, 1647–1648* (Oxford, 1987), p. 349.
2. Lilburne was scathing of the 'big swolne blar[t]herly [blathery] priviledges' of the House of Commons which possessed no privileges in relation to the king except 'freedome of speech and debate': *The Juglers Discovered*, 28 Sep. 1647, E409(22), p. 7 (pages misnumbered).
3. *Clarke Papers*, I p. 234. The words are Ireton's.
4. *Vox Plebis, or, the Peoples Out-cry against Oppression, Injustice, and Tyranny*, [19 Nov.] 1646, E362(20); frontispiece; John Saltmarsh, *Smoke in the Temple*, [16 Jan.] 1646, E316(14), 'Liberty for printing and speaking' and 'Free debates and open conferences'.
5. *Vox Plebis*, p. 1.
6. 'As thy sword hath made women childless, so shall thy mother be childless among women', which was the justification for Samuel to slay King Agag.

7. *Vox Plebis*, pp. 2–3. The structure and concerns reveal a familiarity with Machiavelli's, *Discourses*. Machiavelli's third and fourth chapters discussed the emergence of the plebeians in Rome from the destruction of the rule of the Tarquins: for example, from the opening of Chapter 3 – 'it is necessary for anyone who organizes a republic and institutes laws to take for granted that all men are evil . . . and when such wickedness remains hidden for a time, this is due to a hidden cause that is not recognized by those without experience of its contrary; but then time . . . will uncover it.'

8. Nigel Smith, *Literature and Revolution in England, 1640–1660* (Yale, 1994), pp. 9–10; David Norbrook is currently compiling a major study of the sense in which the rhetoric of republicanism preceded its political form. I am grateful to Dr Norbrook for allowing me to see parts of the manuscript prior to publication.

9. Smith's analysis is an exception – see *Literature and Revolution*, pp. 9–10, 138, 150, 382 n.78. Henry Marten is another suggestion for the author, but his style, which is so recognisable, is not present here, and some aspects are distinctly un-Martenesque. Levellers William Walwyn, Edward Sexby and John Wildman have been suggested. The attribution to Nedham has been made by Blair Worden.

10. John Lilburne, *Innocency and Truth Justified*, E314(21); Gardiner, *History*, II p. 195; III pp. 124–5.

11. *LJ* viii p. 429; Gardiner, *History*, III, pp. 124–5.

12. [Richard Overton], *A Remonstrance of Many thousand Citizens and other Free-born People of England, to their owne House of Commons*, [7 Jul.] 1646, E(11). Overton was arrested on 11 Aug.1646 and committed to Newgate on 3 November.

13. [Henry Marten], *An Vnhappy game at Scotch and English*, p. 23.

14. Brailsford, *Levellers*, pp. 240–1; Wolfe, *Leveller Manifestos*, pp. 11–12.; Woolrych, *Soldiers and Statesmen*, pp. 190–4; Pauline Gregg, *Free-born John*, p. 195 and *passim*; John Lilburne, *Two Letters written by Lieut. Col. John Lilburne*, 13 and 15 Sep. 1647; Lilburne, *A Copy of a Letter written to Col. Henry Marten*, 20 Jul. 1647, 669.f.11(46) E407(41), and *Rash Oaths unwarrantable and the breaking of them inexcusable*, 31 May 1647, E393(39); Leeds, ML MSS Box 78, f.1, Marten's draft reply to Lilburne, unpublished, called *Rash oaths uncharitable*; Richard Overton, *An Arrow against All Tyrants*, [12 Oct.] 1646, E356(14).

15. *Argvuments proving that we ought not to part with the Militia*, broadsheet, point 1.

16. One attempt to articulate a wider sense of England's liberties forms the basis of the following chapter.

17. While the Levellers were at the forefront of women's petitioning, the majority of their leaders and writers (except Kate Chidley who does not appear in this study) were men, and in order to avoid the clumsy repetition of 'him or her', this study uses him throughout, unless specifically referring to a woman.

18. See the discussion on the recovery of liberties and ancient constitutionalism in Chapter 1 above, p. 21.
19. [Overton], *Remonstrance*, p. 7.
20. This was Lilburne's 'general proposition' stated as a preface to *The Freeman's Freedom Vindicated* (1646), and traced to a religious principle of the equality of all mankind as a result of their descent from Adam.
21. [Overton], *Remonstrance*, p. 3.
22. Brailsford, *Levellers*, pp. 129–30, 535–6; Christopher Hill, 'The Norman Yoke', in his *Puritanism and Revolution* (London, 1958), pp. 50–122; Johann P. Somerville, 'History and theory: the Norman conquest in early Stuart political thought', *Political Studies*, XXXIV (1986) 249–61.
23. [Overton], *Remonstrance*, p. 4.
24. [John Lilburne], *Regall Tyrannie discovered: or, a Discourse, shewing that all lawfull (approbational) instituted power by GOD amongst men, is by common agreement*; Thomason dated it 6 Jan. 1647 and added 'by Lilburne' with the title – E370(12), pp. 15–16.
25. [Lilburne], *Regall Tyrannie*, p. 16, who wrote of the 'French ungodly proceedings' at Westminster Hall; *Petition of March 1647*, in Wolfe, *Leveller Manifestos* p. 139. Overton, *An Appeale*, in Wolfe, ibid., p. 192; *Large Petition of the Levellers*, 1647, clause 7.
26. John Hare, *Plaine English to our Wilfull Bearers with Normanisme* [4 Nov.] 1647, E412(24); Brailsford, *Levellers*, p. 141 n. 43, who rather dismisses Hare's contributions as romantic pedantry with no social value.
27. [John Lilburne], *Englands Freedome, Souldiers Rights*, 14 Dec., E419(23), in Wolfe, *Leveller Manifestos*, p. 244.
28. Robert Parsons, *Severall Speeches delivered at a Conference concerning the power of Parliament to proceed against their King for Misgovernment*, 31 Jan. 1648, E521(1), p. 69.
29. [Lilburne], *Regall Tyrannie*, p. 34.
30. [Liburne], *Regall Tyrannie*, pp. 7, 20, 27, 32, 41, 58, 59, 60, 61, 98.
31. [Lilburne], *Regall Tyrannie*, p. 10.
32. [Liburne], *Regall Tyrannie*, p. 57 and contents page.
33. *To the Right Honourable, the Trustees of the English Nation Assembled in Parliament . . . the petition of divers Englishmen*, 29 Sep. 1648, 669.f.13(24); William Godwin also denounced the 'moderated sovereignty' implied by mixed government, see John Morrow, 'Republicanism and public virtue: William Godwin's *History of the Commonwealth of England*', *HJ*, 34.3 (1991) 645–64, p. 651. It was also implied by the difficulty of wanting to describe commonwealths as organic, while superimposing a contractual relationship; Harro Höpfl and Martyn P. Thompson, 'The history of contract as a motif in political thought', *Am Hist Rev* 84.4 (1979) 919–44, pp. 928–34.
34. Machiavelli, *Discourses*, Ch. 3.
35. [Overton], *Remonstrance*, p. 114, 115. Ironically, this was partly because the people were diverted from their consideration of the fundamentals because they were living in affluence, wealth and ease.

36. [Marten], *Vnhappie game*, title page.
37. [Marten], *Corrector of the Answerer*, p. 7. Maugre, meaning 'in spite of'.
38. [Overton], *Remonstrance*, p. 4.
39. *A Cal to all the Souldiers*, p. 6.
40. The metaphor and play on words associated with poor eye-sight, blindness, clouded vision, etc. and the inability to see the truth of an argument was well used in the 1640s. There appears to have been a particular relationship between Scotland and spectacles, which so far no expert in the history of medicine and science or of trades has been able to fathom. Marten chided that 'Brethren might doe well with their next papers to send us a paire of *Scotish-spectacles* that are fit for our eyes, and their caractar' (*An Vnhappie Game*, p. 5) and Thomas Scot is accredited with the pamphlet ridiculing the Scottish Commissioners, called *A New Paire of Spectacles of the old Fashion for the Scots Commissioners to helpe their Eye-sight, when they are returned to the Parliament at Edenburgh*, [18 Dec.] 1648, E476(30) and again at 5 Mar. 1649, E546(3) [wrongly catalogued as E539(11)]. The type of spectacles pictured on the front of Scot's pamphlet are known as Nuremburg spectacles.
41. *Remonstrance*, Wolfe p. 115.
42. Marten, *Corrector*, p. 5.
43. Lucy Hutchinson, *Memoirs of Colonel Hutchinson* (London, 1965), p. 3, who in an interesting but mixed metaphor equates William's conquest with a poison in the English bloodstream (which sank the vessel).
44. [Overton], *Remonstrance*, p. 5.
45. [Overton], *Remonstrance*. p. 6.
46. [Marten], *Vnhappie game*, p. 10; the extended, unpleasant metaphor is repeated in *A True Copie of the Berkshire Petition*, 2 Dec. 1648, E475(2).
47. *An Agreement of the People for a firme and present Peace*, [3 Nov.] 1647, E412(21), p. 13; [John Lilburne], *Foundations of Freedom or an Agreement of the People*, [15 Dec.] 1648, E476(26).
48. Richard Overton, *An Appeale from the Commons to the Free People*, 1647, p. 4.
49. With the sole exception of a threat to march northward being countered by Fairfax's army moving southwards: [Marten], *Vnhappie game*, p. 26.
50. John Morrill, 'Mutiny and discontent in English provincial armies, 1645–1647', *P&P* (1972), and reprinted in *The Nature of the English Revolution*, (London, 1993), pp. 332–358; this is the argument advanced by Mark Kishlansky in several articles and his book, *The Rise of the New Model Army* (Cambridge, 1979); 'The army and the Levellers: the roads to Putney', *HJ*, 22.4 (1979) 795–824; 'The case of the army truly stated: the creation of the New Model Army', *P&P*, 80 (1979) 51–74.
51. The sequence of events is confusing, but Marten, having been banned in 1643 from taking up his Berkshire seat for three years, seems to have been returned as a recruiter member for Abingdon in 1645. Having arrived in the House for Abingdon, he was allowed to resume the shire seat and thus helped Ball to the vacant borough place.

52. Bodleian Library Tanner MSS 60 f.491, Ball to Lenthall, 1 March 1645(6); *CJ*, IV, p. 397.

53. *Vindication of the Officers of the Army*, 27 April 1647; there is no more sensitive and comprehensive account of the political pressure movements in the army than Austin Woolrych, *Soldiers and Statesmen*.

54. *Apologie of the Common Soldiers of Sir Thomas Fairfaxes Army*, 28 Apr. 1647, E385(18).

55. The terms 'agent', 'agitator' and 'adjutator' are synonyms.

56. Gardiner, *History*, III, pp. 280–1; Woolrych, *Soldiers and Statesmen*, p. 117ff.

57. Such as it had in the declaration of 14 Jun. 1647, *Representation of the army*, published 16 June 1647, E392(26).

58. Kishlansky, 'Army and the Levellers', p. 795: 'the English Revolution began in the summer of 1647', and p. 797; Ian Gentles, *The New Model Army in England, Ireland and Scotland, 1645–1653* (Oxford, 1992), p. 197.

59. Brailsford, *Levellers*, pp. 205–6; BL Add MSS 71532 f.23: it is unfortunately undated, but is almost certainly from 1647.

60. Leeds, ML MSS 78/51, 53. There is surprisingly little information available about the family of Richard, first Baron Lovelace, into which both Marten and Wildman married. Marten married Margaret, daughter of Richard, Lord Lovelace, and widow of William Staunton, around 1635. The *DNB* has Wildman married first to Frances, daughter of the Catholic peer Sir Francis Englefield of Berkshire. It is believed Wildman's first marriage took place during the first civil war. By 1655, Wildman had married Lucy, a daughter of John, the second Lord Lovelace of Hurley. The exchanges of letters between Marten and Wildman indicate that Wildman was married to Lucy by 1650. H. A. Doubleday and Lord Howard de Walden (eds), *The Complete Peerage* (13 vols) (London, 1932) VIII pp. 229–32, 271–2.

61. Because there was a specific reference to the centre of sectarianism, the Isle of Ely, given the cipher Y.

62. There were possibly two men with similar names who may be confused, but this is almost certainly William Eyres who was a yeoman of Berkshire known to Marten. His name can also be spelt Ayers or Ayres.

63. It may possibly have been the divine, Hugh Peter, but he would have been more likely to have been in the camp of suspects. The appearance of the name at the end of the friends and start of the enemies in a document which lacked punctuation makes the precise placing problematic.

64. House of Lords, House of Commons, City of London, the Scots, the Commissioners, the Committee for Both Kingdoms, the French, Irish, Welsh and Dutch.

65. *The Case of the Armie Truly Stated*, presented to Sir Thomas Fairfax by Edmond Bear and William Russell, 15 Oct. 1647, E411(9), but probably the work of John Wildman, with additional contributions.

66. Maurice Ashley, *John Wildman: Plotter and Postmaster*, (London, 1947), p. 29ff. Wildman was often known as 'major' during the 1650s, but I am inclined to agree with Ashley that there is no evidence of military rank prior to 1649, although a role in Henry Marten's unofficial regiment of 1648 may have been a possibility – see Chapter 3; Ashley, *John Wildman* p. 9.

67. Ashley, *John Wildman*, p. 200.

68. Gardiner believes that this last section of practical proposals was added by Cromwell; Gardiner, *History*, III pp. 280–1.

69. Murray Tolmie, *The Triumph of the Saints: the Separate Churches of London, 1616–1649* (Cambridge, 1977), pp. 164–5.

70. Ashley, *John Wildman*, p. 15; Wolfe, *Leveller Manifestos*, p. 223; Gentles, *New Model Army*, p. 204.

71. *An Agreement of the People for a firm and present Peace*, [3 Nov.] 1647, E412(21), p. 7.

72. On a more practical note, five of the nine cavalry regiments and five of the seven artillery regiments (not counting Colonel Rainsborough's) which were named in the cipher of agitators held by Marten are named as regiments subscribing to the *Agreement*.

73. Höpfl and Thompson suggest the German Calvinist, Johannes Althusius, as a possible antecedent of the idea that civil society was an association of lesser associations which began with the family and ended with a presupposed fundamental law, sustained by common consent and approval; 'History of contract', pp. 935–6.

74. Alan Craig Houston, ' "A Way of settlement": The Levellers, monopolies and the public interest', *HPT* IVX.3 (1993) 381–420, p. 407.

75. *Agreement of the People*, p. 9.

76. *Agreement of the People*, p. 7.

77. *Agreement of the People*, p. 3.

78. *Agreement of the People*, p. 9.

79. BL Add MSS 71534 f.11.

80. The most probable would seem to have been Edmond Bear and William Russell, the representatives of these two regiments who had been appointed to take the *Case of the Armie* to Fairfax. Woodhouse, however, identifies Robert Everard, the other agent of Cromwell's regiment, as the buff-coat who remained unknown throughout the first day's debate. Although this seems likely, the text is still not quite precise about whether Everard brought the other two debaters or was himself one; A. S. P. Woodhouse, *Puritanism and Liberty* (London, 1974 edn), p. 42; Gentles, *New Model Army*, p. 204.

81. Most of the original agents of the five regiments of horse had been replaced by new ones. Brailsford suggests that this may have been overseen by Edward Sexby and·that the new agents were more willing to see the end of negotiations with the king and a comprehensive purge of parliament to ensure that this was secured: Brailsford, *Levellers*, p. 256.

82. John Lawmind pseud., [John Wildman], *Putney Proiects. or the Old Serpent in a new Forme*, [30 Dec.] 1647, E421(19). Cromwell and Rainsborough had

had to leave the House on the day of the vote to send further addresses, though Cromwell had been a teller on the side which subsequently voted for further addresses when a division had arisen the day before.

83. [Wildman] *Putney Proiects*, pp. 39–40. *Putney Proiects* also contained a further reference to Lilburne's efforts to free himself from imprisonment.
84. *Clarke Papers*, I, p. 228.
85. *A Cal to all the Souldiers*, [29 Oct.] 1647, pp. 4–5.
86. *Clarke Papers*, I, pp. 227–34. See Chapter 1, p. 22.
87. *Clarke Papers*, I, pp. 227–8.
88. *Agreement of the People*, pp. 7–8.
89. *Clarke Papers*, I, pp. 236–7.
90. Thomas Rainsborough at Putney, *Clarke Papers*, I, p. 301.
91. See Petty's speech, *Clarke Papers*, I, p. 351.
92. *Clarke Papers*, I, p. 318.
93. *Clarke Papers*, I, pp. 323, 325, 330.
94. *Clarke Papers*, I, pp. 318–20.
95. C. B. Macpherson, *The Political Theory of Possessive Individualism* (Oxford, 1962); Christopher Hill, 'Pottage for freeborn Englishmen: attitudes to wage labour in the sixteenth and seventeenth centuries', in C. H. Feinstein (ed.), *Socialism, Capitalism and Economic Growth* (Cambridge, 1967); Richard Ashcraft, *Revolutionary Politics and Locke's Two Treatises of Government* (Princeton, 1986), pp. 149–65, sets out a convincing case that with the exception of Petty, the Levellers were arguing for a radically extended franchise amounting to adult male suffrage, and Houston's case against Macpherson is equally strong: Houston, 'Way of Settlement', p. 382.
96. J. G. A. Pocock, *The Machiavellian Moment: Florentine Political Thought and the Atlantic Republican Tradition* (Princeton, 1975), pp. 374–5.
97. 'God hath given no man a talent to be wrapped up in a napkin and not improved, but the meanest vassal . . . is equally obliged and acceptable to God with the greatest prince or commander under the sun, in and for the use of that talent betrusted to him': *Case of the Armie truly Stated* from the letter to Fairfax, cited in Pocock, *Machiavellian Moment*, p. 373; Ashcraft, *Revolutionary Politics*, p. 163.
98. See above, p. 48.
99. The point was not explicitly made, but it would be, literally, a commonwealth.
100. Patrick Riley, *Will and Political Legitimacy: A Critical Exposition of Social Contract Theory in Hobbes, Locke, Rousseau, Kant and Hegel* (London, 1982); John Locke, *The Essay Concerning Human Understanding*, ed. A. C. Fraser (New York, 1959), pp. 328–9.
101. *To the Supream Authority of England, the Commons in Parliament assembled*, 23 Nov. 1647, 669.f.11(98), broadsheet.
102. William Eyres, William Bray et al., *Englands Freedome, Souldiers Rights: Vindicated against all arbitrary unjust Invaders of them, and in particular against those new Tyrants at Windsore*, 14 Dec. 1647, E419(23).

103. *Englands Freedome*, p. 10; *The Peoples Prerogative*, pp. 42–4; *To the Supream Authority of England*, broadsheet.

104. *CJ*, V pp. 415–16.

105. John Wildman, *Truths triumph*, p. 3, which argued that the article about tithes had been dropped because too large a section of possible support would not agree.

106. *To the Supream Authority of England, the Commons Assembled in Parliament*, described by Lilburne as the petition of 19 Jan. 1648, in *An Impeachment of High treason against Oliver Cromwell*, [10 Aug.] 1649, E508(20), citing a cry of Zephaniah.

107. Zeph. 3: 1, 3: 6–7; Ezek. 58: 4–7; Mic. 6: 6–8.

108. *The mournfull Cryes of many thousand poor Tradesmen, who are ready to famish through decay of Trade*, 22 Jan. 1648, 669.f.11(116), broadsheet; The Lamentations of Jeremiah 4: 3. Lamentations 4: 9 reads 'they that be slain with the sword are better than they that be slain with hunger'.

109. Robert Ashton, *Counter-revolution: the Second Civil War and its Origins, 1646–8* (Yale, 1994).

110. *A full Relation of the murder committed upon Col. Rainsborough, 29 Oct.*, 29 Oct. 1648, E470(4); Thomas Alleyn, *An Elergie upon the Death of Col. Rainsborrow*, 669.f.13(41); see also 669.f.13 (39), (40), (45), (46).

111. *To the Right Honorable, the Commons of England in Parliament assembled*, the petition of 11 Sep. 1648, E464(19), Wolfe, *Leveller Manifestos*, p. 285; Brailsford, *Levellers*, pp. 350–3.

112. Wolfe *Levellers Manifestos*, p. 289, article 25. This particular sentiment does not appear to be a direct citation of the Bible.

113. *A Remonstrance of his Excellency . . . and of the General Councell of Officers, held at St Albans the 16. of November 1648*, presented to the parliament 20 Nov. p. 48; Janelle Greenberg, 'Our grand maxim of state, 'the King can do no wrong'', *HPT*, XII.2 (1991) 209–28.

114. *Mercurius Pragmaticus*, 12–19 Sep. 1648, E364.

115. [Lilburne], *Regall Tyrannie discovered*, The Table, and p. 57.

116. John Lilburne, *Legal Fundamental Liberties*, 8 Jun. 1649, E560(14), p. 19.

117. [Lilburne], *Foundations of Freedom*, p. 4.

118. John Evelyn claimed to have crept into the army council debates in disguise and to have witnessed the discordant debate over the second *Agreement*; William Bray (ed.), *Diary and Correspondence of John Evelyn* (London, 1854), p. 550, 18 Dec. 1648.

119. John Lilburne, *Legall Fundamentall Liberties of the People of England revived, asserted and vindicated*, 8 Jun. 1649, E560(14).

3

The Expense of Blood and Treasure

Finding a name by which to identify the activists which have emerged in the course of Chapters 1 and 2 is fraught with difficulty. Most seventeenth-century names were epithets which began life as risible attacks coined through opposition. Titles were like mud, slung by hostile forces, but subsequently rationalised by proud and defiant adoption. In the summer of 1647 the main 'parties' were described as Royalists, Presbyterians, Independents and Covenanters[1], but during negotiations between them all, some noted a group in the Commons (the Independent-ultraists of Chapter 1), together with Levellers and agitators in the army (the 'populist faction' of Chapter 2), which constituted a separable party. Lucy Hutchinson thought of the emergent third group in terms of allies of, though not synonymous with, the Levellers, and declared her parliamentarian husband to have been sympathetic to their cause:

> the two factions of presbytery and independency being so engaged to suppress each other, that they both ceased to regard the public interest; insomuch, that at that time a certain sort of public-spirited men stood up in the parliament and army, declaring against those factions and the ambition of the grandees of both . . . The lords, as if it were the chief interest of nobility to be licensed in vice, claimed many prerogatives, which set them out of the reach of common justice, which these good-hearted people would have equally to belong to the poorest as well as to the mighty; and for this and such other honest declarations, they were nicknamed levellers . . . men of sober principles, of honest and religious ends, and therefore hated by all the designing self-interested men of both factions.[2]

Professing an ideology of responsibility for and towards the common weal, they opposed themselves to so-called private interest. They stood against privilege by birth, which seemed to license amorality, and were instead 'good-hearted', 'honest', 'sober' and 'religious'. David Underdown placed particular emphasis on the word 'honest', in that it came to mean the 'honest party', the identifying mark of a particular political stance.[3]

Previously, Underdown had referred to them as 'extreme Independents',[4] but this does not satisfy, since this group sought to avoid the impression that they were allied to any pre-existent political faction. In part, their stance, independent of even the Independents, was playing politics, righteously placing themselves above distasteful factionalism. Faction was the politics of interest, and these few sought to represent the many by defining themselves as honest people whose reading of individuals, actions and events could be trusted by the ordinary person who was excluded from the channels of political power. For doing so they were ridiculed, barred from the Commons, imprisoned, cashiered or censored, and the action of the authorities to stifle them was used as proof that they were indeed martyrs to the truth. Of course, all parties claimed to be speaking truth and their opponents to be pedlars of lies and falsehoods.

The figures described here emerged in 1649 as 'worthies' of the Commonwealth government. At some level, therefore, they possessed a commitment to the non-monarchical regime which emerged after Charles' execution. Worthies could be members of the Commons or local administrators. Underdown called the latter 'intendants' or managers of the public business.[5] Within their vicinity, these were the political movers and fixers, who ensured a continuing commitment to the cause. Edmund Morley in Sussex, John Lisle in Hampshire, John Pyne in Somerset, Luke Robinson in Yorkshire and Miles Corbet in Norfolk are distinguished by their activism through local channels such as the county committees, and emerge in 1649 as the worthy gentlemen who were the local fount of power and patronage. Underdown's work on the West Country has particularly teased out the working relationship of figures around John Pyne of Curry Mallet.[6] They were men who during the 1640s struggled against faint-heartedness or neutrality; the 'radical rank and file in the country'.[7] All of these attempts to define what these men had in common during the 1640s are flawed. Underdown is caught in the trap which faces historians of republican activity prior to 1649: these figures emerge as the local powers in 1649, but evidence for their ideas or activities prior to 1649 is often shadowy and circumstantial. He is in much the same position as those he is trying to define: they knew who they were, and their most violent opponents seemed to know precisely who they were, but seldom explicitly named names or gave reasons. Clement Walker believed that the anti-authoritarian elements in 1648 were 'Independents, Sectaries, (and) Antimonarchists' and William Prynne identified 'the Sectaries, Republican, Anabaptistical, Jesuitical, Levelling party'.[8]

The personnel of this group emerged through practical activism and there is therefore a paucity of evidence for the way in which pragmatic and expedient manoeuvring was rationalised into philosophical postures and shared cultural attitudes were expanded into a common bond.[9]

During the 1640s, many were too busy being active to write down for historians what it was they were doing, planning to do or thinking of doing.[10] One excellent reason for caution was security. George Wither was thankful to the Commonwealth government that after 1649 he could write 'truth, without fear of halter, pillory, or whip now, when I can remember . . . that to call a *Spade* a *Spade*, was counted no lesse than Treason.'[11] However, without the evidence of what he would have written before 1649, we cannot assume anything of Wither or his colleagues. After 1650, a number of connections emerge which are suggestive that a network of like-minded individuals existed before 1649/50. Levellers John Wildman, William Wetton, Maximilian Petty, William Eyres, Samuel Chidley, William Cockayne, George Bishop and Edward Sexby can all be tied to Henry Marten by 1650, but only Wetton and Eyres can certainly be placed in Marten's circle earlier, and then only to 1648.[12] Thomas and James Chaloner were working with Thomas Westropp in the anti-Scottish campaign of 1646, and Westropp was a close confidante of Marten by 1650. Also in 1650, the year he died, the historian of the Commonwealth, Thomas May, was part of the administration of Chaloner's estates in North Yorkshire. The Lilburne *manqué*, John Musgrave, moved in the circle of Alexander Rigby, MP for Wigan, and both Marten and Rigby were well regarded by the Leveller leadership.[13]

Gerald Aylmer identified a common social background among these figures. Far from being empathetic with the Southwark poor, the Levellers were often apprenticed to London guilds and expected to employ their trade skills within prominent mercantile circles. Their social status already gave them a certain prominence among local gentry or the trading circles of the capital, but their politics were not typical of their station.[14] Pyne was of a higher social status than his opponents liked to paint him, but he chided John Gorges for being a 'man of yesterday'.[15] Aylmer called his protagonists 'gentleman levellers'. Edward Sexby was the son of Marcus Sexby, a London gentleman, apprenticed to the Grocers' Company in 1632. Squire John Petty of Tetsworth, Oxfordshire, apprenticed his son, Maximilian, to the same company two years later.[16] The more obscure Thomas Westropp and John Musgrave were also landowners of some wealth and prominence in their areas and the owners of fine houses and demesnes.

Henry Marten was perhaps the biggest landowner of this group.[17] His lands ran along the southern and eastern side of the rivers Cole and Thames, from Shrivenham in the west to Longworth in the east. Marten was potentially a very rich man indeed. Thomas Chaloner and his brother James kept a house at Steeple Clayton, Buckinghamshire, and had extensive estates around Guisborough in North Yorkshire, under the occupation of the Scots in the early 1640s. The family was in decline and their influence under attack.[18] The others were not quite so landed, men of some standing within their community but far from prestigious in London political circles. Edmund Ludlow's father, Sir Henry, was a friend and parliamentary ally of Henry Marten early in the decade, was said to have spoken in the Commons just once. He took his opportunity and received Speaker Lenthall's censure, for 'the Words which he spake were Words that had an Aspect towards the King; and when Words fall from him, that may reflect upon his Sacred Person, he ought to weigh them.'[19] The Ludlow family had county gentry status within Wiltshire, despite its Commons' tradition. The family of Thomas Saunders were county gentry of Derbyshire, with connections which went back three hundred years. Saunders' father had purchased the estate at Little Ireton, Coldwell and Coton-in-the-Elms, dismantled by German Ireton in 1611.[20] Thomas Saunders was educated at Repton and at the Inner Temple. Maximilian Petty could also boast parliamentary links through his uncle. John Pyne was a man of landed influence in Somerset and within his circle were similar figures such as John Preston, Sir Thomas Wroth and Edmund Prideaux.[21] The most prestigious, but not the wealthiest, was Thomas, Lord Grey of Groby, son of the earl of Stamford. Grey's political journey took him furthest away from his social background and early politics.

Most of the members of the House of Commons in the 1640s were from a gentry background. Most of them had strong affiliational links with their locality (most often expressed as a county loyalty) and were part of kinship networks in which the geographical and social aspects of such localism were combined. I would suggest, however, that there were specific ways in which the social and geographical backgrounds of these men illuminated their radical politics. Their localism was an aspect of insular, nationalistic parochialism which informed the concept of England's liberties. Their relative wealth and pretensions to social standing gave them a quantifiable material stake in the settlement of their area and the outcome of the war. As Marten and William Strode suggested in the 1643 debate on taxation, those who did not contribute financially to the war effort should be barred from having a say in making peace.[22] Their radical anti-monarchical politics dictated that they had to be successful in their war aims, because to allow the king any say in the future peace was to risk losing their lives and their posterities' estates for their treasonable politics. Our group shared, by 1648, a deep mistrust of Charles, a belief that the constitution of England could be settled without him and a willingness to envisage government without kings. The political isolation of Charles Stuart in the late 1640s increasingly identified either his person or monarchy in general as the cause of the honest party's failure to secure a peace formula which defended their liberties. The path of this mistrust can be followed in the votes of the Commons, the writings of the Levellers and the disillusionment of the rank and file of the army.

The cause which they followed can be defined as consistency. It became self-defining. The battle against the forces of oppression grew as individuals' commitment to the war tailed away and the radicals appeared a shrinking faction fighting against a growing enemy. The Scots moved into opposition when they abandoned the war party and embraced the peace process. The Presbyterians, as they represented the desire to find an accommodation with Charles (though not necessarily as they were an expression of religious practice), became part of the forces ranged against the honest party. The House of Commons' commitment to the Newcastle Propositions made it a suspect institution, and despite some members' initial enthusiasm for Fairfax and the New Model Army, the grandees promoted the *Heads of the Proposals* and were not always to be trusted. There was a certain sympathy with the Levellers, as Lucy Hutchinson admitted, and also with the rank and file of the soldiery. This was because the gentlemen leaders of, or speakers for, a community and the ordinary soldier could both demonstrate their continued commitment to the honest cause – the soldier by risking his life and the gentleman by risking his fortune. Sexby at Putney illustrated the point:

> We have engaged in this Kingdome and ventur'd our lives, and itt was all for this: to recover our birthrights and priviledges as Englishmen . . . There are many thousand of us souldiers that have ventur'd our lives; yett wee have had a birthright . . . If wee had nott a right in this Kingdome, wee were mere mercenarie souldiers. There are many in my condition, that have as good a condition . . . , itt may bee little estate they have att present . . . I am resolved to give my birthright to none.[23]

The continued exclusion of individuals and groups from the ranks of the honest allowed these gentlemen to become self-appointed figureheads, who used their status to speak on behalf of a community of 'oppressed' people, but neither the gentlemen nor the wider community of the oppressed whom they claimed to represent were a majority in terms of numbers. A combination of the claim to honesty, the exclusion of 'dishonest' elements and the belief that the dishonest had hidden the truth from the people at large, could lead to an assertion that they were, in fact, representative. The definition of the group offered by Thomas May evocatively picks up the mixture of materialist and principled motivations which operated through practical political action. They were those who 'in a most just cause, had valiantly adventured their lives and fortunes: that nothing was now left for them to do, but to take care for the safety of themselves and their friends, and settle the Commonwealth . . . without a King.'[24] For brevity and at the risk of introducing another title which is open to challenge, I have chosen to call them 'gentry republicans'.[25]

It is within this form of discussion, identifying the common social and cultural status of the gentry republicans, that we now encounter the hitherto little-remarked fact that England was in the midst of a civil war. The attitudes of localism, gentry materialism and (consequently) radicalism were most clearly visible in the practicalities involved in defending their communities, through the particular need to raise militia forces and the wider calls on their purses. The most famous and derided slogan of the radicals in the later 1640s, *Salus populi, suprema lex*, did, after all, refer to the *safety* of the people as the supreme law. The New Model Army was successful because it offered a centralised command network and rigorously disciplined troops: the breakdown of centralisation, which produced the agitator unrest of the later 1640s, has been examined for the ways in which it fostered radical politicisation. Another way in which radicalism could flourish was in areas where military discipline was least tight. A lack of clarity about the delimitation of authority left room for personal and political disagreements to take the form of factional political campaigns.

The East Midlands provides a good example of a region in which military centralisation was lacking and there was room for autonomous action and an individual interpretation of the nature of military authority. The Association of the East Midlands proved 'stillborn'.[26] It is perhaps for this reason that the region which offered the least successful example of an army association and contained some of the greatest royalist aristocrats also proved a forging ground for radicals. The East Midlands was so geographically fragmented and factionally divided that there was room for extremists to emerge. It lacked internal, geographical cohesion, comprising rather those counties which did not seem naturally to fall into any other region, from Lincolnshire in the north to Buckinghamshire in the south. Almost as soon as the association was born, the Buckinghamshire committee detached itself and joined the Eastern Association, followed by Huntingdonshire in May 1643. Petty parochialisms interfered with a vigorous prosecution of the war effort and even the region's gentry republicans did not cooperate with each other.[27] At a personal level, relations between Thomas, Lord Grey of Groby in Leicestershire, Thomas Saunders in Derbyshire and John Hutchinson in Nottinghamshire were strained.

The region contained only one family of aristocratic parliamentarians, and thus lacked a sense of communal outrage at the actions of courtiers. It was soon obvious when royalist forces established themselves along the river Trent, surrounded by supporters with such noble power as the Cavendishes and Hastings, that this was not promising parliamentarian soil. The East Midlands could not be considered a bulwark of parliamentarian support, nor a region in which military resources could be concentrated in order to turn it to parliament's advantage. It was virtually abandoned to royalism. Only one major family in the area declared for parliament, and military command was therefore given to the Earl of Stamford and, at a precocious age, to his son, Thomas, Baron Grey of Groby. Grey of Groby was only seventeen when elected to serve for Leicestershire in the Long parliament and nineteen when placed in charge of the regional association. Probably following the lead of his father, he started the war as a supporter of Essex, but travelled a huge distance in political terms. When he died in his early thirties, he was a republican Fifth Monarchist. His role within the East Midlands Association has been described as a 'cipher', a man who presided over counties which continued to organise themselves with a fair measure of autonomy. The charge most often made against him was his unwillingness to serve outside Leicestershire, though ties to one's county was a feature of the characters outlined here.[28]

Localism was blamed for the sluggishness of the parliamentary war effort during the first two years of the fighting. Grey was accused of it by Thomas Saunders, and the Presbyterian, Sir John Gell, made the same charge against Saunders, who refused to escort the parliamentary commissioners from Peterborough to Derby because he 'would nev^r goe in any service where the Lord Grey com[m]anded in cheife'.[29] Lincolnshire felt particularly aggrieved at the failure of the association to come to its aid. Attempting to buttress the gain of Crowland in the far south of the county and to intercept a convoy of arms and ammunition sent from Oxford by Henrietta Maria to strengthen royalist resistance in the area, the parochial concerns of the East Midlands Association came to the fore. Cromwell blamed Grey for not leaving Leicestershire. The Lincolnshire Committee blamed both Grey and Cromwell, for the same reason:

> There hath not at any time this three weeks passed one day that we have not writt to Colonel Cromwell, the Norfolk gentlemen and my Lord Grey to appoint a place of meeting, and we would march with them wheresoever it were; their answer alwayes was they would meet, but something of importance was first to be done in those counties they were in.

There was certainly evidence that the military leaders were not pulling in the same direction. Cromwell's resources were stretched to the limit.

He was able to proffer the excuse that he was expected to be in several places at once as a general-purpose saviour of the cause. Grey and the Norfolk Committee were guilty of more blatant parochialism. It was perhaps unbecoming for a man who had been given overall command of a region not to move away from Leicestershire, but Grey's reluctance is more appreciable in view of the strength of royalist hostility in the county which threatened his own estate at Bradgate. The Hastings and Grey families had long viewed each other with violence across the eastern hills of the county. Although Grey's protection of his own estate might seem selfish, in view of the ruination of the lives of smaller farmers whose land was being trampled by rival armies the loss of the Bradgate estate would deprive the Midlands region of a centre of parliamentarian resistance. It would seem equally bad military practice to embark on tentative manoeuvres northwards, only to leave one vulnerable to a rearguard counter-manoeuvre. Cromwell did not agree and challenged Grey with obstructing the common good. The solution to the crisis in Lincolnshire was to blame the local command, and father and son, Sir and Captain John Hotham, became the first casualties of a purgative process whereby men who became lacklustre in their commitment to the cause fled or were pushed into royalism.[30]

At some point in the mid-1640s – around 1646, though the records for Grey's activities in the war years are virtually non-existent – Grey underwent a political transformation and became a stalwart of the populist faction. The most likely cause is as a consequence of his 'conversion' to sectarian religion. He did not join the Fifth Monarchists until shortly before his death, and the path of his religious views is difficult to trace in the interim.[31] He was certainly a sectarian, not a predestinarian but a believer in the power of the universal spirit, and in the second half of the 1640s had developed religious views which placed him much closer to Saunders and Hutchinson, though relations between all three were never cordial. Certainly by 1648 his politics were radically altered from the days of his moderate parliamentarian support for Essex. One of the keys may have been his isolated position within the East Midlands and his localist sense of patronage towards his tenants. It manifest itself in the need to defend his patrimony, particularly in view of the inability to secure a safe and secure peace and, after Naseby, the presence of the Scottish army in the English Midlands.

Thomas Saunders of Little Ireton also had a semi-detached relationship with the command of the East Midlands. He was frustrated at Grey's localism and with his command, but because he believed that he was left isolated and vulnerable in Derbyshire. He was commissioned with only the rank of major,[32] directly through Essex's authority and he owed a nominal allegiance to the Presbyterian, Colonel Sir John Gell, with whom he had a stormy relationship. Saunders, however, had secured the agreement of the county committee that he should be responsible for raising his own troop, officered by men of his choosing.[33] Gell's authority was threatened and he ensured that his forces would be free from Saunders' influence. As early as February 1644, Fairfax had cause to reprimand Saunders for not following Gell in his day-to-day instructions.[34] From an early stage, therefore, Saunders was a loose cannon who could use the blurred lines of authority to play individuals and factions off against each other.

By November the rift between colonel and major was personal and antagonistic.[35] It was also detrimental to military discipline. There seems little to gainsay Gell's conviction that Saunders deliberately precipitated mutiny in the ranks in order to subvert the colonel's authority. Saunders accused Gell of using 'slanderous words' towards him – that he was a brownist, coward and knave – and responded by accusing Gell's brother, Thomas, of being unfit to be Recorder of Derby 'in respect of his meane estate, want of learning, lawe [and] honesty; his conversation being soe scandalous . . . swaring, [and] hating all honest [men]: he favored malig[nancy] [and] enemyes in armes: and [was not] to be trusted or confided in'.[36] Thomas Gell had been keen to make peace with the Duke of Newcastle. All 'honest [men]' would resent the affairs of Derbyshire being controlled by Sir John Gell, Thomas Gell and Gell's sons-in-law, Henry Wigley and Henry Wigfall.[37] Saunders employed the strategy which had been used by Musgrave, Westropp, Chaloner and Rigby in order to discredit mainstream parliamentarians in the localities.[38] The men in power displayed leniency towards malignants.[39] The Gells placed Saunders under house arrest while charges of insubordination were drawn up and Saunders dispatched letters to Fairfax in order to play his authority off against his accusers.

These exchanges are littered with expressions of insularity. Saunders was accused of tying his forces to Derbyshire, as Grey was deemed to have sacrificed the greater interest on the altar of local (or personal) materialism.[40] Saunders' cavalry troops failed to join the rest of the Derbyshire forces at Eginton Heath, where an attempt was being made to halt Prince Rupert's progress from Ashby de la Zouche. When Gell commanded his major into Nottinghamshire to liaise with Fairfax's horse besieging Newark, Saunders refused, went instead to London, and 'questioned what authority the deputie leivtenants had to com[m]and him, he said they had noe power to command any but such as were raised by vertue of the Ordinance of Militia, wch he said hee was not.'[41] The localist accusation against Saunders was effective because it was a tool to expose radical politics and sectarian religion. In contrast, the Nottinghamshire man, Colonel Francis Thornhaugh, was considered best placed to oversee the siege of Newark, 'as good reason hee hath his whole estate' bordering the town itself. Thornhaugh's material interest was considered justifiable. Localist sentiment encouraged Lucy Hutchinson to be glowing in her praises of her fellow Nottinghamshire man. Colonel Thornhaugh led soldiers who were 'as brave men as any that drew swords in the army'. Saunders was considered a poor soldier, with extremist politics, whose semi-autonomous status allowed him to raise officers in his own mould. Royalists in 1648 scoffed at 'Independent cowards and vermine' and highlighted Saunders in particular, who had deliberately encouraged his troops to mutiny whenever there seemed need to take them out of the county and whose greatest contribution to the war effort, it was claimed, had been to shoot an unarmed prisoner in the arm.[42] His religious stance and political outlook were similar to Hutchinson's, so he was considered 'a very godly, honest, country gentleman', but he was 'a Derbyshire man' and 'had not many things requisite for a great soldier'.[43]

Saunders' free commission to raise junior officers produced unswervingly loyal partisans who were prepared to lead the chorus of demands for Gell's removal and to have his commission vested in Saunders. Gell's charges centred around Saunders' insubordination and cowardice, two qualities antithetical to military command, while Saunders' supporters stressed the major's devotion to public service, in the language of the 'honest radicals'. Petitioners argued that to ask him to relinquish his commission in favour of a new one, albeit on terms similar to other commanders, would deprive Derbyshire of 'one of the bravest Regiments of horse in the North p[ar]ts'.[44] A subsequent draft enlarged on this theme:

> Wee make bould to advertize you that Maio[r] Sanders, whoe hath raysed one of the best Regiments of horse in theise parts of the Kingdome; and donne singuler service w[t]h them, is now confined by S[r] John Gell, whereby the service is like to bee neglected and the Regiment to bee dissolved and distroyed (w[ch] maye bee the designe of them that can confine him) and the good party here that have adhered to the Parliament discouraged.[45]

Localised letter-writing and petitioning campaigns turned a cause with little general appeal into one which seemed to command wider support. An ill-judged bombast from Gell to Saunders' rebellious junior officers began, 'I am more beholdinge to S[r] Thomas ffairfax then to yo[w] for he acknowleges me to be yo[r] Colonell, w[ch] is more then yo[w] doe', in which he chided captains Swetnam – 'that vaine ungratefull ffellow' – Daniel Watson, Battley, Hardstaffe, Sleigh and one Lieutenant Wetton.[46] This last junior officer was the Leveller, William Wetton, who three years down the line would be a disputant of the *Agreement of the People* and a trusted confidante of Henry Marten, whose Derbyshire estate he administered with the man he called his 'comrade', Maximilian Petty.[47]

Captain Joseph Swetnam, who may have been Saunders' own minister at Muggington and who was vicar of All Saints', Derby, was dispatched to Fairfax in York to plead on Saunders' behalf.[48] He found Fairfax encouraging and wrote back to his colleague, Captain Ralph Sutton, asking him to convey the news to the Derbyshire Committee. Sutton could inform the committee that Saunders had friends in high places and his allies on the committee would have support should they unite to pressurise the Gell faction. 'Sir John', he opined, 'is extreamely odious heare.'[49] Swetnam's support was useful in the parallel campaign which denied Saunders' brownist tendencies. He vigorously refuted the claim, to the extent of obtaining a petition from more orthodox local ministers. Charles Broxholme, the minister at South Darley, Peter Whiting, John Compton, Thomas Bakewell and Everard Poole, all ministers of the gospel, sent a message of support to the major, encouraging him that should authority call them to testify to Saunders' orthodoxy, they would 'conceive you to be noe seperatist [*sic*] or independent: and this opinion we will have of you dureing yor p^{r}sant practise amonge us [and] profession to us.'[50] Saunders was clearly both, though not a brownist.[51]

Saunders' regiment was incorporated within the New Model Army in March 1646. His supporters resisted it, seeing an attempt to stifle his potential for radical, independent action. Parliamentary managers were trying to muzzle by accommodation what Gell had failed to do by confrontation. Saunders became a major under Sir Francis Thornhaugh and subsequently took over the regiment when its colonel was killed at the battle of Preston. Hutchinson believed that Cromwell, in support-ing Saunders' command, was insinuating himself with Saunders in order to purchase Little Ireton, so that he could return it to the Ireton family. Henry Ireton had recently married Cromwell's daughter, Briget.[52] Under its new colonel, Saunders' regiment, along with that of Colonel Adrian Scrope, lobbied hard for justice against the king and for a radical political settlement. There was, however, no evidence that this was a regiment in which specific Leveller influence had been exercised through the agitators. It issued an implied criticism of the New Model (and presumably garrison forces) because officers whose commissions came from parliament would be stymied in any attempt to press for redress of their soldiers' grievances. The officers were aware that the soldiers had knowingly broken the existing law but would not be seen to defend them because they were of the 'ruder sort'. Saunders' soldiers, on the other hand, defended individuals who had uttered statements against the king and had themselves, revealing an awareness of the person/office distinction:

> had meditations concerning the Kings coming in to be King over us, whether by any rule from God or the election of the people, or by the Sword: but we found no other but that his inheritance came through William the Conquerer by the Sword. Neither do we find in the Law of God any such Command, that *this man* should be King in England'.

Scrope's and Saunders' regiments even put forward their own version of an *Agreement*, in which the parliament would be made up of two MPs elected from each county and two from each regiment.[53]

Saunders was to be one of the New Model officers most hostile to the rule of Cromwell, believing that the issues of the mid-1640s offered a history lesson which could prevent the repetition of mistaken authority. Military force administered by a central authority – an institutionalised state – would always be detrimental to liberty. The single exception was a state governed by an accountable, representative 'peoples parliament'. In 1642, the question of a single person's sovereignty over parliaments had led to a fight

> over . . . a *Militia*, as the late king durst claim; that is to say, *A standing Army*, which may in a short tract of time, by the policy of any Single Person that shall succeed, be made wholly Mercenary, and be made use of to destroy at his pleasure the beings of Parliaments, and render all the blood and treasure expended in this cause, not only fruitless, but us and our Posterities under an absolute Tyranny and Vassallage, both in our consciences, persons, and estates, the danger being beyond comparison higher . . . then it could have been to have allowed the late Kings Claim to that *Ancient Militia*, which was, *to command the Country to Array*, the Arms being in the Countryes own custody, and themselves, or men of their own chusing to bear them, who had no particular interest to oblige them to obey any of the kings illegal commands.

There were two options open to the honest party in the country. Either the militia was under the control of a government which was accountable to the people and represented the public interest – as defined by the honest party – or the honest party retained the right to protect its independence and posterity from state interference.[54]

In the north of England, parochialism expressed itself in unwillingness to march away from one's locality for any military commander, royalist or parliamentarian. There was a strong streak of neutralism in the rugged hills of the North Country, which expressed itself in terms of defence of local rights and privileges. The most reactionary and the most radical were united in their resentment of the presence of the Scottish Covenanting army. While the Scots insisted on a say in the peace negotiations, the expense of keeping a foreign army in the north of

England, and its behaviour, was the hottest political topic.[55] Once the country was at peace, pressure grew to send the Scottish army home, but the English parliament was behind in its payments. Independents were in a small minority in the far north and the experience of heavy taxes and lenient treatment of malignants and Catholics had the effect of radicalising those few. Money which it was felt ought to be raised from the sequestration and taxation of Catholics and malignants came instead from crippling demands for taxation made on those who had shown unswerving commitment to the parliament. They would be expected to continue to dig deep into their resources – their birthright – while, it was claimed, the parliament was negotiating it away. Thus parliament left itself open to further charges that it was alienating its own supporters by charging high rates of tax and not pursuing malignants' estates with sufficient vigour.[56]

In the North East, the campaign against the Scots was led by Thomas Chaloner. Both contemporaries and subsequent historians have sought to cheapen his stance against the king with the claim that it sprang from bitterness and envy, but the Stuarts' dealings with the Chaloners may well have provided an example of a single action which could spark the chain of republican reasoning. The Stuart kings were accused of arbitrary treatment of the Chaloner family's patent on alum mining, the revocation of which left their posterity 'destitute of all present convenient means for their maintenance'.[57] The Animadvertor claimed that Chaloner's Speech without Doors was 'out of some Ancient discontent of his against the King', or the product of 'revenge' as Aubrey put it.[58] In the mid-1640s, disproportionate numbers of complaints about the behaviour of the Scots came from Chaloner's estates – six square miles of Cleveland. From nearby Newham Hall, the Cleveland gentleman, friend and creditor of Henry Marten, Thomas Westropp,[59] and Thomas Chaloner's younger brother, James, shuttled between home and London, organising a campaign against the Scottish Commissioners and their army.[60] One of the earliest actions of the Chaloner brothers after the establishment of the Commonwealth was to enlist the help of Thomas May to witness the family's campaign to restore its sole interest in the mining rights which it believed had been arbitrarily taken from them by the crown.[61]

John Musgrave's parallel campaign also had its roots in a local gripe about ill-treatment, this time against the Vaux family.[62] His wider campaign extended his own case, contrasting the political power and continuing financial buoyancy of malignants with his own sufferings and in particular his imprisonment for daring to speak out against such injustices. His definition of malignancy was sweeping. He used as violent language against Richard Barwis, the loyal if moderate MP for Cumberland, as he did about Sir Philip Musgrave, chief English ally of

Montrose, Charles' champion in Scotland. John Musgrave's four tracts called *A Word to the Wise* led to his appearance before the Commons' committee on parliamentary privilege. The chair of the committee, John Lisle, was unable to help him, especially because Musgrave refused to speak and was therefore clearly in contempt of parliament.[63] From the Fleet, however, he inveigled Sir Arthur Haselrig and Alexander Rigby to plead his case. Musgrave reminded Rigby of the latter's cousin, Elizabeth Worsley, who had invested all her estate towards the recovery of English birthrights and had seen little return. Worsley had written to Rigby:

> I have often heard of Magna Charta for which (and Religion) I have freely ventred all I have, so that when we sent in the beginning of these times, all the little plate we had, I durst not in confidence keep back so much as the handle of my Fanne . . . but being free-borne subjects, I humbly petition for the benefit of that great Charter.[64]

Rigby had his own reasons for citing the rights of the free-born and the degree of sacrifice which had been made for the cause. He chaired the committee which deemed that MPs whose personal livelihood was so compromised by the war that they were no longer able to function should be entitled to a weekly allowance of four pounds.[65] Rigby was one of its beneficiaries, but subsequently came under suspicion for embezzling public funds and felt compelled to compose an extraordinary letter, justifying every penny and horse which he had had during the war, and outlining the degree to which he had abandoned his own profession and willingly ruined his estate for the public cause.[66] In accounting for the loss of 'the greatest pte of the pfitt of my estate for my service for the Parliam' oftentimes to the hazard of my life', he identified his own sufferings with those of the unpaid soldiery, widows and orphans.[67]

In the West Country, the strength of royalism during the war delayed the setting up of centralised parliamentarian forces, though following the battle of Naseby, the area west of Oxford saw much of Cromwell and Fairfax's forces during the campaign to capture the region.[68] The last royalist stronghold, Oxford, fell on 24 June 1646. The forces under the Presbyterian peace-party stalwart, Colonel Edward Massey, were disbanded in favour of soldiers of the New Model. This, along with the disbandment of other provincial forces, was a defeat for the Presbyterian moderate faction.[69] However, localised forces outside the New Model were not necessarily a sign of anti-Independent activity, and the ability to operate outside centralised structures offered opportunities for radicalism as well as reaction. Returning to the bogus printing campaign of 1646 which played with the name of Evan Tyler – 'Printer to the Kings most excellent Majestie, as was the Scottish papers lately published and dispersed in London' – there is evidence of localism for more radical purposes. Several of the tactics used in the other tracts, which claimed to come from Tyler's Edinburgh press in the autumn of 1646 and which were, in reality, pro-Chaloner defences of the Speech without Doors, reappeared in a seemingly mainstream suggestion for a Western Association. This was published shortly after Massey's opponents had succeeded in new modelling the western forces at the expence of Massey's brigade.[70] Initially, this seemed an uncontroversial account, which recommended Wiltshire as an good example of a local defence force, formed by dividing the county into twenty-four squadrons based around groups of parishes. It offered self-defence as its justification, since without them, should they 'be invaded by *French* or *Irish*, then we cannot provide for our own safety'.[71] The language then gave away increasing evidence of extremism. The forces would be officered by local men, elected by the rank and file.[72] There followed a stirring piece of patriotic, Levellerish recruitment:

> What makes them here ['foreign' forces, to be understood in its widest sense], cumbring this English ground? We are English men, and cannot beare any other government, but what is approved by consent to be free, just, and rationall . . . let us lay aside all delusions of the Enemies of our naturall Rights and liberties and resolve to stand by this Parliament against all opposers whatsoever . . . continue to stand firm as free men borne, free to live and so to dye, and live as doth this honourable Parliament, whom we have intrusted for our preservation.[73]

As if to drive home the point, George Thomason wrote on his copy that these were 'Independant Propositions'. There are few textual clues to the individuals behind it. Edmund Ludlow was closely associated with raising the militia in Wiltshire. Two parishes – Inglesham (Squadron XIII) and Buckland (XXI) – fell within the estates of Henry Marten, the prime exponent of such drolleries using Tyler's name. The phrase 'against all opposers whatsoever' is one which we will encounter again.

The gentry's interest in protecting their estates and recouping their losses and the material welfare of the ordinary person were moulded together. Local control over the militia was the way to ensure the maximum commitment to the cause while preserving the integrity of the people and their environment. Should there be need to fight 'foreign' invaders, local people protecting their own would be the surest way to keep the spark of commitment to the fight alive and 'other charge is little, yes, as nothing, in respect of our security we shall injoy, there by, our Officers and Soldiers are of our selves.' '[S]uppose we never are disturbed,' and there was no need to fight, local people who had not been pressed into service to defend other areas would be left free to pursue the right to employment and material sustenance, so 'our labour and charge is not lost, with our Horses we may dayly plough, sow, to carriage and all other necessary worke that may be'.[74]

During the second civil war, local materialism came into its own as a means of supplementing New Model forces while maintaining a high degree of autonomy for radical action and statements.[75] Sir Arthur Haselrig wrote to Lenthall, that in the face of the Scottish army mustering on the English border, the Commons was slow to offer encouragement to the people of the North East 'to Joyne in main-tenance of o[r] ould Cause or for to defend themselves'.[76] The material interest of self-sacrifice defined the public interest and the righteous cause, bonding commanders and men. All ranks in these forces were risking their lives and their livelihoods – the commanders in investing estate and the men in deserting the harvest. John Pyne levied a militia force to defend Somerset[77] thereby igniting the smouldering resent-ment of his opponents, who charged him with demagogic, illegal and unrepresentative behaviour. Charges were made retrospectively against Pyne, in 1649, similar to those of Clement Walker in the *History of Independency*, and he seems the most likely organiser of the campaign.[78] Pyne's ability to manipulate local administration allowed him to assume an independence which his opponents referred to as petty tyranny. He enforced *ex officio* oaths, ruled through a faction on the county committee, applied heavy assessment on those who opposed him, 'mutinously and seditiously by power carried and indeavoured to carry *Elections of parliament men* for his favourites, and wilfully disobayed many *Orders, and Ordinances of Parliament*:

> and when we hoped for peace by the late Treaty, whilst it lasted, he declared in the Country, *that the Parliament should make no peace with the King, but that the Kings life should be taken from him*: And for that purpose, he and his confederates have listed and raised divers new forces without the authority of *Pa[r]liament, to alter the fundamentall Lawes and government of the Kingdome, disinherit the King and his issue of the Crowne*, and inslave the free people of *England* to Martiall Law and Government, and the County to his tyranny and violence.[79]

From the vantage point of 1649, his opponents accused Pyne of having been in the same camp as fellow gentry republicans, Marten and Chaloner, in being one of the earliest incendiaries to separate the English from the Scottish Commissioners.[80]

The most notorious local regiment of the second civil war was raised by Marten in Berkshire in the summer of 1648. Marten was well aware that the New Model Army was the 'bulwark of all our liberties', but equally clear that its centralising tendencies and the influence of the grandees gave it the potential to oppress.[81] In May 1648, he composed letters to Fairfax and to the Derby House Committee on behalf of sections of the Berkshire Committee. Resolving to prevent the county from joining in the local risings for the king, he informed them that he was raising a defensive militia force before he had secured the agreement of either the Commons or Fairfax.[82] It was a *fait accompli* which placed the onus on the authorities to assert themselves and have it disbanded, and should they attempt this, he could respond that parliament or army did not have the security of the people at heart, that they disrespected the opinions of local people and acted in a high-handed, arbitrary and oppressive fashion. Parliament did regarrison Reading and levied fresh troops, but tried to prevent Marten's independent action because he was rallying 'the holy tribe of levellers'.[83] Defiant, Marten presumed that the House would 'rather bee served than waited on' and would not answer to it in person. Instead, he sent a 'justification' to the Speaker, that he had raised cavalry troops and 'by ye help of some friends & my own care & cost I have gotten up a troop of honest men . . . resonably well appointed, notwithstanding ye strange obstructions I mett with from those that owed their contrey as much assistance as my self.'[84]

Marten recruited William Eyres, who had been active in promoting the *Agreement of the People* among the regiments.[85] Others deserted established regiments, lured by Marten's egalitarian principles, so that the troop was rumoured 1,500 strong by the end of August.[86] Their horses were 'commandeered' from travellers, with the repeated sneer that malignants ought to make greater contributions to the war effort. One in particular, Lord Craven, was one of Marten's (many) creditors.[87] In August the Commons reported to Fairfax that it had demanded Marten's attendance, his officers' arrest and the return of stolen, or in Marten's eyes, commandeered property.[88] His soldiers displayed little respect for the Houses or the New Model.[89] Their authority was the sword. Their justification was material – the oppressiveness of tithes.[90] Marten was aware of the latitude with which his men interpreted *salus populi*, and 'I presume ye House will consider that ye extraordinariness of ye occasion in this iunture of affairs may excuse a little over-acting in a service of this nature, for which I do not doubt . . . but I shall receive ye happines of being favourably understood, if not well accepted by ye House'. *Mercurius Pragmaticus* denounced

> their imbellished colours beautified with this misterious motto, 'For the People's Freedom against all tyrants whatsoever,' . . . the rusticks of Berkshire resorting to him in great numbers, being mightily taken with [the] novell doctrine, that the supreame power & authority is inherently in the people, & to them doth Harry daily preach in the habit of a Leveller.[91]

The Presbyterian, Sir John Maynard, reinterpreted Marten's slogan as 'parity and Anarchy'.[92] Another opponent wrote a clever account which wove together the pamphleteering campaign – 'thick Vellome' that hung 'in the smoaky Chimney of Rebellion' – agitation, and the sponsorship of Henry Marten, whose notoriety for licentious living encouraged a plethora of scabrous references to the 'Gunnerea of Martiall authority'.[93]

Thomas, Lord Grey of Groby, raised a force in Leicestershire imbued with the radical principles of its commander.[94] One newsletter, encouraged that the county was so forward in promoting the common safety and in

> such a formidable posture, that I think they may be the patterne to the rest of the Counties of England, for they have chosen their Officers, and formed their Regiments, *viz.* six Regiments of Horse and Dragoones, three hundred in each; the Foot are not as yet completed, my Lord *Grey* is chosen Commander in chiefe, so that now there wants nothing but power from the House, to inable my Lord *Grey* to give Commissions to the officers thus chosen by the Countrey.[95]

Grey had returned to Leicester from London in order to settle the militia, and it had been the decision of the 'well affected party of that County' that Grey's force be raised and be the 'ways and meanes, as might put the said county into such a posture, as should be for the defence of themselves, and render them most serviceable to the peace and safety of the Kingdome'.[96] These soldiers demonstrated that 'old English blood boyl(ed) afresh in Leicestershire men'. They were fired by zeal for the cause, a sense of community liberties and patriotism for their native soil, which encouraged gentlemen to give up their horses and tenants to abandon their farm work, supposedly, according to the propaganda version, without a thought for the material sacrifice this represented:

> we understood that our *proclaimed enemies* (the Scots) were drawing towards us, even to fall upon this Nation when it was weak . . . wee tryed what volunteers would appear, which were not a few, that tendred themselves and their own horses, and those that wanted wee horsed upon those that were dissenters, insomuch that . . . we have mounted a considerable number for so inconsiderable a County . . . not waiting upon the customary way of pay and quarter, which would retard us, and such a work as this.
>
> We had our men so willing to goe forth as if they should finde their *wages in their worke*, yea though in the highest of this harvest, and this unseasonable weather; At our meeting a March being propounded, they cryed, ONE AND ALL.[97]

Grey's troops continued the tradition of localist reluctance to come to the aid of the rest of the country. Rossiter's offensive in Nottinghamshire was only finished by Grey when the royalists fled into Leicestershire.[98] When Cromwell informed the Committee for Both Kingdoms of the dire state of the siege of Pontefract, Grey was encouraged to march north, but returned word to the committee that while his forces were at 'great readiness to serve the public' he required £500 for arms. The committee reported the request to the Commons.[99] However, when Grey sent a copy of his communication with Skippon to radical sectarian printer, Giles Calvert, the urgency for pay and provision was suppressed and his troops were ready to serve in 'all our neighbouring Counties'.[100] It was not until early September that the Leicestershire forces reached Pontefract, and only then did the Committee of Both Kingdoms recommend that Grey's request for maintenance be fulfilled. Two weeks later the committee was still dealing with calls from local commanders, including Grey, to provision their forces.[101]

Miliary action was coupled with pamphleteering and petitioning.[102] Henry Marten redoubled his efforts in the first two months of 1648, following his successful promotion of the Vote of No Addresses.[103] In February, he addressed his 'fellow citizens' with a message which John Wildman and Thomas Saunders were later to address to Cromwell in the petition of the three colonels.[104] The military had to be controlled by a representative parliament or by local representatives with a concern to protect their own.[105] Thomas May claimed it was the Leveller petition of 11 September which 'broke the Ice', followed 'by many other Petitions of the same kind, from divers Counties of *England*, and several Regiments of the Army; namely, from the County of *Oxford*, on the 30th of *September.* from the County of *Leicester*, on the 2nd of *October.* from many Commanders in the Army, on the 4th of *October.*'[106] Sections of the gentry in Leicestershire were the first to demand that parliament put the king on trial.[107] Rutland and Northamptonshire – 'other Counties . . . which have formerly felt the miseries of a Civill War' – established a force based on that of Leciestershire and, led by Lieutenant Freeman and 'three Gentlemen of Rutland', the county's well-affected complained to Fairfax of parliament's neglect of petitions from Hull, York, Leicester and London. They feared being massacred 'as our beloved Rainsborough was', and of 'our undone estate if our greatest enemies shall be made our Judges and chiefest Governour (or King)'.[108] The connections between Marten and Grey were noted[109] and in December 1648 – while Marten, Wetton and Wildman were debating the *Agreement of the People* – sections of the well-affected of Berkshire presented a petition to the Council of War, minded of 'our Countreymen of Leicestershire, [who] in behalfe of themselves and the whole Nation, did fully impresse our Sense of the present Condition of Affaires'.[110] They would expend the last of their lives and estates for the public good, called for '(either by this present Parliament purg'd, or another and more equall Representative chosen) to have a true Accompt requir'd of all the Bloud spilt, and Treasure spent', and warned the New Model not to become one of the oppressors.[111] The heavy hand of Marten's prose was evident: the petitioners admonished parliament that readmitting Charles to the peace negotiations would be like a dog returning to its vomit.[112]

A petition from Taunton of 9 February 1648 reminded parliament of its support for the 'true cause', which it would continue to defend it to the point that 'no Danger in the world may cause us to desert'.[113] In January 1649, the well-affected of Somerset suggested that the new Commonwealth would soon stabilise, provided the Vote of No Addresses was not forgotten.[114] Somerset moderates called Pyne a regicide and a republican, who lobbied his minority views by promoting 'scandalous and seditious Petitions in the Country, [sending] them up in the Counties name'.[115] The Presbyterian response to the petitioning campaign and the levy of county militia was to recall twenty-six MPs, described as 'doing ill services in their Counties'.[116] This corresponds closely with the numbers who voted against further addresses – though unfortunately it is not possible to demonstrate the correlation of the names for only Marten is specifically mentioned in both instances.

By stretching their actions beyond the point acceptable to the majority, gentry republican responses made explicit the notion of necessity and transformed tyranny into a universal concept. Pyne's supporters would defend Somerset against any 'danger in the world'. Marten recruited 'against tyranny and oppression', without specifying the source of his people's oppression, for as Maynard expressed it, he demanded freedom 'against all tyrants whatsoever'. Petitioners in Buckinghamshire vowed to fight against 'all opposers'. This is the language of the honest party – it was they who decided the nature of honesty and since honesty represented the natural state of public interest, anything which opposed them provided a definition of coercive tyranny. Tyranny could come from king, lords, parliament or army. Malignancy could be found anywhere. The 'common, plain, general and universal reason and moral principles' were, in fact, defined by very few, justified by the safety of the whole.[117] Any number of factions and institutions could be defined around and through the honest minority. Even though they directly represented a minority cross-section of their communities, they could claim to be speaking for the people. Henry Ireton warned that men 'frame pretences of public danger and extremity thereof, and from thence immediately to assume a liberty to break, or else neglect and fly above, the due bounds of order and government, and stir up others to do the same, pleading privilege from that vast large rule of *Salus populi*.'[118] Not only was the safety of the people the only law: but *salus populi, solus rex*.[119]

The primary concern of gentlemen of local standing was to protect their patrimony: a question of both principle and materialism. It is futile to try to separate them. On the side of principle, they would defend their area to the death in the face of royalist, Presbyterian or Scottish threat. There was a genuine concern for the safety of the people – their people. On the other hand, their protection of local interests involved defending their own demesne, an unwillingness to leave their area to assist another, and a keen awareness of their personal contribution to the cost of saving the nation from arbitrary government. Gentry republican rhetoric repeated so often the idea that its adherents had risked both their lives and their fortunes for a hard-won ideal that it developed all the characteristics of a cliché.[120] Pragmatic concerns about the need to defend one's patrimony were allied to a stirring language of political principle which spurred soldiers to a new level of radicalism. These were men who would '[throw] their Lives and Fortunes into hazard against a common Enemy'.[121] Initiating autonomous action did several things. It established and bolstered a power base within their localities, which in turn gave the defenders of England's liberties more leverage on the national political scene.[122] The way in which their personal position had been threatened was used to highlight injustices in the system, and marked them out as test cases, figureheads, and in some cases martyrs to the cause of individual rights.[123] As Rainsborough demonstrated at Putney, it made them a focus of attention and gave them status among those of more humble background, giving them common cause with those who believed that they had not received what they had fought for all this while.

NOTES

1. The nature of these parties much exercised civil war historians during the mid-1960s. A few of the pieces to emerge then were those of Lotte Glow, 'Pym and Parliament: the methods of moderation', *Journal of Modern History*, 36.4 (1964) 373–97; 'The manipulation of committees in the Long Parliament 1640–1642', *JBS*, 5.1 (1965) 31–52; Lawrence Kaplan, 'Presbyterians and Independents in 1643', *EHR*, 84 (1969) 244–56; Valerie Pearl, 'Oliver St John and the "middle party" in the Long Parliament', *EHR*, 81 (1966) 490–519.
2. Lucy Hutchinson, *Memoirs of Colonel Hutchinson* (London, 1965), p. 251.
3. One possible source for the debate between the honest representation of the general interest and what was personally beneficial was the Ciceronian disinction between *honestas* and *utile*, discussed by Richard

Tuck, *Philosophy and Government, 1572–1651* (Cambridge, 1993), p. 7. 'Honest' would be a rather crude translation of *honestas*, meaning rather honour or integrity. Nevertheless, the sections of Cicero's *De Officiis* (bk I.55–6) give an indication of the way in which 'good men of similar conduct' might form an association and (bk I.57) the sense in which 'of all fellowships none is more serious, and none dearer, than that of each of us with the republic' (p. 23). I have consulted the translation and edition made by M. T. Griffin and E. M. Atkins, *Cicero: On Duties* (Cambridge, 1991).

4. For example, by David Underdown, *Pride's Purge: Politics in the Puritan Revolution* (London, 1971), p. 163. The difficulty presented by the term Independent is amply demonstrated by the index to *Pride's Purge*, in which Independent has to be split into political and religious varieties with subcategories.

5. And gives a convincing critique of the rise of several of the politicians mentioned here, through the network of county communities and local power elites: Underdown, *Pride's Purge*, pp. 24–44.

6. David Underdown, *Somerset During the Civil War and Interregnum* (Newton Abbot, Devon, 1973).

7. David Underdown, "'Honest' radicals in the counties, 1642–1649', in Donald Pennington and Keith Thomas (eds), *Puritans and Revolutionaries* (Oxford, 1978), pp. 186–205, p. 188.

8. Clement Walker, *The Compleat History of Independency upon the Parliament begun 1640* (London, 1661) and p. 81 above. To which we can add those cited by Underdown, ' "Honest radicals", p. 187: "the Faction', the 'Levelling Faction', the 'Holy Beggars' (Marchamont Nedham in his royalist days)'.

9. Underdown also noted a shared stance which emerged out of the clash of antitheses: *Pride's Purge*, p. 24. His antitheses, however, clashed and formed new positions. Here, the relationship between the different elements is designed to be one in which one aspect fed another.

10. The most infuriating of which was Henry Marten, who, also by temperament, would begin to write down his opinions and then abandon a draft pamphlet with little more than a title page: Leeds, ML MSS 64/137; 78/10.

11. G[eorge] W[ither], *Respublica Anglicana or the History of the Parliament*, [28 Oct.] 1650, E780(25), to the reader, A3.

12. Petty, Wildman and Wetton were employed as agents on Marten's estates; Bishop, Cockayne and Chidley sent him ideas for reform and Cockayne in particular seemed to absorb the ideas and language of Marten; Eyres was part of Marten's county troops in 1648 (see below). Sexby was employed as a spymaster in Marten's great French connection of the 1650s and they may have collaborated in the authorship of *Killing no Murder* (1657). These links are detailed in my forthcoming study of Marten.

13. [Richard Overton], *An Appeal from the Commons to the Free People*, 1647; John Lilburne, *Legal Fundamental Liberties*, 1649; Lilburne, Overton and

Thomas Prince, *The Picture of the Councel of State*, [11 Apr.] 1649, E550(14), p. 22.

14. Another branch of the Saunders family were staunch royalists, who followed Prince Charles into exile; John L. Hobbs, 'The Saunders family and the descent of the manors of Caldwell, Coton-in-the-Elms and Little Ireton', *Journal of the Derbyshire Archaelogical and Natural History Society (DAJ)* 1XVIII (1948) 1–23, p. 10.

15. *Thurloe State Papers*, III pp. 237, 248; J. Richard Williams, 'County and municipal government in Cornwall, Devon, Dorset and Somerset, 1649–1660', Ph.D., Bristol (1981), pp. 135, 341–2.

16. G. E. Aylmer, 'Gentlemen Levellers?', in Charles Webster (ed.), *The Intellectual Revolution of the Seventeenth Century* (London, 1974), pp. 101–8, and also in *P&P*, 49 pp. 120–5.

17. Underdown, *Pride's Purge*. Thomas Chaloner and Henry Marten are described as declining greater gentry, Grey of Groby as greater gentry, Edmund Ludlow and John Pyne were 'county gentry'. Blair Worden has described Chaloner as an 'aristocratic republican'. His fortunes had been waning for three decades by the time the war broke out: Blair Worden, 'Classical republicanism and the puritan revolution', in A. B. Worden, V. Pearl and H. Lloyd Jones (eds), *History and Imagination: Essays Presented to H. R. Trevor Roper* (London, 1981), pp. 182–200, pp. 189, 191.

18. N. Yorks Record Office, ZFM Alum Deeds Nos 1–5. His country seat in Buckinghamshire, at Steeple Clayton, meant he was the neighbour of the Verneys of Middle Clayton.

19. *CJ*, II, pp. 563–4; Clarendon, *Rebellion*, V, p. 280, 7 May 1642; Ludlow, *Memoirs*, I p. 38 and n.1.

20. Hobbs, 'The Saunders family', p. 8. Little Ireton Hall was demolished in 1721: OS ref. SK313416. It was taxed at nine hearths in 1664; Michael Craven and Michael Stanley, *The Derbyshire Country House* (2 vols) (Matlock, 1984), II, p. 87.

21. See Underdown, *Somerset* and *Pride's Purge* where he is described as 'county gentry'.

22. Robert Ashton, *The English Civil War: Conservativism and Revolution, 1603–1649* (London, 1978), p. 198.

23. *Clarke Papers*, I, pp. 322–3.

24. Thomas May, *Breviary*, in Francis Maseres, *Select Tracts Relating to the Civil Wars in England* (2 vols) (London, 1815), I, p. 108.

25. The term is not my own and I owe it to Nigel Smith for distilling my ideas so aptly.

26. Clive Holmes, *The Eastern Association in the English Civil War* (Cambridge, 1974), p. 1.

27. There was also, as Lynn Beats has noted, an issue of wider principle at stake, which neatly illustrated the way in which the failure to delineate local responsibilities could be used by opposing parties. The East Midlands Association showed how parliamentary control of the trained

bands and the authority of the lord-lieutenants was sometimes at odds with the soldiers raised under commissions from Essex, the Lord General; see Lynn Beats, 'The East Midlands Association 1642–1644', *Midland History*, 4 (1978) 160–74.

28. Cited in Holmes, *Eastern Association*, p. 73; 'Believe me, it were better in my poor opinion, Leicester were not, than there should not be found an immediate taking of the field by our forces to accomplish the common ends', Cromwell to the Lincolnshire Committee, cited by Samuel Gardiner, *History*, I, p. 143; J. Richards, 'The Greys of Bradgate in the English Civil War: a study of Henry Grey, first Earl of Stamford, and his son and heir Thomas, Lord Grey of Groby', *Transactions of the Leicestershire Archaeological and Historical Society*, LXII (1988) 32–52.

29. Sanders MSS, Derbyshire Record Office, Matlock, D1232M/024; P. Young and R. Holmes, *The English Civil War: A Military History of the three Civil Wars* (London, 1974), pp. 107–10; Hastings MSS, *Historical Manuscripts Commission* 78, vol. II (London, 1930) p. 101; Lynn Beats, 'Politics and government in Derbyshire, 1640–1660', PhD, Sheffield (1978), pp. 180–227.

30. Holmes, *Eastern Association*, p. 74; Gardiner, *History*, I, pp. 105, 141.

31. *Thurloe State Papers*, III, p. 148; VI, p. 829.

32. That is above captain and below lieutenant-colonel.

33. Sanders MSS, Derbyshire Record Office, D1232M/031, in which citizens of Derbyshire argued to Essex that the money that they had invested in a regiment was dependant on Saunders' autonomous commission. Saunders was supported by Nathaniel Hallows, MP for Derby, who was a quiet member but one who retained his seat until 1653, did not stand for the Protectorate Parliaments and was returned in 1659; see Mary Frear Keeler, *The Long Parliament, 1640–1641: A Biographical Study of its Members* (Philadelphia, 1954), p. 201; Underdown, *Pride's Purge* p. 281 n.1.

34. Sanders MSS, Derbyshire Record Office D1232M/04 and 06.

35. Relations are detailed by Lynn Beats, 'Politics and Government in Derbyshire, 1640–1660', PhD, Sheffield (1978), pp. 180–227, 267–99.

36. Many of the papers in the Sanders MSS are Saunders' copy-letters, in which he uses a form of shorthand. Words such as 'not' and 'man' are usually replaced by a single character and are transcribed in full, using square brackets in the text.

37. Sanders MSS, Derbyshire Record Office, D1232M/09a and b.

38. See pp. 77–9.

39. Denzil Holles bewailed the fact that the 'moderate party' should be accused of favouring malignants: Holles, *Memoirs*, in Maseres, *Select Tracts*, I, p. 266.

40. Ibid., I, p. 270.

41. The charges laid by Colonel Sir John Gell against Major Thomas Sanders, Sanders MSS, Derbyshire Record Office, D1232M/024, clauses 4–6; Beats, 'East Midland Association', pp. 162–5.

42. *A Paire of Spectacles for the Citie*, [4 Dec] 1647, E419(9); *A Case for the City Spectacles*, [6 Jan.] 1648, E422(7); Hobbs, 'Sanders family'. pp. 11–12.
43. Hutchinson, *Memoirs*, p. 256; Underdown, *Somerset*, p. 121, notes of Pyne that '[t]ough talk . . . concealed military incapacity . . . Pyne was no soldier. His moment came at the end of the war: he was a politician and above all a local one.' There is certainly a good case to be made of Saunders, Grey, Marten and Pyne that another significant thing which these men had in common was military incompetence, at least in the eyes of other commanders, especially in the New Model. Their soldiers thought different.
44. Sanders MSS, Derbyshire Record Office, D1232M/015a.
45. The draft of the petition, which practises the same phrase, is Sanders MSS, Derbyshire Record Office, D1232M/015 and the finished draft at 018, dated 8 Feb. 1644(5), endorsed in Saunders' hand 'the Com[m]ittes letter to the Com[m]itte of boath kingdomes'.
46. Sanders MSS, Derbyshire Record Office, D1232M/020, Derby 10 Feb. 1645.
47. This throws up some interesting, but as yet unanswerable, questions about the rationale of awards of land to parliamentary supporters during the early 1650s. Were people given lands in an area in which they already had contacts? Was there a correlation between their wartime activities, those royalists with whom the victors had come into contact, and the estates which were sequestered and reallocated? Marten Loder MSS dealing with the estate management of Richard Peters: Leeds, ML MSS Box 56/ unfol.; 66/11; 68/1+2; Berkshire RO D/ELs F18 B5; Derbyshire Record Office, 1235/p. 3. Wetton had risen to the rank of colonel by the time the republic was established and was described as being from Covent Garden; John Lilburne, *Legal Fundamental Liberties*, reprinted in *Clarke Papers*, II, pp. 257–8; Aylmer, 'Gentlemen Levellers?', p. 107.
48. Derbyshire Record Office, D1232M/071b, petition of the inhabitants of Muggington to the House of Lords that Mr Joseph Swetnam be presented to the rectory in place of Sir Andrew Kniveton, a delinquent, n.d. All Saints was the main church in Derby and subsequently became the cathedral.
49. Sanders MSS, Derbyshire Record Office, D1232M/014, York, 4 Feb. 1645. From the members of the Committee for Derbyshire, Saunders received support from Colonel Robert Eyres, Ralph Clarke, John Mundy, Rowland Morewood, Edward Charlton and Randle Ashenhurst.
50. Sanders MSS, Derbyshire Record Office, D1232M/023, 18 Feb. 1645.
51. H. N. Brailsford, *The Levellers and the English Revolution* (Nottingham, 1961), p. 31, has him as an Anabaptist, along with Robert Lilburne, Hutchinson, Alured, Rich and Okey.
52. Hutchinson, *Memoirs*, pp. 257–8; Hobbs, 'Sanders family', pp. 10–11. They were married in June 1646: Gardiner, *History*, III, p. 109.
53. *The Declarations and Humble Representations of the Officers and Soldiers in Colonel Scroops, Colonel Saunders, Col. Wautons Regiment*, [7 Dec.] 1648,

E475(24); *A moderate and cleer Relation of the private souldierie of Colonell Scroops and Col. Saunders Regiments*, [15 Dec.], 1648, E476(25), n.p.; Brailsford, *Levellers*, p. 334, who dates the *Moderate and Cleer Relation* earlier than mid-December (p. 345 n.4); Underdown, *Pride's Purge*, p. 131. It was not clear, however, whether it was expected to first remodel the army in order to create county militias, or whether MPs would be returned direct from the New Model Army.

54. [Wildman], Thomas Saunders, John Okey, Matthew Alured, *To his Highness the Lord Protector*, 18 Oct. 1654, 669.f.19(21).

55. I am currently preparing an article on the nature of the Anglo-Scottish relations which shaped this view.

56. Bodleian Library, Tanner MSS 59/2 ff.705, 712, 714, 716–716ᵛ, 718, 752, 811.

57. N. Yorks Record Office, ZFM Alum Deeds No. 3, 27 Sep. 1627.

58. *The Justification*, p. 11; the point does not appear directly in the *Animadversions*, though this tract also seems to have been written by a member of the House of Commons, who specifically states that the most insulting parts about the king were not printed up in the written version but uttered within the safety of Commons' privilege; *An Answer . . . or Animadversions*, p. 2; Aubrey, *Brief Lives*, p. 158; William Page (ed.), *Victoria History of the County of York: North Riding*, (2 vols) (London, 1968), II, p. 355.

59. Newham Hall was rebuilt in the mid-nineteenth century, but the original was a house and estate of considerable size; T. Bulmer, *History, Topography, and Directory of North Yorkshire* (Preston, 1890), p. 176; OS map 1857, N. Yorks Record Office MIC 1803/255. The Marten/Westropp evidence dates from 1650. The closeness of the Westropp/Marten relationship by 1650 and the degree of Westropp's indebtedness, which led to him preceding Marten in the Upper Bench prison, would tend to demonstrate that Westropp was one of Marten's many creditors during the 1640s. Marten was already close to Chaloner by 1646 and it is unlikely that Westropp had not been introduced to Marten by or before then; Leeds, ML MSS 43/unfol; 64/137; 64/145–7; 64/149; First series 1/unfol, articles of agreement 25 May 1664 between John Wildman and John Loder; George Marten Letters/2 and 9.

60. *CJ*, IV, p. 711; *A Remonstrance concerning the Misdemeanours of some of the Scots Souldiers in the County of Yorke*, dated 20 Nov. 1646, printed 6 Dec. 1646, E365(9).

61. *Victoria History – York: North Riding*, II, p. 355; N. Yorks Record Office, ZFM Alum Deeds, No. 5, 16 Apr. 1650.

62. [John Lilburne], *Englands Birth-right Justified*, [10 Oct.] 1645, E304(17), p. 18.

63. *CJ*, IV, pp. 419, 451, 682; V, pp. 316–17; Worcester College, Oxford, Clarke MSS XLI ff.164ᵛ–165ᵛ; [John Musgrave], *A Word to the Wise*, [26 Jan.] 1646, E318(5); *Another Word to the Wise*, [20 Feb.] 1646

E323(6); *Yet another Word to the Wise*, [1 Oct.] 1646, E355(25); *A fourth Word to the Wise*, [5 May] 1647 E391(9), *A declaration of Captaine John Musgrave*, [23 Oct.] 1647, E411(20).

64. [Musgrave], *Yet another Word*, p. 36.

65. *CJ*, IV, p. 141, 14 May 1645; p. 161, 3 June 1645.

66. Bodleian Library, Tanner MS 59/2 f.683a, 25 Jan. 1646(7).

67. BL Egerton MSS 2648 f.126, 26 Jun. 1646, to Sir John Barrington, produced in court in 1654 in a claim that Rigby had embezzled a charitable bequest. His defence was his estates should not have been burdened during wartime: BL Egerton MSS 2648, f.126–8, 130; Egerton MSS 2649 f.41b.

68. Ian Gentles, *The New Model Army in England, Ireland and Scotland, 1645–1653* (Oxford, 1992), pp. 61–86.

69. Gentles, *New Model Army*, p. 144; Gardiner, *History*, III, p. 147; *CJ*, IV, p. 697; Bodleian Library, Tanner MSS ix f.566, Ludlow and Allen to Lenthall, 22 Oct. 1646.

70. Gentles, *New Model Army*, pp. 143–4.

71. *Propositions for the Westerne Association*, [14 Nov.] 1646, E362(8), p. 3.

72. *Propositions*, p. 2, clause IV.

73. *Propositions*, p. 4.

74. *Propositions*, p. 3.

75. *A New Engagement or manifesto . . . seeing all present Authorities to be perverted . . . are necessitated to . . . put themselves into a Posture for Defending their own and Countries Liberties*, [3 Aug.] 1648, 669.f.12(97).

76. Bodleian Library Tanner MSS 57/1 f.85, Newcastle, 18 May 1648.

77. He was MP for Poole in neighbouring Dorset.

78. Walker, *History of Independency*, pp. 5–6; Underdown, *Somerset*; *CJ*, V p. 565; Humphrey Willis, *Times Whirligig or, the Blew-new-made-Gentleman mounted*, Thurs., 9 Feb. 1647; Sarah Barber, "A bastard kind of militia', localism and tactics during the second civil war', in Ian Gentles, J. S. Morrill and Blair Worden (eds), *Soldiers, Writers and Statesmen*; Underdown, *Pride's Purge*, p. 222.

79. *Articles of Treason and high Misimeanours [sic], committed by John Pine of Curry-Mallet, in the county of Somerset*, Thurs., 2 Apr. 1649, 669.f.14(15), articles 1, 2 and 6. Another copy is published in the Thomason collection dated by Thomason 2 Mar. 1649 at 669.f.13(94); Underdown, ' "Honest" radicals', p. 193.

80. Underdown, *Somerset*, p. 122; *Articles of Treason*, p. 3; *Mercurius Aulicus*, 23 Feb.–2 Mar. 1645.

81. [Marten], *A True Copie of the Berkshire Petition*, p. 6.

82. Bodleian Library, Tanner MSS 57/1 f.111, signed by Marten, Daniel and John Blagrave, George Woolldridge, Timothy Avery, Reading, 26 May 1648.

83. *Mercurius Pragmaticus*, 6–13 June 1648, E447(5); *LJ*, X, p. 302, 3 Jun. 1648; *The Remonstrance or Declaration of Mr Henry Marten and the whole*

Society of Levellers (a satire), [25 Sep.] 1648, E464(37); Chris Durston, 'Henry Marten and the High Shoon of Berkshire: the Levellers in Berkshire in 1648', in *Berks Archaeological Journal*, 70 (1979–80) 87–95.

84. Bodleian Library, Tanner MSS 57 f.197, dated 15 Aug. 1648.

85. In Pusey is an area which bordered Marten's holdings along the Thames, nowadays called 'Ayers Common Plantation'. Unfortunately, the Pusey parish records for this period are unavailable.

86. *Mercurius Elenticus*, 23–30 Aug. 1648, E461(20).

87. Leeds, ML MSS 66/116; 85/32; 90/1. The attack on Forster was described in some detail in a complaint to parliament, signed by Francis Smith, John Wright, Thomas Grove, James Veare, John Aubrey and John Young: Robert Ashton, *Counter-revolution: The Second Civil War and its Origin, 1646–8* (Yale, 1994), p. 161; Barber, ' "Bastard kind of militia" ' (forthcoming).

88. Worcester College, Clarke, MSS cxiv f.67.

89. Bodleian Library, Tanner MSS 57/1 f.199, dated 16 Aug. 1648.

90. Bodleian Library, Tanner MSS 57 f.199; Deposited MSS C.168; Portland MSS f.103. Bulstrode Whitelocke claimed to have been a guest of Sir Humphrey Forster on the night of this alleged event and made no mention in his diary; Ruth Spalding (ed.), *The Diary of Bulstrode Whitelocke 1605–1675* (Oxford, 1990), p. 221.

91. *Mercurius Pragmaticus*, 22–9 Aug. 1648.

92. 'A Speech in answer to Mr Martyn who railest against ye king Lords & Commons. Said to be Sr John Maynards for ye wch he was turned out of ye house'. In manuscript in Thomason's hand; E446(19); W[illiam] Turvil, *Terrible and bloudy Newes from the disloyall Army in the North*, [11 Sep.] 1648, E462(28) p. 1. Turvil's letter was dated 7 September; *Mercurius Pragmaticus*, 22–9 Aug 1648, E461(17), n.p.; *CSPD*, 1648–9, p. 268, Inter 10E, pp. 117–21.

93. *An Agitator Anotomiz'd: or the Character of an Agitator*, [30 Mar.] 1648, E434(6), n.p.

94. Leics. Record Office, Common Hall papers, DXXX/xii/184, n.d.

95. *Two Letters sent out of Scotland . . . with another Letter written from a Friend concerning the affaires in Leicester, Rutland and Northamptonshire*, [24 Jun.], E449(24), p. 5. Another at E449(29), dated 22 June, repeats the same material except for the inclusion of Market Harborough.

96. *A Petition presented at a Common-Hall in London on satturday last concerning the Kings Majesty*, [28 Jun.], 1648, E449(35), p. 3.

97. Thomas, Lord Grey of Groby, *Old English Blood boyling afresh in Leicestershire men*, [24 Aug.] 1648, E461(7), p. 2; Ludlow, *Memoirs* I, p. 202.

98. *CSPD*, 1648–9, pp. 168, 177–8.

99. *CSPD*, 1648–9, p. 236, 8 Aug. 1648.

100. Grey, *Old English Blood*; for Skippon's role in London, see Ian Gentles, 'The struggle for London in the second civil war', *HJ*, XXVI (1983) 291–9.

101. *CSPD*, 1648–9, pp. 247, 269, 19 Aug., 4 and 19 Sep.
102. *To his Excellency the Lord Fairfax. A Petition presented at a Common-hall in London*, 24 Nov. 1648, 669.f.13(47), p. 4, mistakenly catalogued (Fortescue, p. 639) as in favour of the Personal Treaty.
103. Henry Marten, *The Independency of England endeavoured to be maintained*, [11 Jan.] 1648, E422(16), p. 15; Hutchinson, *Memoirs*, p. 265.
104. See Chapter 8.
105. Henry Marten, *The Parliaments proceedings justified, in declining a Personall Treaty with the King*, [7 Feb.] 1648, E426(2), p. 15.
106. May, *Breviary*, p. 127; *The Humble Petition of the Committee, Gentry, Ministry and other Inhabitants of the County of Leicester*, to the Commons, 2 Oct. 1648, E465(36).
107. The 'well-affected' of Leicestershire continued to petition in the early months of the Commonwealth government: *The Humble Representation of the Committee and other well affected Persons in the County of Leicester, to the Lord Fairfax and the Generall Councell of Officers in reference to the Agreement of the People as touching Religion*, 22 Feb. 1649, E545(22); *The humble representation of the committee, gentry, ministry, and other well affected persons in the county of Leicester*, [19 Mar.] 1649, E345(22); and also as *To the Supreme Authority the Commons of England . . . Petition from the well affected in Leicestershire*, 19 Mar. 1649, 669.f.14(6): 'That the Militia may be speedily setled and put into good hands, Tythes may be taken away, and relief sent to our brethren of Ireland', published by Giles Calvert.
108. *A Petition presented at a Common-Hall in London on satturday last concerning the Kings Majesty*, p. 4.
109. Turvil, *Bloudy Newes*, p. 3. Marten chaired the committee on major-generals, which decided in March 1648, that Grey had fulfilled the post of major general for 640 days, at £8 a day, and ordered his pay to be made from the sequestered estate of the Earl of Chesterfield: *CJ*, V, p. 506.
110. *A True Copie of the Berkshire Petition*, 30 Nov. 1648, E475(2), p. 1.
111. *True Copie*, pp. 5–6. They professed the army to be a bulwark of the people's liberties, a phrase particularly used by Marten, who called the army 'the greatest Bulwark, under God, of our Liberties', *Independency of England*: p. 8.
112. See Chapter 2, n. 46.
113. *The Humble Petition and grateful Acknowledgement of the town of Taunton*, 9 Feb. 1647(8), printed by order, 17 Feb., E427(21).
114. *To the Honourable the Commons assembled in Parliament*, the petition of the gentlemen, ministers and well-affected of Somerset, ordered to be printed and published 5 Jan. 1648(9), 669.f.13(68).
115. *Articles of Treason*.
116. Oxford, Worcester College., Clarke MSS CXIV f.80.
117. As David Underdown put it, '(t)he leaders of the Commonwealth believed in liberty, but they also believed in defining it themselves': *Pride's Purge*, p. 266; Hutchinson, *Memoirs*, p. 263.

118. [Henry Ireton], *A Remonstrance of Fairfax and the Council of Officers*, 16 Nov. 1648.

119. The name of a pamphlet issued in October 1648; *Salus populi, solus Rex. The Peoples Safety is the sole Sovereignty; or, the Royalist out-reasoned* (a reply to judge David Jenkins), 17 Oct. 1648, E467(39). I am not convinced by Brailsford's attribution of the tract to Hugh Peter. I am, however, certain that the author was not a gentry republican: the tone of contempt for the views of the people is not theirs: Brailsford, *The Levellers*, p. 345 n.8.

120. Marten, *Independency of England*, p. 25. It was usually expressed in the four basic principles which the war was fought to defend – 'their religion, lives, liberties and estates': Ludlow, *Memoirs*, I, p. 143. It was satirised in *A satyrical Catecisme betwixt a Neuter and a Roundhead. Also how the Round-head converted the Neuter and promised him an Excise Office*, [20 Jun.] 1648, E449(1).

121. May, *Breviary*, p. 97.

122. Denzil Holles provides a list of those Independents whom he considered to have benefitted materially from public office: Holles, *Memoirs*, in Maseres. *Select Tracts*, I, pp. 267–70.

123. A characteristic which persisted. In 1819 the editor of the newspaper, *The Republican*, Richard Carlile, was arrested. From Dorchester jail he wrote that he was 'fully aware of the aspect of the times: but unless they are met by a boldness equivalent to martyrdom on the part of writers and publishers, the press will become that destructive engine in England which it has proved to be in other countries.' *The Republican*, address to the readers, 30 Dec. 1819.

4

King Ahab

In tracing the gentry republicans, we have followed a debate about the king and kingship which travelled from the particular to the general. The starting point was a specific action by Charles which demanded a specific response. The argument then moved on to discuss the ways in which Charles had demonstrated a continuous history of immorality and finally concluded that this was the behaviour which could be expected from all kings. It was expressed in largely civilian and secular terms. However, a parallel debate was taking place, chiefly amongst the soldiers of the army, which was an apocalyptic expression of biblical exegesis. This account reversed the logical process which travelled from the particular to the general. It started from general biblical parables about the magisterial office and came finally to rest with a highly personalised condemnation of Charles Stuart.

Every man who enrolled in the parliamentary army was furnished with a copy of the *Soldiers' Bible,* containing passages of Scripture which encouraged him 'to fight the Lords Battels, both before the fight, in the fight, and after the fight'.[1] In 1645, the New Model thus emerged out of a pre-existent culture in which the soldiery were appraised of their own religious role.[2] Religion was an important means of keeping morale high. A mixture of Old and New Testament texts reminded soldiers of God's gracious promises to his army and to think of their enemies 'as nothing, and the men that warre against thee as a thing of naught, (Isa. 54: 17).' Recent historians have counselled against too literalist a view of the New Model Army 'filled with preaching, praying and psalm-singing soldiers inspired by their chaplains': the testimony of contemporaries, like Thomas Edwards, that the army was a breeding ground for sectarian anarchism, is suspect hyperbole.[3] However, comforting resort to the word of God could ameliorate the physical and emotional insecurity fostered by the itinerant life of a soldier. Despite being warned against too literalist an interpretation of contemporary sources, there is no reason to doubt John Vicars' account that the chaplains at Edgehill encouraged the soldiers to fight for 'their Religion, Lawes and Christian Liberties'.[4] England's liberties could be both civil and religious, but the religious response had a tendency to stress the soldiers' special relationship with God, which distinguished and therefore separated them from their fellows. '[T]he worde doth hold out in the Revelation', proclaimed William Goffe in apocalyptic language which presaged the Fifth Monarchism of the next decade, 'that in this worke of Jesus Christ (the destruction of Antichrist) hee shall have a companie of Saints to follow him . . . Now itt is a scruple amonge the saints, how farre they should use the sworde, yett God hath made use of them in that worke.'[5] These saints had a more noble and Christian motivation than the desire for regular pay or military reputation.

The soldiers sought the Lord down a number of different sectarian routes, fed by the availability of pamphlet literature within the ranks.[6] There were those whose views incorporated some form of (generally Calvinist) predestination, believing they belonged to an elect group of saints favoured by God. There were also many who posited free will, believing God's love to be universally bestowed, and that Christ and Antichrist, spirit and flesh, was a struggle which took place within the heart of every man and woman, not between individuals. Belief in free will was invariably described as Arminian, that is Arminian in its widest context, meaning a believer in universal grace.[7] These coexisted with a current of millenarianism, which equated the chaos and carnage of the war with the conditions required for the end of the old world of the flesh, announcing the new world of the thousand year reign of Christ which would herald the rule of the saints.[8] Later in the 1650s it often referred to Christ's literal second coming.

The corollary of seeing religion as a morale-booster was that it was also a means to analyse defeat, despair and confusion. The lives of ordinary people had been turned upside down by the call to fight an incomprehensible war which would 'surprize a man on the sudden, force him from his Calling, where he lived comfortably, from a good trade; from his dear Parents, Wife or Children, against inclination'.[9] Parallel to the intellectual debate about Charles' acceptability to control the militia and the duration of his seclusion from power which would restore his suitability, was another, more emotional reaction. This was all the greater because it arose out of civil bloodshed rather than being the rationalised consequence of martial glory abroad or defence against invasion. It was partly resolved by referring to the alien imposition of the Norman

Yoke, but was more aptly and colourfully expressed as a spasm within the body politic:

> We never did, not doe regard the worst of evills and mischiefes that can befall our selves in comparison to the consequence of them to the poore Nation, or to the security of common right and freedom, we could not but in (reall not formall fained) trouble of heart for the poore Nation of oppressed people, breake forth and cry, O our bowels! our bowels! we are troubled at the very heart to heare the peoples dolfull groanes, and yet their expected deliverers will not heare or consider, they have run to and fro, and sighed & even wept forth their sorrowes and miseries, in petitions, first to the King then to the Parliament, and then to the armie, yet they have all been like broken reeds.[10]

The idea of a civil war cut deep into the self-confidence of the English people, reflective of wounds and scars within the nation itself.[11] The soldiers who had to leave their families, their communities and their employment, were anxious to discover the cause of the nation's misery, and to remedy it.

This chapter is therefore a study of the religious language employed against Charles in particular and monarchy in general. In particular, questioning the reason for war involved searching for its origins. The evil which caused men to fight and kill each other could be a result of mankind's fallen nature. It could be the result of the malign influence of individuals – evil counsellors such as bishops, prelates, Laud, Strafford or the Presbyterians who issued such caustic and overblown threats of the consequences of sectarian religion in the army.[12] It could be the fault of the person whose sovereign power gave him the power to declare war, and who, by being given a veto and a personal say in the peace negotiations, was being given the same prerogative back again. In 1646, some (in the main anonymously) tried out a rhetoric of culpability and inquisition after blood-guilt: '[f]or God is a God *that taketh vengeance*'.[13] One anonymous pamphleteer believed that:

> to give [or debate upon giving] the *Militia* to the King at the end of twenty yeares, is very dangerous, and apt to beget an opinion in the people that he hath some right to it, and that at present is onely kept from him, for his abusing it, when . . . he hath no right at all in the least to it, *Salus populi* having already run such hazards of an utter ruining, by the *Militia's* being in his single hand, for which he ought, *according to Protestations, Oaths, and Covenants*, to be brought to exemplary, & condign punishment, he being the greatest & most notorious Delinquent in the whole Kingdome, yea, the originall fountain and Wel-Spring of all the Delinquents, giving Commissions to all the rest, to kill, murther and slay the innocent People.[14]

In 1646 Charles was seldom explicitly named: instead, reference was made to 'a king', 'him' or to kings as a class of people.[15] There was, nevertheless, an undercurrent of personalised retribution, for 'the warre might in the beginning have been prevented, if yee had drawn a little more blood from the right veine'.[16]

During 1647 the leadership of the army attempted to accommodate and neutralise lobbying from both inside and outside its ranks, wary of emotional outbursts. They searched for a settlement which included Charles almost as hard as the parliamentary commissioners, who carried to Newcastle their Covenant commitment to the king's person and the reformed religion.[17] When the grandees promoted their own peace formula, the *Heads of the Proposals*, the army agents spoke of betrayal, even by the gathered churches.[18] Indeed, leaders of Particular Baptist churches could be found supporting the *Heads*, which relied on extracting a pledge from Charles that he would guarantee (limited) religious toleration.[19] Nevertheless, the outward expression of their feelings remained secular.

The secular campaigns and the language of religious crusade dove-tailed at the end of 1647, when, despite the continuing negotiations with MPs, commissioners and grandees, Charles signed an *Engagement* with the Scots, and by the spring of 1648 it appeared likely that there would be a second civil war. The Particular Baptist, William Allen, described a prayer meeting held by the New Model Army at Windsor on 29 April 1648. After a whole day of thought, prayer, introspection and self-analysis, and then another two days' reflection, the soldiers concluded that the cause of the country's miseries was their continued negotiations with the 'man of blood'.[20] The army suffered 'iniquities of unbelief' and 'base fear of men'. The soldiers' lack of conviction had stymied progress, obscuring the 'right' path, defined as that which they would have taken had they been carried along by trust in the will of God.[21] With prolonged prayer, they passed through the three stages of knowledge – 'searching for, being ashamed of and willing to turn from our iniquities', also described as 'serious seeking his face'. This engendered 'a very clear and joint resolution'. They would stop looking to Charles for an end to the war.

Allen's is a stirring and dramatic account which stands out as a record of army decision-making, but his words were written eleven years after the event and were designed to rekindle emotions.[22] The intervening years may have made the recollection different, more straightforward or rosy tinted. We do not know how united were the views within the New Model in April 1648. It was unlikely to have been quite as unanimous as Allen remembered. Nevertheless, another account, written at the time, claimed that the prayers lasted from nine in the morning to five in the afternoon and would 'direct them (the army) in the great businesse now in hand That they may bee Instruments that

Justice may bee done uppon those who have caused soe much bloud to bee shed, and that righteousness [and] Judgemt may flowe in the land. Itt is incredible', continued Clarke's informant, 'how wonderfully God appeares in stirring uppe and uniting every man's heart as one in the prosecution of this busnesse.' As if to confirm the decision taken at Windsor, two hours after the meeting dispersed, petitions calling for justice on the man of blood arrived from soldiers in South Wales and northern England.[23] We are presented with a picture in which soldiers, to a man, knelt with each other, silently wept, and with one accord realised the error of their previous policy and the clarity of their new.[24]

The numbers calling for justice against Charles and the passion of their cry, rose sharply in the summer of 1648. It may have been no coincidence that one of the most zealous accounts of the change of heart was given by a Particular Baptist, William Allen. Guilt at their churches' previous involvement in promoting negotiations with Charles may have pushed members of Baptist congregations into overblown statements of repentance.[25] Edward Sexby knew that there were some 'both great and small (both Officers and Souldiers)' who had wavered on the straight path to a righteous and just conclusion about the war, having 'lean'd on, and gone to Egypt for helpe'.[26] The numbers of evil counsellors left to blame shrank even further, leaving (within England) the isolated figure of the king – 'that man of blood'.[27]

The saints only took a decision after intense and often prolonged introspection and emotional anguish. Only when a policy, a point of view or an action could be said to accord with the will of God could it be considered 'valid'. Cromwell wrote long, self-examinatory letters, surely as much to clarify his own ideas as to persuade his recipients. One such was addressed to his friend, Colonel Robert Hammond, in charge of Charles' confinement on the Isle of Wight. Hammond had doubts about the policy which seemed increasingly to demand retribution towards the king, but Cromwell advised him '[i]f thou wilt seek, seek to know the mind of God in all that chain of Providence, whereby God brought thee thither, and that person to thee . . . And, laying aside thy fleshly reason, seek of the Lord to teach thee what it is; and He will do it.[28] Cromwell was counselling his friend to rely on God's will, and not to make independent judgements of his own, for 'our fleshly reasonings ensnare us'.

Discord among the saints clearly flagged a problem. Since God's judgement allowed only one right and a series of wrong courses, lack of agreement implied that at least one group promoted a view discordant with God's harmony, provoking claim and counter-claim that one side or other was acting from fleshly, self-seeking motives.[29] The greater the sense of unanimity, therefore, the less reason for self-reflection and the consequent conclusion that confusion must be caused by God having abandoned them. When the Putney debates were adjourned for prayer, the outcome was an expression of solidarity – that the army should not talk to the king.[30] Having allowed this decision to recede into the background, it returned with renewed fervour in the spring of 1648 as Charles prepared to launch a renewed war. The prayer meeting at Windsor was a major propaganda coup, creating the impression that the decisions of the army were still unchallenged – internally, at least. So great was the force of God among it, leading it to follow His path, that eventually there was none who could deny that it was God's will that the army be the instrument to bring Charles to judgement. It was an easier task to present the renewed resolve which was the purpose and consequence of prayer, when one began praying from a positive – and majority – position. The opposite stance – that the negotiations ought to be given a chance to succeed – was predicated on caution. Those who favoured continued negotiations were in retreat and conservative officers found their position increasingly uncomfortable. They were either pushed out of the army or felt the only option was to resign, both of which courses increased the impression of homogeneity in the ranks.

The result of such deliberations was a decision which had, by definition, to be absolute. Measured against the will of God, resolutions could only be right (in accordance with God's will), or wrong (politic reasonings contrary to it). The saints, both Arminian and predestinarian sectaries, promoted a dialectical view of the world, culled from an interpretation of the Pentateuch in which good was distinguished from evil, the spirit from the flesh.[31] For Arminians, the battle was fought out within each person's soul as it had been outlined in the creation story of Genesis.[32] For the latter, the battle between good and evil was one between saved and damned individuals, taken from God's covenants with Abraham and Moses.[33]

There was an obligation on all saints to make themselves humble before the Lord so as to be passive recipients of the will of God. They attempted to divest themselves of all human vanity or will, becoming empty vessels which God would direct. But this was a difficult task when flushed with military success which thrust them into the centre of the political stage.[34] Their certainty was self-defeating. They combined the arrogance of belief in their own grace with shrewd political manipulation, effective organisation and the ability to churn out the propaganda to disseminate their message, which allowed them, towards the end of 1648, to overshadow all opposition points of view within the army. They also interpreted the Bible selectively, seizing on an apposite

text or phrase which throughout 1647 and 1648 came almost exclu-
sively from the Old Testament[35] and reflected the sense of the
imminent, revolutionary dawn of a new millennium. The Old Testament texts can be grouped into four types: those which picked out
individuals drawn from the books of the Pentateuch, and in particular
Adam, Cain, Ham and Nimrod; the origins of Judaic kingship, outlined
in I Samuel 8; examples of non-Judaic kingship, found chiefly in
Chronicles and Kings; and finally, as the saints tried to envisage their
future, they turned to the prophets.

During the early years of the war, a parallel for a fundamental division
of mankind into good and evil was most often found in Adam's two
sons: Abel was blessed, Cain was cursed to live east of Eden, hunted by
the righteous for the distinguishing mark which he bore for his brother's
murder.[36] The author of *The Subjects Liberty set forth* believed that
'Royall power began with Cain, and the Giants of the Earth sprang by
mixture, and were men of renown, (Gen. 6: 4)',[37], and an author
Thomason described as a 'High German' claimed that England's rulers
were responsible for 'Cain-like, fierce, nay Diabollicall contentions'.[38]
This division of mankind, tending towards the idea that it reflected
fundamental differences between people or types of person was
described by the Swiss divine Giovanni Diodati.[39] In the same year
that the range of pamphlets using the Cain parallel hit the presses,
Diodati published his *Pious Annotations*, a commentary on the Geneva
Bible.[40] His gloss on the Book of Genesis ran:

> There came two branches from Adam, the one by Cain, and the other by Abel
> . . . The first of the children of the world, accursed, abandoned in the state of
> sin and condemnation, having the devill for its head . . . These two bodies have
> even from the beginning continued in enmitie, trained up in much cruelty and
> fiercenesse of the evill, against the good one, the first always strengthening
> himself, and increasing in power and number and exceeding in wickednesse,
> and iniquity . . . For the accursed one quickly grew mighty and powerfull in
> the world, by setting up great, and tyrannicall empires; and was corrupted by
> idolatries, pride, violence, and other vices.[41]

The distinction between the children of Abel and those of Cain was that
between the saved and the damned, but Diodati also described the
behaviour or actions of those children on earth. Those predestined to
damnation applied their sinfulness to the oppression of their fellows and
the glorification of themselves through the exercise of pride, violence
and idolatry. It was a description of heroism, military strength and
aggression, characterised as 'mighty', 'glorious' and 'powerful'. While
these comparisons – the forces of good represented by Abel, and the evil

of Cain – relied on distinctions drawn between individuals, it was also appropriate to use the biblical individuals as a metaphor for all subsequent human behaviour. 'Lordly' behaviour may mean acting like a lord, but could indicate a universal presumption.[42] Royal power could mean pride and arrogance in anyone. All men were subject to Cain-like contentions.

As the generations of Adam multiplied, so did mankind's iniquity. Noah, however, was chosen, and God having seen that mankind created ever more generations of sinful 'men of renown', he purged his creation with a flood. God settled a new covenant on humanity, through Noah, in which mankind was given dominion over land, sea, produce and animals, but should any person be killed, God required the murderer to give up his or her own life, for 'whoso sheddeth man's blood, by man shall his blood be shed: for in the image of God made he man'.[43] Despite the covenant, Noah's sons, Shem, Ham and Japheth, divided in the same way. Shem and Japheth were blessed. From 'the loynes of the cursed Ham' came 'the Kings of the Nations'.[44]

The man of renown descended from Ham was Nimrod, a more fitting representation of a powerful and evil individual, for he was 'a mighty one in the earth . . . the mighty hunter before the Lord'.[45] An image of greater populist force, it was particularly taken up in the later 1640s. In *The Parliaments Proceedings Justified*, Henry Marten attacked the way in which the Presbyterian-dominated parliament pandered so much to the will of the king, by shrewdly combining biblical image with the personal experience of those whose material hardship was a result of the king's attempts to revive feudal privileges over woodland. The conservative parliament would even have voted 'for the making a Forrest of all England, and a God of Nimrod'.[46] John Cook, Charles' prosecutor, repeated the phrase at the king's trial, claiming that prerogative made Charles 'that great *Nimrod*, that would have made all *England* a Forrest'.[47] William Erbury, former chaplain to Ingoldsby and Lambert's regiments and a believer in universal redemption, published *The Lord of Hosts* or *The Armies Defence* in December 1648, with a reminder that Nimrod had been the first king and the first oppressor.[48] Within a general framework in which he attacked the spirit of oppression and lordliness in anybody, and in particular opposed the second *Agreement of the People* for formalising worldly authority, he drew a distinction between historical kingly power and the saints who, when they came to govern, would do so remembering that God ruled them.[49]

A more providentialist and predestinarian approach was fostered by citations which explained the history of individual, named kings, and in particular Ahab and Nebuchadnezzar, responsible for tyrannising the

Israelites.[50] Both made frequent appearances in petitions which called for Charles to be brought to justice. Ahab was king of Israel, whose rule was related in the first Book of Kings. He married the infamous Jezebel, and, despite Elijah's warnings, fostered the worship of and gave protection to the idolatrous priests of Baal, which may have been a reminder of the Laudian church and the unpopularity of Henrietta Maria.[51] For the officers of the northern regiments, the godly who demanded Charles be brought to justice were the 'thousands . . . that have not bowed their knee to Baal and are yet . . . firme and untainted with the poysonous principles of Oppression and Tyranny'.[52] A similar example was used by George Cockayne, the preacher of St Pancras, Soper Lane, in his sermon to parliament at the end of November 1648. The story of Ahab was a lesson that 'if God do not lead you to do Justice upon those that have been the great Actors in shedding innocent Blood, never think to gain their love by sparing of them'.[53] When Matthew Barker left his congregation at Mortlake in October 1648, sponsored by Colonel Edmund Harvey[54] to preach to the Commons, he chose to remind the House of

> the foure great Monarchies of the world, though their firm-nesse and strength be like that of Gold, Silver, Brasse, Iron, as they were represented to Nebuchadnezzar in his dreame (Dan. 2).
>
> Yet because they were not erected upon a true foundation, the Stone cut out of the Mountaine breakes them to pieces . . . And so Great Babylon the throne of the beast being erected without Christ, yea against him, as falling down every day before him.[55]

It was a characteristic of the ungodly that, even after their power had been cut down, they would rebuild themselves. The forces of evil had to be entirely extirpated: to leave any opportunity for aggrandise-ment would be sufficient for tyranny to resurrect itself. 'Verity Victor' – a pamphleteer whose very name revealed an acute awareness of the coupling of military might and divine providence – argued that to restore Charles' negative voice would be like cutting down Nebuchadnezzar's mighty tree and leaving the root behind.[56] No matter what degree of power was left to the king, he would always be able to tyrannise the saints. A mere chink of potential power was, in the hands of those inured to tyranny, a sufficient opportunity for them to exploit it.[57]

But the saints of Israel also had kings, the model for which was provided by the eighth chapter of the first book of Samuel. God agreed to the Israelite's request for a king, copying the (heathen) nations which surrounded them. The royalists were fond of quoting I Samuel 8 to prove that monarchy was sanctioned by God, and John Cook was later to admit it was 'one passage which the King would have offered to the Court'.[58] Anti-royalists, on the other hand, maintained that I Samuel 8 did not constitute divine blessing on all monarchy, but was a situation specific to the Jews. The parallel did not cross boundaries of geography or time. Customs applicable to Judea were no longer relevant and Edmund Ludlow retrospectively claimed that it was at the point at which the Commons voted no addresses that republicans urged that I Samuel 8 was an argument proving monarchy 'was not desirable in itself'.[59]

Confining the sanctified elements of kingship to that specifically ordained for the Jews was one way of attacking Charles' pretensions to the divine right of God-ordained power. It was an argument with potentially radical consequences. Since the Israelites were the only people with a direct bond with God, their appeal for a king, like the heathen nations, was a breach of covenant. They were warned, through the prophet Samuel, of the nature of ungodly rule:

> This will be the manner of the king that shall reign over you: He will take your sons, and appoint him captains over thousands, and captains over fifties; and will set them to ear his ground, and to reap his harvest, and to make his instruments of war, and instruments of his chariots . . . He will take a tenth of your sheep: and ye shall be his servants. And ye shall cry out in that day because of your king which ye shall have chosen you; and the Lord will not hear you in that day.[60]

The first king of the Jews was Saul, but he was chosen at the people's peril. Though God sanctioned earthly rule, he did not approve it: kings received God's permission, but not His approbation. Although the concept of kingship was allowed, all those who held the office would prove to be unjust and oppressive.[61] God had instituted kingship/tyranny as a means to punish the children of Israel for their breach of faith.

A combined attack on both tyrants who were non-Jewish and a wider notion of Judaic kingship was prefigured in the parallel of Saul and Agag. Saul's rule was characterised by continuous warfare, but when the Lord instructed Israel to entirely destroy the Amalekites, Saul elected to spare the life of their king, Agag. The rout of the Amalekites, while their king remained a captive, seemed pertinent in the autumn of 1648. Charles had been twice defeated, and providential victory had demonstrated that God did not sanction the royalist cause. Despite such indications, there were still those in the army and the parliament keen to conclude the war by a personal treaty.[62] In the pamphlets which flooded the presses in support of no further addresses, Charles was Agag and his royalist supporters the people of Amalek.[63] If the army treated with Charles, 'shall not Agag, and the fattest malignants be only spared against all lawes of justice and equity: but must these have swords put into their hands again?'[64] George Cockayne drew attention to Ahaziah, the son of Agag, who also 'did evil in the sight of the Lord . . . For he served Baal, and worshipped him'.[65]

This was a potential attack on all kings who did wrong, and not just on specific kings who lacked divine sanction or who fostered evil. Agag, the heathen king of the Amalekites, does not feature heavily in the Bible, but for such a brief appearance in the Scriptures, the passage carries a heavy import. Saul had failed to follow God's clear instructions, sparing the king and his beasts for sacrifice to the Lord, but in doing so he presented 'burnt offerings'.[66] Saul was rejected as king of the Israelites because he had not followed the word of God, and the task of slaying Agag was left to Samuel, who told his victim 'as thy sword hath made women childless, so shall thy mother be childless among women'.[67] Here was a sense in which confused ordinary people, wrested from their families by the need to fight a civil war, could make sense of their sacrifice. It provided an emotive image which appealed to soldiers separated from loved ones. Innocents had been the victims of the civil war and families had been destroyed.[68] Henry Marten chose it for its impact:

> Because Agag by drawing his sword, had made many women child-less, it seemed to be Sauls opinion. That the putting up his sword again would restore the children to their mothers: But the ways of God were more equal in that case . . . One of the Kings had his own thirst after mans blood quenched with his own; and the other, for thinking that Laws did not extend to the punishing of Kings, was himself punished with being unkinged.[69]

Citizens of London echoed this sentiment in July 1648, but from a more orthodox religious position, counselling that God dealt directly with the disturbers of the peace. Whereas for Marten the text was a resonant parable, for these citizens it was a directly analogous situation, which warned that the war would be perpetuated if the people subjected themselves to the wills of the king and his courtiers:

> For as the lives & estates of Saul & Agag were taken, the one for sparing Agag King of Amaleck and the other Benhadad King of Syria, so it is likely and possible, and it is just and equitable, that God wil in the first place so deale with those who have justly accused the grand enemy of our peace, if they instead of prosecution, make an unjust agreement, contrary to the revealed will of God. I Sam. 15: 8 &c. I King. 20: 42. Isai. 14. 18. 19. 20.[70]

Divine institution was insufficient sanction of kingship if the king's actions were in contravention of the law of God.[71]

Prophets, such as Samuel, were the means by which the children of Israel were shown the ways in which they veered from the righteous path and the direction they needed to take to return to godliness. They were internal critics who presented a conditional situation – either people followed their advice or God would exact vengeance. The sins of the Israelites, in breaking the covenant of Moses, brought the terrible consequences of oppression and slavery upon themselves. The idea that the civil war in England was God's punishment for the sins of his people operated in even the most convinced of the saints.[72] If military victory was cited as evidence of God's support, military defeat was analysed for the point at which the vanquished had left the path of righteousness and brought defeat on themselves.[73]

The attack on Charles in 1648 employed the prophets to great effect, but not as analysts of the contemporary situation. The prophets were seldom used self-critically, especially when the army continued victorious – 'if God be pleased to owne us in Counsell as he hath owned us in the Field'.[74] The prophets were a rich source of other, more uplifting messages. The saints portrayed themselves as direct parallels of the Israelites who suffered the burdens of enslavement under Babylon or Syria, and the prophetic books implied that salvation was imminent.[75] The prescience of the prophets sourced the dramatic language and heightened emotion which seemed to make the metaphors of Christ's rule and freedom from Charles Stuart less hyperbolic. Quotations from Isaiah, Jeremiah and Daniel built up the anticipation of liberty and provided a sense of hope after years of despair, as the original prophets had heightened the language of doom in order to increase the remnant's anticipation of freedom. Isaiah was most frequently used, though the original may have consisted of three separate and variable writers using the same name.[76] Isaiah of Jerusalem was a prophet of doom, an analyst of society, and a means to restore the ways of Yahweh. Thomas Brooks preached the funeral oration for the murdered Leveller hero, Rainsborough, to the text '(t)hy dead man shal live (together with) my dead body shall they arise. Awake, and sing you that dwell in the dust; for thy dew is as the dew of herbs, and the earth shall cast forth her dead' (Isa. 26: 19).[77] The prophetic books were also quarried for the blood-curdling language of vengeance against the oppressor. Most of the pamphlet literature of late 1648 which emerged from publishers which specialised in sectarian pieces was illustrated with a passage from the prophets. John Redingstone used Zechariah to parallel Charles' transgressions with those of Saul: 'but our King hath slain and destroyed the Lords dearest friends, his first borne, his peculiar treasure and jewels, most dear and tender to him, "He that toucheth them, toucheth the apple of his eye".'[78]

Cromwell found comfort in Isaiah as he struggled during 1648 to reach conclusions about the future. In June he was clear God would smash England's 'yoke of bondage'[79] and break 'the rod of the oppressor, as in the day of Midian, not with garments much rolled in blood, but by the terror of the Lord'.[80] The frontispiece text of the *Case of the Armie* had likened the petitioners to Gideon who conquered the Midianites.[81] By September, as the New Model crushed the renewed royalist assault, Cromwell counselled Oliver St. John and Sir Henry Vane, still seeking accommodation, not to have too much to do with the defeated.

> Remember my love to my dear brother H[enry].V[ane]. [he wrote]. I pray he make not too little, nor I too much, of outward dispensations. Let us all not be careful what use man will make of these actings. They shall, will they, nill they, fulfil the good pleasure of God, and so shall serve our generations . . . This Scripture has been of great stay to me; read it: Isaiah eight, 10, 11, 14.[82]

Although Cromwell was counselling Vane and St. John not to associate with Charles, the tone of these passages is different from the stridency he utilised in the midst of the fighting. In moments of quiet reflection he was confused about the correct political path to take, and at the end of November he still searched for guidance and was among the last to decide in favour of trying the king.[83] Such hesitancy at the enormity of the decisions required of the victors was reflected in *The Peoples Eccho*, which cited Isaiah 59: 9: 'judgement is farre from us, neither doth Justice overtake us. We want for light, but behold obscurity; for brightnesse, but we walke in darknesse.'[84]

As the soldiers of the New Model found solace, fortitude and encouragement in the pages of the Old Testament, so they looked to its Judaic moral law for solutions. The Decalogue – the Ten Commandments handed down from God to Moses at Sinai – was divided into the first and second tables, or tablets. The first contained the strictures which guided mankind's true worship of its God, and the second human relationships. In an uncorrupted natural state, or in a state of grace in which mankind automatically followed God's path without the mediation of civil government, godly behaviour was considered 'natural' conduct. The moral law was prohibitive, but since man had been created in God's image, the soldiers claimed it was natural for man to eschew these sins. Charles' actions which violated God's law were an unnatural subversion of the divine order and against conscience.[85] To commit crimes which violated the moral law, such as theft or murder, required a knowing, conscious intention to sin. It was unnatural and evil to worship anything other than God, to create idols, to blaspheme or to worship in an incorrect way. Similarly, it was aberrant to subvert the traditions of family life or community.

The force with which Judaic moral law could be implemented in the England of 1648 was not an uncontroversial argument, even amongst the leaders of the army, as was amply demonstrated by the second of the major General Council debates at Whitehall. The disputants were concerned with the role of the civil magistrate in spiritual affairs, to be represented in the revised *Agreement of the People*. The protagonists were divided on the issue of the moral law's continued legitimate force, as they had argued over the text of the first book of Samuel. Were the strictures given to the ancient Jews of universal application, or were they designed for a specific people in unique circumstances? It was generally, though not universally agreed, that provided the laws being enforced were indeed the moral law – and therefore touched the conscience rather than dictating more specific and transitory forms of worship – then they did remain in force. It was a point made most volubly by Henry Ireton, but a trained divine stated it better:

> When Israell having bin at a losse a longe time had renewed their Covenant with God soe that God accepted them, Hee was pleased to deliver his minde to them . . . in those ten words, commonly called, the Ten Commandements. Now as your good Apostle saith, they consist of two Tables, and the commands of the First Table are all negatives. Now God never gave any rules to the sons of men butt hee gave them to bee in force. For my owne parte I apprehend, that they are morall, and soe a rule to all the sons of men as well as to Israell, butt especially to those who are zealous for their God.[86]

The moral law described man's nature and provided a blueprint for godly behaviour on earth.

Charles was deemed to have broken both tables. His actions in the first war and instigating the second broke the law, but now critics were prepared to rehearse Charles' faults throughout his life. Thus, when Lieutenant Freeman[87] presented a petition of Rutland gentry to General Fairfax, it called on the army to protect truly godly civilians from a personal treaty with Charles because it would violate all the votes previously upheld against him, concerning La Rochelle, the death of king James, the Irish Rebellion, the use of German cavalry and the violence done to the parliament. Thus, they railed, 'how durst our Parliament think of treating with such a man!'.[88] Charles' character was demonstrated through action, but such a long history of misdeeds revealed a man with a flawed nature.

An ethical and legal judgement which was founded in Old Testament principles also dictated that Charles should be punished according to Old Testament criteria; a principle best summed up as 'an eye for an eye', although the precise phrase was rarely used, an exception being William Bridges' sermon, *Babylon's Downfall.*[89] In this respect, divine law parallelled the human law of equity[90] and the use of Old Testament values went beyond a citation of Charles' blood-guilt.[91] The saints, as God's instruments on earth, considered they had the right to judge Charles according to God's law. Levellers, county factions and regiments were 'all urging them (parliament) to . . . bring delinquents, without partiality, to justice and condign punishment, and to make inquiry for the guilt of the blood that had been shed . . . and to execute justice; lest the not improving the mercy of God should bring judgements in their room.'[92] Soldiers under Adrian Scrope, Thomas Saunders and Valentine Wauton were troubled by 'the serious thoughts of the hideous cry of innocent blood crying out for vengeance to Heaven, together with the peremptory command of the Creator, 'whoso sheddeth mans blood, by man shall his blood be shed".'[93] The author of *A Sad Message Threatening Destruction* counselled that 'thy princes are rebellious and companions of Thieves . . . like wolves ravening the prey, to shed blood and destroy, Jer. 6: 10, 11, 13. Isa: 1: 23. Jer. 22: 27.'[94] *The Peoples Eccho* which had likened Charles to Agag, believed that Agags should be 'hewen in pieces by the sword of Justice'.[95] This was the terror of the Lord on the unrighteous and the saints claimed sanction to inflict that terror on earth.

The Old Testament drew a distinction between sanctified and unacceptable sacrifice, the distinction between which depended on the object of veneration. The Bible condoned sacrifice, provided that its object was godly. Sacrifice made to heathen gods broke the First Table, its evil embodying idolatry and the worship of false gods. Charles had sacrificed his people for the worldly cause of his own power: now he was to be the sacrifice. The representatives of two regiments appeared at the Army Council at Windsor in the final week of November 1648. The first presented a petition on behalf of the 'officers and soldiers' of the garrisons of Newcastle, Tynemouth, Hartlepool and Holy Island.[96] The second came from the regiment of Colonel John Hewson. The army in the north-east was of the opinion that judgements against delinquents other than the king were 'to little purpose, as being not an acceptable Sacrifice to the Justice of God', and counselled that a new parliament examine continental republican regimes, 'that we may not idolize any one Creature'.[97]

All of these biblical parallels could either refer to tendencies within each individual or to differences between individuals.[98] The division of mankind represented at the Fall and the subsequent branches of the first family leant itself better to an analysis of human nature. The behaviour of all individuals could be good, or, if they acted in a certain way, display 'Cain-like' characteristics. Sometimes, the characteristics which were exhibited by human beings under the grip of worldliness were more likely to be exhibited by one class of person than another. It was more likely that pride, power, might and glory would be the preserve of kings than commoners, but proud, vainglorious behaviour might be exhibited by anyone. In this vein, Nimrod, the first king on the earth, provided a model for the likely characteristics of his earthly successors, relating a Biblical history in overtly religious language which paralleled the way in which the Norman Yoke argument related a secular history of kings. The republican, Verity Victor, wanted Nebuchadnezzar's tree to be grubbed up 'root and all; that there may be no more remembrance of Prerogative, Tyranny and Norman Bondage amongst us'.[99]

When kings performed specific actions, the genus could be analysed with more focus. The actions of Nebuchadnezzar were evil by definition, predetermined by his opposition to Yahweh and his oppression of Israel. But examples of evil behaviour could be extended to include the kings of Israel, which reflected the controversy among Hebraists over the status of kingship in the Old Testament. This was, in its turn, the same fundamental dilemma that had been expressed in classical scholarship, in which the Euripidean definition of tyranny – rule by any single person – was superseded by the Ciceronian moralism which distinguished kings (good men) from tyrants (immoral men).[100] Both types of ruler would, nevertheless, be punished in the same way – with equity – should they transgress God's law. Heathen kings, or tyrants without title, could also be defined as tyrants by nature. All of their actions were and would be aberrant. Their unbelief prescribed the inevitability of their punishment. When the kings of Israel assumed the right to make law for themselves, they ignored the will of God. They were tyrants by practice. They were otherwise legitimate rulers, judged according to specific and individual actions.[101] Reference to Scriptural example, however, allowed the two to become confused and elided, because God's law judged the morality of every person made in His image. All men, even kings with divine sanction, should receive the same punishment if they transgressed the Law of God. As such they were reduced to being mere men.

It was possible, therefore, for an interpretation of these biblically inspired arguments to reach a conclusion which was either an indictment of rulers (kings) in general or of one ruler (king) in particular.[102] On the whole, however, the use of the texts in the later 1640s follows a

rough chronology of the Old Testament. A general moral line against all
pretensions to rule (Cain, Ham) developed into an attack on kings
(Nimrod). The attack on heathen conquerors which demonstrated the
evil nature of kings (Ahab, Agag, Nebuchadnezzar) was extended to
take in Hebraic kings (Saul, David), which demonstrated God's
punishment of a king who would otherwise have reigned with
God's permission. When the second civil war returned the soldiers
to action and forced them to fight again a battle which they thought
God had given them in 1646, bitterness and emotion pushed them
towards the conclusion of this chain of parallels. Charles Stuart was
the chief delinquent, responsible for the bloodshed, and the general
criticism of kingliness and kings turned into a vicious, regicidal attack,
homing in on Charles as an individual. It eventually arrived at the
most personalised attack possible. Charles was unlike other men, all of
whom possessed the sins of the flesh. He was Ahab. He was
Nebuchadnezzar.[103] He was Belshazzar, at whose pagan feast the
hand of God wrote 'Mene, mene tekel upharsin . . . God hath
numbered thy kingdom, and finished it . . . Thou art weighed in
the balances, and art found wanting.' For Charles the writing was on
the wall.[104] A prophesy of Lady Eleanor Douglas was reprinted in
August 1649. Sanctioned with an imprimatur from Theodore Jen-
nings, the pro-Commonwealth printer added marginalia which
glossed her original vision of Belshazzar's feast. The wall of the
Whitehall Banqueting House should be terrible to Charles, 'as the
writing on the wall was to Belshazzer, which proved true, for there he
was beheaded'.[105]

NOTES

1. *The Souldiers pocket Bible: containing the most, if not all those places contained
   in holy Scripture, which doe shew the qualifications of his inner man, that is a fit
   Souldier to fight the Lords Battels*, [3 Aug.] 1643, C.54.aa.1.(2).
2. The complexity of the relationship between the New Model Army and
   religious practice is too great to enable a long discussion here, but has
   been skilfully outlined in Ian Gentles, *The New Model Army in England,
   Ireland and Scotland, 1645–1653* (Oxford, 1992), pp. 87–119. See also
   Derek Massarella, 'The politics of the army, 1647–1660', PhD, York
   (1978).
3. Thomas Edwards, *Gangraena: or a Catalogue and Discovery* (1646) (Rota
   Press reprint, Exeter, 1977); Anne Laurence, *Parliamentary Army
   Chaplains, 1646–1651* (Woodbridge, Suffolk, 1990), pp. 76–81, plays

down both the extent of sectarianism in the army and the influence of chaplains.

4. John Vicars, *Jehovah Jireh. God in the Mount*, various editions beginning in 1641, this from the 1644 edition, p. 200; *The Picture of Independency*, [15 Mar.] 1645, E273(11); *The Schismatick Sifted*, [22 Jun.] 1646, E341(8), the reply by Marchamont Nedham, M.N., *Independencie no Schisme*, [16 Jul.] 1646, E344(24); Laurence, *Parliamentary Army Chaplains*, pp. 76–7.

5. *Clarke Papers*, I, pp. 282–3; Revelations 17–19.

6. Laurence, *Army Chaplains*; Christopher Hill, *The Experience of Defeat: Milton and some Contemporaries* (London, 1984), pp. 84–117.

7. Edwards, *Gangraena*, I, pp. 16–17.

8. Laurence, *Army Chaplains*, p. 83.

9. Laurence, *Army Chaplains*, p. 125.

10. [Wildman], *The Case of the Armie Truly Stated*, p. 13. It is not clear whether this is a reference to a specific text. If so, the most likely is Jeremiah's lamentation for Judah, which was unable to secure peace because it had turned away from the ways of the Lord: 'My bowels, my bowels! I am pained at my very heart . . .' (Jer. 4: 19). Bowels were often a biblical reference for the seat of pity, but in a metaphorical sense referred to a civil war within the midst of the body politic.

11. See Cowley, 'Poem on the late civil war', 1643, in Ruth Nevo, *The Dial of Virtue: A Study of Poems and Affairs of State in the Seventeenth Century* (Princeton, 1963), p. 39.

12. Edwards, *Gangraena*, I, pp. 16–17, 61–3; Richard Baxter, *Reliquiae Baxterianae*, ed. Matthew Sylvester, pp. 41, 50–1, 53.

13. [Richard Overton], *The Remonstrance of many Thousand Citizens*, p. 18.

14. *Argvments, proving that we ought not to part with the militia*, point 10 of 11.

15. An exception is a passage in [Overton], *Remonstrance*, p. 6: 'King Charles his wickednesse' should lead parliament to 'declare *King Charles* an enemy' and thus deal with 'this originall of all Oppressions, to wit *Kings*'.

16. [Overton], *Remonstrance*, pp. 17–18.

17. See Overton's acid comment in *Remonstrance*, p. 17.

18. *Clarke Papers*, I, pp. 226–56; see Chapter 2.

19. For a text of the *Heads*, see *GCD*, pp. 316–26; Murray Tolmie, *The Triumph of the Saints: The Separate Churches of London, 1616–1649* (Cambridge, 1977), pp. 164–5, who draws a distinction between the leaders of the churches, especially William Kiffin, and the rank and file members.

20. William Allen, *A Faithful memorial of that remarkable meeting of many officers of the army of England, at Windsor Castle, in the year 1648* (1659); Patricia Crawford, 'Charles Stuart, That Man of Blood', *JBS*, XVI.2 (1977) 41–61.

21. See also *The Peoples Eccho to the Parliaments Declarations concerning a Personall Treaty with the King*, [18 Aug.] 1648, E459(25), p. 4.

22. He was addressing himself to the army's then commander, Fleetwood, as part of a particular political campaign. Allen was part of the so-called Good Old Cause, which in the late 1650s aimed to rally republicans to the banners which had seemed so successful in the previous decade. See the Epilogue.

23. At Windsor, the General and the officers 'sought God earnestly for a Blessing uppon their Councills'. Part of this communication in short-hand reveals that as of 26 November, the correspondent was confident that the Presbyterians would join against the king. Perhaps the feeling engendered by the prayer meeting was overconfidence. I am grateful to Frances Macdonald of New College, Oxford, for deciphering the shorthand; Oxford, Worcester College, Clarke MSS CXIV ff.110, 112.

24. *The None-such Charles his Character: extracted out of divers Originall Transactions, Dispatches and the Notes of several Publick Ministers, and Councellors of STATE,* [6 Jan.] 1651, E1345(2), p. 174.

25. While Tolmie tries to distance Allen from the Particular Baptist leaders' wavering in October 1647, he admits his reticence at Putney: *Triumph of the Saints,* pp. 164–5, 167. Allen made few, short and ineffectual interjections at Putney, the last arguing for some form of negotiations with Charles: *Clarke Papers,* I, pp. 376–7.

26. Putney debates, 28 Oct. 1647: *Clarke Papers,* I, p. 227.

27. It also imparted a new venom into the attacks on the Scots who were now in alliance with Charles.

28. W. C. Abbott, *Writings and Speeches of Oliver Cromwell* (4 vols) (Harvard, 1939), I, p. 696; *Clarke Papers,* I, pp. 238–9; Mayfield, 'Puritans and regicide', pp. 279–81.

29. This was a potent idea within an army, for which unity of purpose was also vital to morale and the effectiveness of its actions.

30. A. S. P. Woodhouse, *Puritanism and Liberty* (London, 1986 edn), p. 38ff.

31. Of the first five books of the Bible, Genesis and Deuteronomy were by far the most widely used; Genesis for the origins of good and evil in the world and Deuteronomy for the origins of Judaic law.

32. Man in the state of grace was innocent as in the Creation: Gen. 2: 17, 'But of the tree of the knowledge of good and evil, thou shalt not eat of it.'

33. Deut. 29: 21: 'And the Lord shall separate him unto evil out of all the tribes of Israel, according to all the curses of the covenant that are written in this book of the law.'

34. A good example is the confidence displayed in the newsletter *Mercurius Militaris, or the Armies Scout,* during late 1648: 31 Oct.–21 Nov. 1648, E470–3.

35. Or as *Mercurius Pragmaticus* sought to satirise them 'as their Rabbies often teach', 22–9 Aug. 1648, E461(17).

36. Gen. 4.

37. *The Subjects Liberty set forth,* [8 Jun.] 1643, E101(19).

38. *A Discoverie, what God, the Supreme Judge, through his Servant hath caused to be Manifest*, [21 Nov.] 1643, E76(17), from the title.

39. He was claimed as an influence on John Milton, who met him while on the European tour, and John Cook, who made a reference to his friendship with the theologian during his 'speech' at Charles' trial; John Cook, *King Charls his Case: or, an Appeal to all Rational Men*, [9 Feb.] 1649, E542(3), p. 32; John Cook, *A True Relation of Mr Justice Cooke's Passage by Sea from Wexford to Kinsale*, Thurs. 5 Jan. 1650.

40. The quotations used here, and those made by contemporaries, come from the Authorised Bible of 1604. It seems strange that sectaries so opposed to the Anglican orthodoxy should quote from its bible.

41. Giovanni Diodati, *Pious Annotations upon the Holy Bible* (London, 1st edn 1643; 2nd edn 1648), 'the argument upon Genesis'.

42. This form of moral decadence was the lesson learnt by William Godwin about monarchical regimes. Moral regeneration would be possible in a republic: 'he that lords it over me, and would persuade me that he is not of the same ignoble kind as myself, ought perhaps to be clad in robes, and covered in ermine and gold' (*History of the Commonwealth of England*, pp. 342–4) cited in Morrow, 'Republicanism and public virtue', p. 649.

43. Gen. 9: 6.

44. *Englands Satisfaction in Eight Queries of the place of a King*, [8 Jun.] 1643, E105(14), p. 7.

45. Gen. 10.9. For some discussion of the use of the Nimrod image, see Christopher Hill, 'God and the English Revolution', *History Workshop*, 17 (1984) 19–31, pp. 23–4.

46. Henry Marten, *The Parliaments Proceedings justified*, [7 Feb.] 1648, E426(2), p. 16.

47. Cook, *King Charls*, p. 13.

48. William Erbury, *The Lord of Hosts or God guarding the Camp of the Saints and the beloved City*, 24 Dec. 1648, E477(22). The titles are alternatives. Hill, *Experience of Defeat*, pp. 84–97; Laurence, *Parliamentary Army Chaplains* p. 124; *Clarke Papers*, II, pp. 178–9 and *passim*; Tolmie, *Triumph of the Saints*, pp. 122–3.

49. Erbury, *Lord of Hosts*, wrongly numbered as p. 31. He maintained this line at the Whitehall debates: 'Itt is nott minded or thought in my heart to destroy any mans person, noe nott to destroy the person of the Kinge, soe his power bee downe . . . [I speake of] the destroying of those oppressive principalls both in powers and persons, and in courts and lawes' (*Clarke Papers*, II, p. 178).

50. The king of Babylon who captured Jerusalem in 597 BC.

51. There are no references to the queen in the many petitions for justice against Charles and it is only at Charles' trial that Henrietta Maria's role in fostering Catholicism resurfaces. However, since many of the arguments used against Charles had earlier been formulated in a

different guise to attack the papacy, Catholicism and, later, Laudian innovations, there is little reason to suppose that the resonance was not intended.

52. *A Copie of Two letters*, from the Officers in the North, dated 11 Sep. 1648, 669.f.13(27), broadsheet.

53. George Cockayne, *Flesh expiring and the spirit inspiring in the new earth*, delivered on 29 Nov. 1648, in R. Jeffs (ed.), *The English Revolution I: The Fast Sermons to Parliament* (32 vols) (London, 1971), p. 42 (page 21 of the pamphlet); Mayfield, 'Puritans and regicide', pp. 258–62.

54. Harvey was recruiter MP (1646) for Great Bedwyn, a Wiltshire seat which bordered on west Berkshire. He has received a critical press as a 'time serving profiteer', 'faint-hearted time-server' and 'dishonest racketeer'; a man whose motives were made impure by a materialist concern to protect his purchase of episcopal lands in Fulham. In 1656 he was jailed for embezzling from the customs; David Underdown, *Pride's Purge: Politics in the Puritan Revolution* (London, 1971), pp. 134, 138, 187, 241; Gentles, *New Model Army* pp. 280–1; Ian Gentles, 'The sale of bishops' lands in the English Revolution, 1646–1660', *EHR*, 95 (1980) 589–90; *The Parliament under the power of the Sword*, [11 Dec.] 1648, E476(1), pp. 6–7.

55. Matthew Barker, *A Christian standing and moving upon a true Foundation*, from Jeffs, *Fast Sermons*, 32, pp. 232–302, p. 236, Epistle dedicatory.

56. 'Verity Victor', *The Royal Project*, [20 Oct.] 1648, E468(22), p. 16; the reference is to Daniel's interpretation of Nebchadnezzar's dream: Dan. 4: 4–27.

57. *To His Excellency the Lord Fairfax*, 24 Nov. 1648, 669.f.13(47), broadsheet, a petition from Rutland.

58. Cook, *King Charls*, p. 8.

59. Ludlow, *Memoirs*, I, p. 185.

60. I Sam. 8: 10–12, 17–18.

61. This was Cook's argument in his *post facto* justification of republicanism, *Monarchy no Creature of God's making*, [26 Feb.] 1651(2) (London and Waterford), E1238(1).

62. A repeat of the situation which the army had been in in October 1647, according to Lieutenant-Colonel William Goffe at Putney: *Clarke Papers*, I, p. 284.

63. I Sam. 15.

64. *The Peoples Eccho*, p. 12.

65. I Kgs. 22: 52–3.

66. I Sam.15: 22; John Bond, *Eshcol, or Grapes among Thorns*, sermon to the Commons, 19 July, 1648, in Jeffs, *Fast Sermons*, 31, pp. 55–106, p. 68. See also John Canne, *The Snare is Broken*.

67. I Sam. 15: 33.

68. Thomas Manton, *Englands Spirituall Languishing*, a fast sermon delivered on 28 June 1648, in Jeffs, *Fast Sermons*, 31, p. 51, and Bond, *Eshcol*,

p. 101; Samuel Anneley, *A Sermon*, 26 July 1648, in Jeffs, *Fast Sermons*, 31, pp. 151–85, p. 179.

69. Marten, *Parliaments Proceedings Justified*, p. 8; the structure of this argument can be equated with that of Senecan *controversia*, in which students of rhetoric was asked to weigh the relative merits and demerits of two people, each of which was guilty of a crime; J. Roger Dunkle, 'The rhetorical tyrant in Roman historiography: Sallust, Livy and Tacitus', *The Classical World*, 65 (1971), p. 13.

70. *The Voice of Conscience of all well-meaning Citizens*, [16 Jul.] 1648, 669.f.12(83), broadsheet; see also *The Peoples Eccho*, p. 12. Behnadad was also used by John Bond in his fast sermon in thanksgiving for Parliament's victories in the second civil war.

71. Cockayne, *Flesh Expiring*, p. 25, using the example of David and Jonathan.

72. For example, Robert Parsons, *Severall Speeches*, p. 23.

73. *Lieut: General Cromwel's Letter*, 23 Aug. 1648, E460(24).The officers of the army were even of the belief that their failure to bring Charles to justice after the first civil war had been the occasion for the second, 'which was justly to be charged on the Parliament for neglecting that duty': Ludlow, *Memoirs*, I, pp. 212–13.

74. *A letter from the Head-Quarters, at St Albanes*, 10 Nov. 1648, E470(34), p. 3.

75. Isaiah, in this context, is the more important because it makes specific reference to the coming of the Messiah.

76. R. P. Carroll, *When Prophesy Failed: Reactions and Responses to failure in the Old Testament Prophetic Tradition* (London, 1979), and R. P. Carroll, 'Inner tradition shifts in meaning in Isaiah 1–11', *Expository Times* 89.10 (1978) 301–4; Stephen Marshall, *Emmanuel*, a sermon preached to the Commons on the victory in south Wales, 17 May 1648, in Jeffs, *Fast Sermons*, 30, pp. 229–68.

77. Thomas Brooks, *The Glorious Day of the Saints Appearance*, 14 Nov. 1648, E474(7); Mayfield, 'Puritans and regicide', pp. 261–6.

78. John Redingstone, *Plaine English*, p. 5, Zech. 2: 8; see also Stephen Marshall's Fast Sermon to the Commons, using Zechariah, Ezekiel and Isaiah, *The Sinne of Hardnesse of Heart*, in Jeffs, *Fast Sermons*, 32, pp. 107–50, p. 111; Zech. 7: 12,

79. Isa. 9: 4. There were several layers of meaning to the yoke in the Bible, and the yoke of bondage or slavery was more usually associated with texts in Lev. 3: 27 and Deut. 28: 48. It also provided a point of contact between biblical justifications and Norman Yoke theories of slavery. I have not as yet come across positive evidence, but I should like to suggest that the yoke may have been the negative reverse-image of the balance-scales. The difference between the two was the relative positions of the people and potentially oppressive institutions.

80. Abbott, *Writings and Speeches*, I, p. 619, to Fairfax, 28 June 1648, using the example of the Midianites which had provided the text of *The Case of the Armie*. The text was used in the Fast Sermons of both Stephen Marshall and Thomas Manton: Jeffs, *Fast Sermons*, 30, pp. 229–68, 31, pp. 13–54.

81. Jud. 7: 7.

82. Abbott, *Writings and Speeches*, I, p. 644.

83. Abbott, *Writings and Speeches*, I, p. 717, John Laurans to Nicholas, 21 Dec., 1648: 'the petty ones of the levelling conspiracy' were eager for the death of the king, but Cromwell was 'retreating from them, his designs and theirs being incompatible as fire and water'.

84. *The Peoples Eccho*, the text on the frontispiece.

85. See Milton, *Eikonoklastes*, pp. 14–21, upon the Earl of Strafford's death; Stuart Hampshire, 'Public and private morality', in Hampshire (ed.), *Public and Private Morality* (Cambridge, 1978), pp. 23–53; Stephen M. Fallon, ''To act or not': Milton's conception of divine freedom', *JHI*, XLIX.3 (1988) 425–47.

86. *Clarke Papers*, II, pp. 109–10; Woodhouse, *Puritanism and Liberty*, p. 152. Woodhouse considered the unnamed contributor to be Mr Gilbert. The most likely Gilbert is Thomas Gilbert see Laurence, *Parliamentary Army Chaplains*, p. 129; J. Seers McGee, *The Godly Man in Stuart England: Anglicans, Puritans and the Two Tables, 1620–1670* (New Haven, Conn. 1976).

87. Since Grey's county regiment was not part of the New Model, this is unlikely to be the same man listed elsewhere as Captain Edward Freeman: C. H. Firth and G. Davies, *The Regimental History of Cromwell's Army* (Oxford, 1940), pp. 296–7; C. H. Firth, *Cromwell's Army*, p. 308; *Clarke Papers*, II, pp. 274–5. Neither is it likely to have been Captain Francis Freeman, who was in continuous religious dispute with his colonel, John Okey: Capt. Francis Freeman, *VIII Problems propounded to the Cavaliers for conviction of their consciences. With a discovery of certain Plots*, [6 Jul.] 1646, E343(6), and *Light vanquishing Darknesse, or, A vindication of some Truths formerly declared*, [29 Oct.] 1650, E615(7).

88. *To His Excellency the Lord Fairfax*, broadsheet. Little is known about the collection of signatories on this petition, but it seems probable that it was at the instigation or with the connivance of Thomas, Lord Grey of Groby.

89. William Bridges, *Babylon's Downfall*, quoted in B. S. Capp, *The Fifth Monarchy Men: A Study in Seventeenth-century Millenarianism* (London, 1972), p. 39.

90. Exod. 21: 24; Lev. 24: 20; Deut. 19: 21; repudiated in Matt. 5: 38–9; *The True Copy of a Petition promoted in the Army*, [19 Oct.] 1648, E468(18), p. 3, and E468(23), p. 3; Representatives of Cromwell's, Harrison's, Pride's, Deane's regiments, *Severall Petitions presented to his Excellency*, [30 Nov.] 1648, E474(5), p. 8.; Nigel Smith, *Perfection*

Proclaimed: Language and Literature in English Radical Religion, 1640–1660 (Oxford, 1989), pp. 170–1.

91. See Crawford, 'Charles Stuart that man of Blood'.
92. Hutchinson, *Memoirs*, p. 265.
93. *The declarations and humble Representations of the Officers and Soldiers in Colonel Scroops, Colonel Saunders, Col. Wautons regiment*, [7 Dec.] 1648, E475(24), p. 2; Underdown, *Pride's Purge*, pp. 131–2. Wauton was MP for Huntington and a relative of Henry Robinson. Thomas Saunders appears in Chapters 3 and 8. Adrian Scrope signed Charles' death warrant.
94. *A Sad message threatening destruction*, [15 Aug.] 1648, E1182(10), p. 1.
95. *The Peoples Eccho*, p. 12.
96. *Two Petitions presented to his Excellency the Lord Fairfax*, 25 Nov. 1648, E473(23); probably influenced by Colonel John Blakiston, who was to sign Charles' death warrant two months later.
97. *Two Petitions*. pp. 4, 8; Nancy Klein Maguire, 'The theatrical mask/masque of politics: the case of Charles I', *JBS*, 28 (1989) 1–22, p. 18.
98. *The Levellers Institutions*, [30 Nov.] 1648, E474(4), pp. 6–7.
99. 'Verity Victor', *The Royal Project*, p. 16.
100. Parsons, *Severall Speeches*, pp. 13–14; Moshe Weinfeld, 'The transition to monarchy in ancient Israel and its impression on Jewish political history', and Daniel J. Elazar, 'Covenant as the basis of the Jewish political tradition', in Daniel J. Elazar (ed.), *Kinship and Consent: the Jewish Political Tradition and its Contemporary Uses* (Washington DC, 1983); William B. Gwyn, 'Cruel Nero: the concept of the tyrant and the image of Nero in western political thought', *HPT*, XII.3 (1991) 421–55; Dunkle, 'Rhetorical tyrant'; Euripides, *The Suppliants*, II. 399–462.
101. See below, Chapter 5.
102. *Englands Troublers Troubled*, [17 Aug.] 1648, E459(11).
103. Marten, *Independency of England*, p. 19.
104. Daniel interprets the writing on the wall at Belshazzar's feast, which says that Belshazzar's kingdom is ended, the king has been weighed in the balance and has been found wanting: Dan. 5: 5–31; Robert Bacon, *The Labyrinth the Kingdom's In*, [7 Feb.] 1649, E541(26), p. 6.
105. Lady Eleanor Douglas/Davies, *Strange and Wonderfull Prophesies by Lady Eleanor Audeley*, [27 Aug.] 1649, E571(28); Ester S. Cope, *Handmaid of the Holy Spirit: Lady Eleanor Douglas, never soe mad a Ladie* (Michigan, 1992), pp. 147–8. Davies was commended for her prescience in foretelling the death of Buckingham in another tract published by authority; *None-such Charles*, p. 10. George Wither also claimed his poetry was prophetic, *Prosopopaeia Britannica: Britans Genius*, 1648, in *Miscellaneous Works of George Wither* (6 vols) (Spenser Society, New York, reprint 1967), 18, pp. 3–118:

> If he, who ownes that name, shall harken to
> Their counsell, who will tell him what to do;

That *name*, at last, much like that *stamp*, may be
Which was preserved, when the *Royall-tree*,
Once, representing *Nebuchadnezzar*,
Was felled down. And, as he did appear
In former Glorie, when he had confest
His failings, and the *living* God *profest*;
So, shall it be with *Charles*, if he repent;
God, will the ruine of his *House* prevent;
Restore him to his *Throne*, and make his fame
To grow the fairer, through its present shame.
But if he shall defer, till 'tis too late,
Let him prepare for King *Belshazzars* fate,
And let all those, who shall to him adhere,
Expect, in his sad *dooms* to have a share.
(pp. 29–30, ll.886–97)

5

Queen Justice[1]

When the gentry of Leicestershire called for Charles to be put on trial and the end of the second civil war, and the petitioners of Berkshire called for an account to be drawn up which made inquisition for the blood spilt and the treasure spent, they petitioned both the parliament and the General Council of the army. They had no doubt that parliament was the correct vehicle for such action, but the composition of the parliament at the end of 1648 was not likely to achieve their aim. Thus, they attempted to lobby the army to put pressure on the Houses and admitted it was necessary to have 'this present Parliament purg'd, or another and more equall Representative chosen'.[2] Despite the possible implications for parliament's claim to representativeness, there were clearly gentry republicans prepared to countenance using force to exclude legitimately elected members. On 5 December 1648 a majority in the Commons voted that the king's answers were a sufficient basis on which to continue to negotiate a treaty. Time for discussion of the relative merits of purge or dissolution ran out. Three 'commonwealthsmen' MPs and three army grandees[3] drew up a list of malignant members of parliament and on the morning of 6 December 1648, they were met at the entrance to the Commons' chamber by Thomas, Lord Grey of Groby, and a battalion of soldiers from the regiment of Colonel Thomas Pride. Grey identified those who had voted to continue the peace process; Pride's soldiers barred their way.[4] Forty-five men were considered possessed of a degree of malignancy which merited imprisonment.[5] A further 186 members were excluded from attendance at the House. Another eighty-six decided to keep away from London and not embroil themselves in a governmental process which had become dangerous and fraught.

Those few who remained were left to devise a settlement which excluded and condemned the chief delinquent. There were only 154 potentially active MPs. Only a fraction of those were 'revolutionaries'.[6] But even amongst this small number, those who drew up the documents of the revolution and sat in the High Court arrived at this dramatic point carrying with them differing concerns. Harry Marten's revolution was nothing like Oliver Cromwell's. Even among figures with a similar political end in sight, there were differences in the route by which they came to a purge and a trial. Diverse individuals were brought together by an expedient. Having traced the different roads down which they had travelled, the glare of publicity surrounding the trial and its aftermath made it possible to view the cracks which were exposed when they tried to mould their concerns into a united whole. Ludlow gives us a flavour of the disagreement between the commonwealthsmen and grandees as soon as the co-operation represented by Pride's Purge had served its turn.

> The King being at Windsor, it was debated what should be done with him: the army were for bringing him to a trial . . . but some of the Commonwealths- men desired that before they consented to that method, it might be resolved what government to establish, fearing a design in the army to set up some of themselves in his room: others endeavoured to perswade them that the execution of justice ought to be their first work, in respect of their duty to God and the people; that the failure therein had been already the occasion of a second war, which was justly to be charged on the Parliament for neglecting that duty; that those who were truly Commonwealths-men ought to be of that opinion, as the most probable means to attain their desires in the establishment of an equal and just government.[7]

In order to expedite the decision-making, the Rump of the Commons voted on 4 January 1649 that, should the Lords refuse to fall in with their plans, the agreement of the Upper House was unnecessary – constitutionally inessential. The Commons then issued a statement of principle, composed by Marten, which encapsulated the twin precepts of the sovereignty of the people and the sufficient balance between the represented and their representatives: 'The people are, under God, the original of all just power (and) the Commons of England, in Parliament assembled, being chosen by, and representing the people, have the supreme power in this nation.' Parliament's justificatory declaration stressed that it was the best judge of the people's safety because it was the people's representative. A joint resolution from the parliament and the General Council of the army chose rather to stress that when the malignants took the step to renew addresses they had betrayed those who had expended blood and treasure, and necessitated 'Revenge both to the Armie, and those well-affected people, who had with grateful acceptance declared their resolutions to live and die there in.' The purge and the vote of the Commons' sovereignty had been necessary 'to weed out those Roots of Faction, and for the time to come to render the

Resolutions of Parliament more fixed, and united'.[8] At the same time, Thomas Scot was placed in charge of collecting declarations from those who wished to take up their seats in the Commons, in which they had to register their dissent from the vote taken on 5 December.[9] The 'honest party' were in power.

The Commons proceeded – with the authority of 'the fundamental power that rests in ourselves' – with a series of acts[10] required to bring the king to trial.[11] On 6 January it set up a High Court of Justice, a body of 135 commissioners drawn from the Commons, Lords[12], Army, the Inns of Court and the Common Council of London. The commissioners were charged with listening to the evidence against the king and the management of his trial. A formal charge was issued on 20 January and sentence passed a week later. Charles was found guilty of High Treason and executed outside the windows of the Banqueting Hall in Whitehall on 30 January 1649. Kingship and the Lords were abolished on 17 and 19 March, and England was finally declared a republic two months later. Ideas of regicide, vengeance, constitutional change and republicanism, which had emerged in the later 1640s, were rehearsed in this six-month period. They sat ill together.

The Act erecting the High Court rehearsed two distinct and seperable histories. One described a long-standing plan, implemented by Charles Stuart, to subvert the fundamental constitution and institute an arbitrary and tyrannical government. This was the reason that Charles was to be tried, not for his actual declaration of war, which had been just one 'evil' way in which he had manifested a 'wicked design'.[13] It was a history which explained the civil war as the culmination of a progressive process in which Charles' ancestors had gradually subverted the rights of the people, openly and knowingly corrupting the natural way of government. The second history was more specific to the war itself, though it had a relevance to the time before the war, and related the forbearance with which the members of the political elite had continued to reason with Charles, continually offering him peace terms. They had been patient with his vacillation, being reluctant to attribute it to more sinister motives.

By the time the High Court came to frame the charge against the king, the emphasis had changed. The change may have been forced on them because the case which the prosecution wanted to make was difficult to frame under common law. The reasons adduced for wanting Charles tried were not concordant with the legal framework necessary to an indictment. The charge was predicated on and relied on the mutual recognition of a specific contract of trust between the king and his people. Charles had 'a limited power to govern by and according to the laws of the land, and not otherwise'. This trust had been breached when he 'traitorously and maliciously levied war against the present Parliament, and the people therein represented'.[14] Even more specifically, it was necessary to recite particular acts of war. The charges, therefore, catalogued the larger battles. The consequence of Charles' act of war was the destruction of the lives, estates, interests and livelihoods of individuals and the nation, and thus he had deliberately acted in a way which ensured that he was not ruling according to his obligation to the public good. His 'wicked designs, wars, and evil practices' were designed to uphold 'a personal interest of will, power, and pretended prerogative to himself and his family'.

A committee was retained to advise on the nature of the charge, composed largely of civilians. Apart from Commissary General Ireton and Colonel Thomas Harrison, both of whom were also MPs, the committee, 'to whom the Counsel might resort, for their further advice concerning anything of difficulty in relation to the Charge against the King', consisted of Thomas Millington, Henry Marten, Thomas Chaloner, Miles Corbet, Thomas Scot, Edmund Harvey, Nicholas Love, John Lisle and William Say.[15] A further, military-dominated committee, of Colonels Ludlow, Purefoy, Hutchinson, Scrope, Deane, Whalley, Pride, Sir Hardress Waller and Sir William Constable was responsible for the logistics of bringing the king to trial, his personal security and the safety of the court.[16] The lists of commissioners who regularly attended to their duties is our best indication of those most committed to the process of trial itself and to its outcome.[17] However, Charles decided not to plead, which circumscribes the written evidence available to the historian about the proceedings. It had been predetermined that should the king refuse to enter a plea or recognise the authority of the High Court, his silence should be taken *pro confesso*.[18]

Great attention was paid to ceremony. The court decided to chose a Lord President to speak on behalf of the commissioners, and he and the prisoner were to be seated on scarlet velvet. The commissioners were surrounded by red drapes and the clerk sat at the Lord President's feet, beside a table covered in a Turkish carpet, on which rested the mace and sword of parliamentary authority and justice.[19] On 9 January the court was ushered in by the crier Edward Dendy, 'being attended with six trumpets, and a guard of two troops of horse, himself with them on horseback, bearing the mace, rideth into the middle of Westminster Hall'. The same ceremony was re-enacted at Cheapside and the Exchange.[20] John Hutchinson presided over a committee to ensure that even the lowliest of court officers were attired in fitting robes.[21]

Care was taken to ensure that the proceedings were 'performed in a solemn manner', by which they would seem as authoritative in law as possible.[22] But it could never be a body which acted according to common law and was not viewed as such. It was a 'new extraordinary court'.[23] The commissioners were both judge and jury. No matter how worthy, they could never be the king's peers. Cheshire lawyer, John Bradshaw, was chosen president, but was reluctant to assume the position. Royalists sneered that his conscience made him fearful, but Bradshaw reasoned against the hierarchy inherent in assuming a title.[24] Nevertheless, not himself wanting to be seen to be refusing the 'authoritative' decisions of his fellow commissioners, he was 'persuaded' to accept. The public attack on the king which was recorded for posterity is therefore in his words.

The other figure who had much to say was the solicitor for the state, John Cook. Cook was a relatively unknown Leicestershire lawyer at the time that he was catapulted to fame. He had been a prolific pamphleteer, publishing on social and legal issues,[25] and his most famous contribution was a defence of the Independents from Presbyterian attack, claiming the uncontroversial, limited and reasonable nature of *What the Independents would have*.[26] At the trial, Charles Stuart's refusal to recognise the authority of the court, and thus Cook's role as prosecutor, denied the lawyer the opportunity of making the speech which he had prepared for Westminster Hall. Like the experienced hack that he was, however, he added a new preface and additional end-notes, and submitted his speech for publication under the title *King Charls his Case*.[27]

The trial of Charles was held in public, so as to hold up the authority of the court to the scrutiny of those for whom it professed to be acting. The court needed to demonstrate that it was the true guardian of English law, Bradshaw finding it necessary to remind the people what the law was, because they had 'sad experience' of the forgetfulness of some.[28] Statute[29] and history[30] were invoked to show that the law was above the king and not *vice versa*. Law, statute and history also demonstrated that parliament should be summoned annually. A long discursive aside described precedents for the deposition of kings, citing classical, continental and British examples.[31] In order to demonstrate that Charles had broken a fundamental bond of trust between himself and his people, it was argued that the kings of England were elective and not hereditary. Charles treated the claim with scorn.[32] Bradshaw's use of the Norman Yoke theory came to a different conclusion than that which had been advanced by Lilburne in *Regall Tyrannie Discovered*. Lilburne had been describing tyrants without title, demonstrating that

Charles' descent from a usurping conqueror had invalidated the titles of all monarchs since 1066 and cast a slur on their ability to rule in the people's interests, according to God's law. Bradshaw, on the other hand, divided monarchs subsequent to 1066 into the legitimate and the illegitimate. Charles I was 'the twenty-fourth king from William called the Conqueror, you shall find one half of them to come merely from the state, and not merely upon the point of descent'.[33] Bradshaw was describing a tyrant by practice, because the regicidal dynamic dictated he demonstrate that a ruler installed by the people could be removed by the people.

The High Court of Justice comprised both soldiers and parliamentarians – ostensibly presenting a united front against the lone figure of a tyrannical king. There was a symbolic theatricality to the scene of the single man at the centre of the court, facing a host of accusers and John Cook professed outrage that Charles would rather have been at the centre of a Jonsonian or Shakespearean tragedy than in the midst of the righteous.[34] Shorn of courts, flunkies, guards, bishops, sycophants and (evil) counsellors, only Charles was left to face the wrath of the godly.[35] Charles was revealed as the 'principal author' of the nation's ills.[36] It was no longer a tenable argument to suggest that he was the unwitting victim of others' selfish agenda for power, given the degree to which Charles had continued to prosecute the war while continually and gradually being deprived of those who had previously been held responsible. Cook chose to trace Charles' responsibility back to his accession. William Laud, Archbishop of Canterbury, had, he said, on the king's orders, left out the clause in the coronation oath appealing for the approbation of the people, and 'from that very day (Charles) had a design to alter and subvert the fundamental laws and to introduce an arbitrary and tyrannical government'. Giovanni Diodati had rebuked Cook for the king's failure to save fellow Protestants at La Rochelle in 1627,[37] but the realisation that Charles had been solely responsible for the nation's failure from as early as 1625 did not dawn on Cook, he claimed, until the recovery of the Naseby letters made a full discovery of the king's perfidy.[38]

Charles' isolation was a practical demonstration of his status as 'mere man', the phrase which Lilburne had promoted in 1646.[39] Charles was liable to be tried for the same crimes and receive the same punishment as any other citizen of England, no matter how lowly.[40] Equality before the law was a godly principle and should therefore be integral to English law. Bradshaw cited the second table of the Decalogue: "Thou shalt do no murder': We do not know but that it extends to kings as to the meanest peasants, the meanest of people; the command is universal.'[41]

The scales of justice were regulated by equity. However, the view that since Charles was a king he was in some way more guilty than an ordinary person, having broken the trust between himself and his people, cut across it. Every time Bradshaw reminded the king that he would have been held in majesty had he ruled as king-in-parliament, he undermined the idea that Charles was a mere man.[42]

While in order to try him for capital crimes Charles was presented as a mere man, his actions had demonstrated that he was not a mere man, but a tyrant. Even here the indictment stood on shaky ground, for it was also intended to show that Charles had evil intentions which predated their tyrannical manifestation. The prosecution sought to make a difference between the trust which defined the office, properly pursued,[43] and the person who manifested a malicious intent to subvert the office. The bold attack on the king's person was not lost on the Scottish Commissioners who reminded the Commons of the Solemn League and Covenant and the *Engagement* of December 1647, and warned that the Court's proceedings were for 'taking away his majesty's life; for change of the fundamental government of this kingdom; and introducing a sinful and ungodly toleration in matters of Religion'.[44] The king was equally aware of the attempt to dissect the various functions of kingship. If he could remind his audience of the connections between person and office he would not save his life, but could sufficiently rescue his reputation to render a subsequent government iniquitous. If he were a mere man then his treatment at his trial and the 'shows of liberty' he received were a benchmark for other citizens and

> truly if it were only my own particular Case, I would have satisfied myself with the protestation I made the last time I was here . . . that a king cannot be tried by any superior jurisdiction on earth; but it is not my case alone, it is the Freedom and the Liberty of the people of England; and do you pretend what you will, I stand more for their Liberties. For if power without law may make laws, may alter the fundamental laws of the kingdom, I do not know what subject he is in England, that can be sure of his life, or anything that he calls his own.[45]

He mirrored the court's concern that unkingly actions released the bond between office and person: 'If that I do say any thing, but that which is for the Peace of the Kingdom, and that which is for the Liberty of the Subject, then the shame is mine.'[46]

Despite this, the temptation persisted for the king to stand on his office. He protested that the king could not be a delinquent and that he was no ordinary prisoner, but this was precisely what the court was affirming. If the king was an ordinary prisoner he should be tried and convicted in the same way as a citizen. If he made himself out to be a special case, he was demonstrating the 'cursed principle of Tyranny, that ha[d] so long lodged and harboured within him', which lifted Charles' character out of the league of the ordinary person.[47] The single figure of Charles, who was not permitted to dispute the legitimacy of the court set to try him, was a physical demonstration that 'Justice knows no respect of persons'.[48] The dualistic notion of balance, in which 'the law keeps the beam even between sovereignty and subjection'[49], represented the High Court on the one hand *versus* a sole figure on the other to demonstrate how out of kilter the current situation had become. Bradshaw turned Charles' claim to be the fount of law on its head: 'For you to set yourself with your single judgment, and those that adhere unto you, to set yourself against the highest Court of Justice, that is not law.'[50] The members of the High Court, as they were ordinary men, had 'weighed the merits of the cause in the Ballances of the Sanctuary, Law and right Reason'.[51] On the day of Charles' execution, William Ball's tract, *The Power of Kings discussed*, reappeared on the streets of London, in which he argued that *salus populi* was the end of English government, not *majestas imperii*.[52] For the one man to seek to be the entirety of one side of the scales was a tyranny of number, presumption of representativeness and a definition of arbitrariness. The court was asserting the notion encountered in the constitutional language of the Levellers. The people and their representatives – usually the House of Commons, but, in this judicial sense, the High Court of Justice – could not, in logic and reason, admit of any power higher than themselves: 'You have indeed struck at the root, that is, the power and supreme authority of the Commons of England, which this Court will not admit a debate of; and which indeed is an irrational thing in them to do, being a court that acts upon authority derived from them, that they should presume to judge upon their superior, from whom there is no appeal.'[53]

In order to set the lone figure of Charles apart from the people of England, it was necessary to reveal the deliberation behind his actions. He must have acted with a degree of malice which set him apart from his fellows because 'every king of England is obliged to act for the people's good: for all power, as it is originally in the People (he must needs be extreme ignorant, malicious, or a self-destroyer, that shall deny it), so it is given forth for their preservation.'[54] He was 'so proudly wedded to his own conceits, as so maliciously to oppose his private opinion against the public judgment and reason of state'.[55] Prosecution language was replete with terms of intent and premeditation. Charles was 'wilful',[56] 'wicked'[57] and 'hard-hearted' to appear unmoved by the blood of 5,000 men shed at Edgehill.[58] He had 'designes, and plots and endeavours'[59] and was a man of 'unmeasurable pride'. His domination was 'invented' so exquisitely as to put the other evil designer, Machiavelli, to shame.[60] In the scales of personal judgement, Charles had failed to regulate his life by conscience. The king, himself, came precipitously close to falling into the trap of declaring himself responsible for the war. In his eagerness to demonstrate himself the champion of the people's liberties he declared 'it was the Liberty, Freedom, and Laws of the subject, that ever I took -'. He thought better of admitting 'took up arms to protect' and reverted to 'defended myself with arms', which threw responsibility for starting the fighting back onto his opponents.[61]

The statements made about Charles during the period of his trial were underpinned with a free-will theology which was unexpected in view of the providentialist and predestinarian language of retribution against Ahab which had characterised the calls for judgement. The implication behind the stress placed on Charles' deliberation was that he had been given the conscionable choice whether to fulfil his trust with the people or to act according to his own volition. He had chosen the latter, acting 'wilfully'.[62] Likewise, when he enacted a piece of bad policy, he was countermanding the will of God and the good of the people: he had, for example, displayed an 'unwillingness' to declare against the Irish rebels.[63] God's will and the law were 'natural' states – 'written in the fleshly tables of men's hearts' – which Charles determined to flout.[64] This natural state was the law used by the High Court, which was 'general', 'unanimous', 'innate' and 'so naturally and necessarily implyed, that it's needless to be exprest'.[65]

The king's 'wit and knowledge proved like a sword in a madman's hand; he was a stranger to the work of grace and the spirit of God: and all those meanders in state, his serpentine turnings and windings, have but brought him to shame and confusion.'[66] Grace was freely bestowed and Charles had been its witting subverter, debasing the fundamental laws and corrupting both the concept and the language of grace. Grace did not guide his actions:

[H]ad we not a gracious king to call a parliament when there was so much need of it, and to pass so many gracious acts to put down the Star-Chamber, &c? Nothing less; it was not any voluntary free act of Grace, not the least ingredient or tincture of love or good affection to the people, that called the short parliament in 1640, but to serve his own turn against the Scots, whom he then had designed to enslave: and those seven Acts of Grace which the king passed, were no more than his duty to do.[67]

The title 'Gracious Majesty' was ill deserved. Such language was blasphemy and its object, by definition, a false idol:

> The Judges and Bitesheeps began to sing lullaby, and speak *Placentia* to the king, that 'my lord the King is an Angel of light:' now angels are not responsible to men, but God, therefore not kings; and the Judges, they begin to make the king a god, and say, That by law his stile is 'Sacred Majesty,' though he swears every hour; and 'Gracious Majesty,' though gracious men be the chief objects of his hatred; and that the king hath an omnipotence and an omnipresence.[68]

He was 'idolized and adored', but the only object of such veneration was God.[69]

The stress on free will – that Charles and his acolytes had chosen to erect a power which blasphemously subverted and challenged that of God[70] – dictated that the judgements which were made about Charles' thoughts and actions were determined by ethics. The moral law did not outline what *was* but what *ought* to be. Charles' actions had given form to his intentions, his 'erroneous principles'. It was with some frustration that Bradshaw entreated Charles that 'you ought to have ruled according to the Law; you ought to have done so'.[71] If Charles possessed the conscience to tell good actions from bad and had chosen the latter, the court was in fact judging his conscience. The fact that he was a king was the justification for his trial on earth; all men's consciences would be weighed at Judgement Day.

A court, acting according to the common law, was a poor vehicle to make ethical judgements.[72] It decided about actions, and then only as they were in breach of pre-existent law. The method for doing so was to call witnesses who would swear that they had seen Charles in person at various civil war battles, 'proving' that he was personally responsible for the blood spilt on the field. The court took thirty statements on the morning of 25 January and a further unnamed witness appeared in the afternoon with the fanciful story that, as early as 1643, Charles had tried to win over the 'Independents' with promises of (presumably) toleration. Charles' letters and papers were produced. All was confounded by the king's refusal to plead, but the commissioners proceeded with a 'Condemnation (that) shall extend to Death'.[73]

Because Charles refused to go along with the display, the court in public session could not condemn Charles' for the degree to which his actions were contrary to law but for the degree to which he possessed an evil intent against the people and their representatives. And, as such, the commissioners could not portray themselves as legally empowered delegates of a common law system, but as the godly instruments of divine will. The 'innocent bloud that has been shed, the Cry whereof is very great for Justice and Judgment' was expressed by 'God who we know is King of Kings, and Lord of Lords'.[74] The court was reminded of the text of blood-guiltiness: 'whoso sheddeth man's blood, by man shall his blood be shed.'[75] God had permitted but not approved '[t]yrants that so domineer with a rod of iron' because '[i]f king Ahab, and queen Jezebal, for the blood of one righteous Naboth, . . . were justly put to death; what punishment doth he deserve, that is guilty of the blood of thousands.'[76] Bradshaw preferred the theme of deliverance, exemplified by the children of Israel who would not worship the false idols set up by Nebuchadnezzar.[77] There was considerable exegesis of I Samuel 8. 'God in his Wrath gave (Charles Stuart) to be a King in this Nation', but God's love would remove him, on account of his 'notorious Prevarications and Blood-guiltiness'.[78] It was Charles' tyranny which entitled the children of God to execute God's vengeance on earth.

The ground had shifted again. This was a very different exegesis to that in which Charles' free will was exercised for the purposes of evil. Now, the emphasis was on the ways in which Charles was bound to act tyrannically because he was an instrument of God's wrath. He was inherently evil. Human justice was sanctioned, but somewhat at odds with the notion that God was the avenger who delivered mankind from blood-guiltiness.[79] In a reversal of the moral imperative in which Scripture instructs a person how one *ought* to govern, I Samuel 8 outlined how kings *would* govern:

> The holy Spirit in that Chapter does not insinuate what a good King ought to do, but what a wicked king would presume to do. Besides, *Saul* and *David* had extraordinary calling, but all just power is now derived from and conferred by the people: yet in the case of *Saul* it is observable, That the people, out of pride to be like other Nations, desired a King, and such a King as the Heathens had, which were all Tyrants: for they that know any thing in History, know that the first four Monarchs were all Tyrants at first, til they gained the people's consent. *Nimrod* the great Hunter was *Ninus* that built *Nineveh*, the first Tyrant and Conqueror that had no Title; and so were all Kingdoms, which are not Elective, till the peoples subsequent consent.[80]

Charles' supporters turned this Old Testament language of blood-guilt and vengeance on its head in order to rebuild his reputation. The faults of which the court accused Charles were redrafted in terms of Charles' Gospel virtues. The court possessed 'ungoverned passion', whilst Charles' 'incomparable patience' was the 'wonder of man'.[81]

Statements made at and about Charles' trial reveal tensions both within and between the arguments of the prosecutors. Were all kings tyrants, instituted by God in his wrath because the people would not trust in divine rule alone? 'The Lord declares his dislike of *all* such kings as the Heathens were . . . the Lord renounces the very *Genus* of such Kings'.[82] Kings were said to be gods on earth 'in no other sence then the Devil is called the God of this world'.[83] Were individual kings tyrants because they behaved like heathen kings? Was Charles Stuart a tyrant because he had breached a fundamental, innate bond of trust between himself and those he governed, wilfully acting against the people's interests? Had he broken a written English statute law or had he breached a covenant with God? Was his rule elective or hereditary? Was his kingship natural or imposed?

None of these questions was resolved by the trial. The forum was ill-fitted to examine questions of common law: Charles could easily point to the lack of precedent.[84] On the other hand, a court trying to appear legitimate according to statute law was ill-equipped to make the case that Charles had been a morally bad king because he had not acted as he ought, or that his actions manifested the real problem of his wilful character. If the court was trying Charles for actual deeds contrary to law – either of England or of God – it was necessary to rehearse the events to which he was privy after August 1642 and to call witnesses. On the other hand, 'before I [Cook] speak of the War, it will be necessary for the satisfaction of rationall men, to open and prove the King's wicked Design', because in the absence of witnesses which would stand up in a common law court, what was on trial was his long-standing and continual desire to subvert the fundamental constitution.[85] This was an attack on the whole of his 'covetous' life and his 'deboysed' [*sic*] character.[86] To make Charles 'sole author and owner of all his ill-ordered or unhappy actions' was not to 'allow him a share in any good deed or act of grace'.[87]

The court would not allow to Charles any virtue, in order to isolate him from the court and the people. The latter were godly and Charles could not, therefore, be allowed to be the champion of their representative rights. Charles had subverted the natural balance of power within the state. He had failed to honour the oath, trust or reciprocal bond between governor and people.[88] Instead, he had not just subverted the balance, but inverted it. Some clergymen of Banbury, Oxfordshire, and Brackley, Northamptonshire, took the issue back to the outbreak of the war. Allegiance was either 'vain, . . . or else obligatory' and made vain as soon as Charles deserted the parliament, set up his standard and levied war.[89] On one side of the scales was Charles' lonely figure. On the other was the people, their representatives, godliness, the common and moral law, justice and trust: 'If the parliament represent the whole kingdom . . . then doth the

King represent onely himself; and if a King without his Kingdom be in a civil sense nothing, then without or against the Representative . . . he himself represents nothing, and by consequence his judgment and his negative is as good as nothing.'[90]

Despite the inadequacies of the public case, the prosecution secured its verdict and sentence. On 30 January 1649 the regicides relished the spectacle of Charles parading under Rubens' painting of James Stuart's 'idolatrous' apotheosis which adorned the ceiling of the Banqueting House in Whitehall. His very public execution took place on a scaffold erected outside its central windows. Charles' death, however, did not end the arguments about the court's validity, the reasons for its actions or the outcome. Indeed, they were exacerbated, because even supporters of the events of December and January were divided about whether to justify the retrospective actions of the court, the current state of kingless government or to project a new settlement.

Charles' execution proved to be his martyrdom, and the speed and volume with which encomiastic accounts of the king's tragic life and heroic death flooded the streets was impressive. The court was branded unprecedented, controversial, and the role of the New Model Army provided the propagandists with a powerful image of might overcoming right. Having taken the most proactive step of the English revolution, the regicides were hurled into reaction. Forms of attack were also defensive. It became necessary to send material to the presses which would retrospectively justify the High Court and its decisions – to champion the regicide. Cook's publication of his unused prosecution speeches, *King Charls his Case*, was one such attempt.[91] During the course of the trial, John Milton composed a defence of tyrannicide, to which he gave the title *The Tenure of Kings and Magistrates*. It was published on 13 February. He so impressed the new governors that he was invited into employment as the state's persuader in foreign tongues.[92] These regicidal tracts made a specific case to a particular purpose: to justify the trial and execution of Charles by reciting resistance theory, biblical texts, Protestant theology and the concepts of blood-guilt and sacrifice.

A 'well-willer to Peace and Truth' rehearsed thirteen reasons why Charles had been deposed (because he had sworn to call a council and failed to do so) and put to death (because he was a tyrannical king who opposed the law, seized estates, was captured and not acquitted by God or man).[93] London citizens, influenced both by secular Leveller demands and also by the need to reform the morals of the people as a whole, were quite convinced that the sole source of England's previous troubles had been the single figure of Charles Stuart. Now he had been removed, however, they were worried by rumours that the reins of government had been taken up by the Army Council. Better that the present laws remain in force until new could be established, and if any of the king's children could be shown to have renounced the actions of the civil wars and signed the *Agreement of the People*, they should be allowed to reign as godly magistrates.[94] Regicidal thinking was reactionary in the sense that it was conservative. If sole responsibility for the crisis could be placed at Charles' door, his removal would restore the *status quo* of balanced and godly magistracy. There was no need to go any further than a search for a godly Stuart to take up the reins at the point where another member of the family had relinquished them. The rhetoric of regicide concentrated on the person-specific evils of one man, the execution of whom would avenge blood-guilt and revive godly magistracy.

Within this continuing rhetoric of regicide, there were, however, signs of republicanism. More precisely, within a discourse of the deposition of the person of Charles Stuart arose the possibility to extend the debate to discuss the possibility of a future administration without a king. The collapse of confidence in the person facilitated a critique of the office which that person had fulfilled. It was possible for regicide and republicanism to coexist within a single source. A regicidal text – one purposely designed to justify the regicide – could contain elements of republican thinking. The way in which Milton elided the two definitions of tyrant without title (usurpers) and tyrants by practice provides an example of the way in which this could arise.[95] Milton chose to stress the object of rule rather than the road to power: irrespective of how they came to the throne, a tyrant was a person who ruled in his or her own rather than the general interest.[96] Milton was guided by expediency. He was seeking to justify the actions of a government which had first seized power by military purge and then confirmed its rule by the unprecedented trial of the former governor.

But Milton was not the first to integrate the two, and the way in which the two branches could become entangled illustrates the interaction between a regicidal and a republican impetus to action. Those who traced a history of ignominy through the Babylonian, Nebuchadnezzar, to the idolatrous kings of Israel, Agag, Ahab and Ahaziah, and finally rested with the kings of the Jews, David and Saul, were engaged in the same exercise.[97] They were both conflating the definitions of tyranny and the distinctive types of kingship outlined in Scripture. A secular version of the same pattern was displayed by those who tangled themselves in knots trying to decide whether Charles was a descendant of William the Usurper or whether the Norman conquest had been subsequently legitimated by the people's consent. Had Charles deliberately left out the part of the coronation oath which called for public acclamation, or had he sworn to this and then broken his promise? The fall of Charles could be deemed to have broken the people's reliance on a monarch, opening the door for an assault on kingship. It was the various events of Charles' life which had eventually led the people to stop their patience with him, but the second civil war 'sufficiently manifest to all men who are not blinded to the name of King' that the evil existed in all kings: 'in him (was) the disabling of the Norman Line for the future'.[98]

The competing respects with which the parliament was dealing both retrospectively with the person of the king and planning a future government without any king were not resolved by the passage of an Act to abolish the kingship.[99] It was a ratification, and extension, of two previous Acts. In order to prevent the immediate proclamation of a successor to Charles, the House, led by Henry Marten, passed legislation prohibiting anybody from proclaiming, or being proclaimed, king.[100] This was followed, on 7 February, by a debate on kingship. Unfortunately, it is difficult to reconstruct the factionalism of this debate. No details survive of the mover of a motion to turn the House into a Grand Committee to debate the kingship question. The motion did not pass, and there is no record of the numbers attending the House that day, though registrations of dissent were well under way. If a large number of members were present on 7 February, it may well have been the case that the move to turn the House into a Grand Committee was opposed by the republican group in order to counter the conservative effect of some of the readmitted MPs. If the membership was low on that day, it is equally possible that the move was promoted by the republicans in order to increase the impression that the result was representative of all of the Commons.

The Act consisted of five clauses, designed to constitute a logically progressive whole, but its seeming continuity disguised unresolved tensions. The text betrayed the continuing concern of some of the revolutionaries to justify the actions which led up to and included Charles' death, and of others to project future constitutional possibilities. Of the five clauses, the first – which justified the past action of trying and executing Charles Stuart for high treason and the consequent disinheritance of his posterity – and the third – which countered the possibility that Charles' son would be proclaimed king – looked back to the regicide. However, the implication which people were expected to draw from the first, regicidal clause was, according to the second paragraph, republican. The second declared that any person, invested with the degree of potential power which attached to kingship, would be tempted to abuse it, because

> it is and hath been found by experience, that the office of a King in this nation and Ireland, and to have the power thereof in any single person, is *unnecessary, burdensome, and dangerous* to the liberty, safety, and public interest of the people, and that for the most part, use hath been made of the regal power and prerogative to oppress and impoverish and enslave the subject; and that usually and naturally any one person in such power makes it his interest to incroach upon the just freedom and liberty of the people, and to promote the setting up of their own will and power above the laws, that so they might enslave these kingdoms to their own lust.[101]

From the particular – experience of the rule of Charles Stuart – came the general – experience tells us that if one man rules in this way, all men will do so. The Act was expressing, in a constitutional form, a return to the Pentateuchal analysis of the origin of man's character: '[n]o man who knows ought, can be so stupid to deny that all men naturally were born free, being the image and resemblance of God himself . . . Till from the root of *Adams* transgression, falling among themselves to doe wrong and violence' they voluntarily erected mutual bonds of authority.[102] These authorities were called kings and magistrates, but they were not to be masters. They should have exercised a covenant, not broken it by oppressing God's people. The fourth clause of the Act announced that the return to the fundamental rule of government by the people necessitated a representative assembly, and made an unequivocal statement that it was intended to dissolve the current parliament and to call fresh elections under a reformed voting system, 'as soon as may possibly stand with the safety of the people that hath betrusted them'.[103]

Charles had distorted the balance of power in three respects, to the point at which experience taught the new governors that they should abolish kingly government for the future. Kings were 'unnecessary, burdensome and dangerous'. Unnecessariness had been demonstrated *de facto*. Since 1642, the government of England had been without kings and the world had not come to an end.[104] The United Provinces of the Netherlands had become a powerful, flourishing neighbour since it overthrew its kings.[105] The covenant, trust or oath of government was that all people had the right to place themselves under that government, and the relationship between the rulers and the ruled had therefore to be circular and self-contained. Anybody outside the circle was, by definition, both arbitrary and unnecessary. The balance was regulated by representativeness and accountability. Since kings were not an integral part of the mutual relationship between the people and those chosen to represent them, they were merely a title, superfluous to the fundamental constitution.

The balance of power could be represented as an account ledger, in which kings stood for the figure nought – ciphers. Keeping a titular, impotent king was ludicrous: having both the tyrannical potentiality of kingship and the worthlessness of his authority. In *Monarchy No Creature of Gods Making* Cook argued, 'I heard many wise men speake of making peace with the King and tyeing him so close to his Lawes, that he should not be able to hurt the people; I thought it was but a kind of dissimulation to make people beyond Sea thinke him to be a great King, and yet in effect to make him stand but for a cypher.'[106] Charles' 'mock' Parliament in Oxford had been an inversion of good government: powerless and, therefore, valueless. The representatives had no authority within it, 'where the Kings consent must be the Figure, and the Representative stand but for a Cypher'.[107]

The same weighing up of the value of the parts of government could be expressed in terms of law. Kingship was customary, and custom was a facet of common law. If the same relationship was expressed in terms of the moral law, kingship was formalistic and ceremonial. Ceremony had a double meaning. It could refer to the pomp and show of kingship, in which 'meer Prerogatives' were 'the Toyes and Gewgaws of his Crown' and copes and surpluses 'the Trinkets of his Priests'.[108] It could also be a reference to the three divisions of Judaic law: the moral, judicial and mere 'Ceremoniall and Circumstantiall formes'.[109] However much men might argue that the moral law was not abrogated by the coming of Christ, it was universally accepted that the ceremonial law was rendered obsolete by the Gospel. In all cases, ceremony defined a worthless and superficial accretion, and insufficient for law, in either spiritual or civil terms.

In 1646, Henry Marten had called for an end to 'King craft, Clergy craft, and Court craft', and though it was never explicitly stated, the power which kings possessed to charm, dazzle and delude had all the appearance of witchcraft.[110] For Cook, the combination of outward inoffensiveness and the potentiality to do disproportionate harm was like virtuous kings who were white witches 'that seem to cure one that they may without suspicion bewitch twenty'.[111] The mask of seeming virtue which attached to kings was a delusion which drew the ignorant into their spell. By the end of this tract, Cook's witch had been transformed into a 'white devill',[112] the external purity of whose dress disguised evil. The white devil was often used to describe the Pharisees, who denied Christ was the prophet, because strict adherence to form and custom had hardened their hearts to the true message.[113] By claiming to be strictly orthodox and by practising right religion, they were, in fact, closing their minds to the true faith. They were hypocrites.

People were 'blinded in affection to the name of king' to the point at which they abandoned their own liberties.[114] The person of the king – and, once he had been executed, his title – acted as a veil to mask true godliness: the 'vail betwixt God and man'.[115] William Cockayne, cousin to the Leveller, William Wetton, railed against the delay in securing no addresses and declared that kings and kingly government were man-made, not instituted by God. Now the Rump would 'remove the vaile from people's eyes, that they would not so much adore the name and person of a King, especially when we see their ambitious nature mounts them up so high, that nothing must content, unless all must be their slaves.'[116]

The idol would retain its ungodly power while the parliament preserved 'the meere useless bulke of his person'.[117] The king's titles were useless 'arrogancies, or flatteries', but the danger and burden of admitting that he had as much right to the titles as any citizen to his inheritance was 'to make the Subject no better than the Kings slave, his chattell, or his possession'.[118] In terms of the metaphor of balance, if a king existed with merely the title, his side of the scales was so lightweight as to be worth nothing. If valueless, why retain it? At the same time, however, the enduring love which people bore the false name was the hairline crack which a king would prize open to enable him to restore his oppressive powers. It was an extension of the argument which 'Verity Victor' had used against the negative voice: it would be cutting down Nebuchadnezzar's tree and leaving the root behind.[119] On the other hand, if a king built himself up to such a height as to tip the balance of power in his favour, the inferior magistrates returned to the position of justifiable opposition to a tyrant.

The example of Charles the man was taken as a lesson about all kings. He was the one man – Agag in this instance – who would 'arrogate so unreasonably above human condition, or derogate so basely from a whole', seeking to balance 'his own brute will and pleasure' against 'so many thousand Men for wisdom, vertue, nobleness of mind, and all other respects'.[120] Marten held all kings possessed of a potential absolutism – 'either an absolute Tyrant over us, or no King'.[121] George Wither balanced the powers the parliament might have allowed to Charles and the importance which he placed on his own authority:

> Suppose the King had agreed to the Propositions, and been set up to hawk, hunt, bowle, and play at Tennis, whilst the Parliament managed the great and publike affairs, had not this been by the Sword, which not only captivated his

Body, but forced his minde to yeeld to part with those things, which he esteemed above the bloud of so many thousands, yea his very owne?[122]

Milton subsequently chose to look back to the militia issue with which the war had begun. Charles should not have had authority over anything except by parliamentary agreement. As soon as he had been given any such power, it signalled the end of all of England's liberties. Charles had been 'idlely raigning', and the years before 1642 were 'either tyranniz'd or trifl'd away', a parallel of the statements made about William the Conqueror, that his rule was secured by both violence and falsehood.[123] Milton's attack on the institution of monarchy was followed, a few days later, by another which compared the godliness of the inferior magistrates with the godlessness of a king. The author of this most caustic and damning example – it was probably Henry Robinson – summed up with vivid clarity:

If we do but cast up our accounts right, we shall find that Kings are but meer chargeable *Ceremonies*, or *Ciphers*, of little use but to contract humors, and promote personal designs destructive to the being, and well-being of *Commonwealths*; for they are neither executioners of justice themselves, nay, scarce (many times) *Counsellors*, nor do any special or publique work; and yet for meer custom and formalities sake, we must have one man adored, having supreme power invested in him, and be maintained in the greatest *State*, and *Glory*, meerly to sit still and have the best, and wisest, and most faithful and gallant instruments bow down, and rejoyce, *but to kiss his hand*.[124]

NOTES

1. The phrase is that of John Cook, 'the Execution of the late king was one of the fattest sacrifices that ever Queen Iustice had': *Monarchy no creature*, title; Nancy Klein Maguire, 'The theatrical mask/masque of politics: the case of Charles I', *JBS*, 32 (1989) 24–43, p. 18.
2. *A True Copie of the Berkshire Petition*, p. 6; see Chapter 3, p. 85.
3. Ludlow's account seemed to imply Ludlow, Grey of Groby and Sir Henry Vane as the MPs and Henry Ireton as one of the grandees: Ludlow, *Memoirs*, I, pp. 208–10.
4. Ludlow also implied that the number excluded (he says around ninety, though that is not an accurate recollection) was roughly the number of MPs who voted in favour of renewing addresses in September 1647: Ludlow, *Memoirs*, I, pp. 210–11; *CJ*, V, p. 312, 22 Sep. 1647.
5. The numbers are taken from David Underdown, *Pride's Purge: Politics in the Puritan Revolution* (London, 1971), pp. 211–21. There is not the space here to rehearse the details of the purge and Underdown's account remains unchallenged and by far the most thorough.

6. Underdown divides the 154 into revolutionaries who actively promoted the purge, subsequent trial and change of government (he numbers them at seventy-one) and the remainder as 'conformists', who did not actively promote the revolution but were prepared to work with it once it was achieved.

7. Ludlow, *Memoirs*, I, pp. 212–13; John Lilburne, *Legall Fundamentall Liberties of the People of England*, 8 Jun. 1649, E560(14), pp. 33–40; Colonel Robert Tichborne, *Petition*, 15 Jan. 1649; *CJ*, VI p. 117; *The Moderate*, 16–23 Jan. 1649, E540(20).

8. *CJ*, VI, p. 111; Ludlow, *Memoirs*, I, p. 213; *A Declaration of the House of Commons in Parliament assembled*, [6 Jan.] 1649, E537(18); *A Joynt Resolution and Declaration of the Parliament and Counsell of the Army. For the taking away of King and Lords*, [11 Jan.] 1649, E538(1*).

9. Underdown, *Pride's Purge*, pp. 165–6 and p. 214 n. 13. Underdown has examined the registrations of dissent with some care, and pieced together a personnel of revolutionaries on this basis. The names of those who dissented, were still alive in 1660 and who feared for their lives should monarchy be restored, were erased by the Commons' clerk in February 1660. Underdown has reconstructed some, and I attempted to bring modern science to the aid of the historian by subjecting the ink with which the manuscript Commons Journals (deposited in the House of Lords Record Office) were written to a number of tests in order to distingish the ink in which the original name was entered from that with which it was crossed out. Unfortunately, the composition of the inks was too similar and the time period between the two layers too short to be able to separate them. Nevertheless, I am grateful to the staff of the House of Lords Record Office, the Metropolitan Police Forensic Science Laboratory and the British Library for their help in making the attempt.

10. These were described as Acts. If one believed that the agreement of the king and the lords was vital in order to make law, then they do not deserve this title. The Commons referred to legislation which had passed only the lower house as Acts, in keeping with the vote of 4 January, and this study will follow this convention; University of Sheffield, Hartlib MSS, 26/13/1A, Lady Ranelagh to Hartlib.

11. *King Charls Tryal: A Perfect Narrative of the Whole High Court of Justice*, imprimatur Gilbert Mabbott, 27 Jan. 1649, E545(4+5), p. 4.

12. The Irish peer, William, Lord Mounson was named and attended ten sessions. There were also four sons of peers, of whom only Grey of Groby was active: Underdown, *Pride's Purge*, pp. 187–8.

13. *GCD*, p. 357.

14. *GCD*, pp. 371–4, pp. 371–2.

15. *The Journal of the High Court of Justice, for the Trial of King Charles the First*, taken by John Phelps, clerk to the court, and transcribed (with modernised capitalisation) in T. B. Howell, *A Complete Collection of*

State Trials and Proceedings for High Treason and Other Crimes and Misdemeanours (33 vols) (London, 1809–26), IV, cols 1045–154, subsequently cited as *Journal* and a column number: *Journal*, 1060–1.

16. *Journal*, 1061. These two committees were set up on 15 January.

17. The differences between those who attended regularly, those who were revolutionary in politics but alarmed or scandalised by the purge and trial and those who absented themselves is made in Underdown, *Pride's Purge*, pp. 187–9.

18. Oxford, Worcester College, Clarke MSS XVI f.66 and CXIV f.160. These are undated, but it is clear from the contents that they were written at the end of December 1648.

19. *King Charls Tryal*, pp. 3–4.

20. *Journal*, 1055.

21. *Journal*, 1065.

22. *Journal*, 1058.

23. Letter of the Commissioners of the Estates of the Parliament of Scotland to Speaker Lenthall, 22 Jan. 1649; *Journal*, 1076; *CJ*, VI, p. 122.

24. *Journal*, 1058.

25. John Cook, *The Vindication of the Professors and Profession of the Law*, [6 Feb.] 1646, E320(17); John Cook, *Redintegratio Amoris or a Union of Hearts*, [27 Aug.] 1647, E404(29); John Cook, *Unum necessarium: or the Poor Mans Case* [1 Feb.] 1648, E425(1).

26. John Cook, *What the Independents would have*, [1 Sep.] 1647, E405(7).

27. John Cook, *King Charls his Case*, [9 Feb.] 1649, E542(3).

28. *King Charls Tryal*, p. 34.

29. *King Charles Tryal*, p. 34; Cook, *King Charls*, pp. 6–7.

30. The jurists, Fortescue and Bracton, and the baron's war: *King Charls Tryal*, pp. 29, 32–33; Cook, *King Charls*, pp. 7, 18.

31. *King Charls Tryal*, p. 34; Cary J. Nederman, 'Bracton on kingship revisited', *HPT*, V.1 (1984) 61–77.

32. *King Charls Tryal*, pp. 5–7.

33. *King Charls Tryal*, p. 38; see Robert Parsons, *Severall Speeches Delivered at a Conference*, 31 Jan. 1648, E521(1), p. 69, and above, Chapter 2, n. 25.

34. Cook, *King Charls*, pp. 6, 7. As if to confirm that the saints were surrounded by loyalists for whom profane literature was more important than the Scripture, Samuel Butler's response to Cook was more concerned that it was Cook who was abusing the literary giants with his 'peasantry of language, especially against such a person': Samuel Butler (or possibly Birkenhead), *King Charles's Case truly stated: in answer to Mr Cook's pretended Case of the blessed Martyr*, in John, Baron Somers, *A Collection of scarce and valuable Tracts, on the most interesting and entertaining Subjects* (16 vols) (London, 1748–52), V, pp. 237–48, p. 238; Klein Maguire, 'Theatrical mask', p. 8.

35. Both the court officers refused to treat Charles with the dignity which he thought befitted his office, and in return Charles refused to

treat the court with the dignity which it felt it was owed: *King Charls Tryal*, pp. 4, 8.

36. *King Charls Tryal*, p. 5; Cook, *King Charls*, p. 5.
37. Cook, *King Charls*, pp. 31–4.
38. Cook, *King Charls*, pp. 7–8, 35.
39. *King Charls Tryal*, pp. 5–7; [Lilburne], *Regall Tyrannie discovered*, pp. 9–11.
40. Henry Marten had argued the same, again in 1646 in *Corrector of the Answerer*, p. 5.
41. *King Charls Tryal*, p. 42.
42. Marten, *Parliaments Proceedings*, p. 10: 'Do you mark how they talk still of mutuality? of equal giving and receiving? As if the Parliament and their Prisoner were upon a Level.'
43. *King Charls Tryal*, pp. 38–9.
44. *Journal*, 1076.
45. Charles Stuart to the High Court, 22 Jan. 1649: *King Charls Tryal*, p. 11.
46. *King Charls Tryal*, pp. 26, 29.
47. Cook, *King Charls*, p. 38. Cook cited his own father as an example of an ordinary person in this context. Cook would provide a marvellous study for those skilled in psycho-history, for there was clearly an interesting relationship between himself and his father which made him acutely aware of the concept of parricide. Most interestingly, in a dream travelling to Munster, he screamed that he did not murder his father: John Cook, *A true Relation of Mr. Justice Cook's Passage by Sea*, 5 Jan. 1650, E598(1).
48. *King Charls Tryal*, p. 18.
49. Cook, *King Charls*, p. 7. Cook uses this as a definition of mixed government, which is clearly a complete change in meaning from the classic definition.
50. *King Charls Tryal*, pp. 31–2, 18.
51. Cook, *King Charls*, p. 40.
52. William Ball (of Barkham), *The power of Kings discussed; or an Examen of the Fundamental Constitution of the Free-born People of England, in answer to several Tenets of Mr David Jenkins*, 30 Jan. 1649, E340(21).
53. *King Charls Tryal*, pp. 24, 27.
54. Cook, *King Charls*, p. 8.
55. Cook, *King Charls*, p. 6.
56. *King Charls Tryal*, p. 24.
57. Cook, *King Charls*, p. 10.
58. Cook, *King Charls*, p. 6; Lucy Hutchinson, *Memoirs of Colonel Hutchinson* (London, 1965), p. 264.
59. *King Charls Tryal*, p. 34.
60. Cook, *King Charls*, to the reader, and pp. 20, 37; *A shrill cry in the eares of Cavaliers, Apostates, and Presbyters, for the Resolve of XIII Queries touching the Primitive state of this Nation, since the Conquest*, 5 Feb. 1649, E341(10),

p. 8; John Warr, *The Priviledges of the People, or Principles of Common Right and Freedom*, 5 Feb. 1649, E341(12), p. 1; *None-such Charles*, pp. 3–4.

61. *King Charls Tryal*, p. 15.

62. *King Charls Tryal*, p. 24; Cook, *King Charls*, p. 6; *None-such Charles*, p. 49.

63. Cook, *King Charls*, p. 28.

64. Cook, *King Charls*, pp. 22–3; 'That which struck most with Abraham about God's command to sacrifice Isaac was this: 'Can I not be obedient, unless I be unnatural?' Was he fit to continue a Father to the people, who was without natural affection to his own Father?'

65. Cook, *King Charls*, p. 23.

66. Cook, *King Charls*, p. 35.

67. Cook, *King Charls*, p. 14, who is referring to the concessions which Charles made during the Long Parliament session of 1641; see also John Milton, *Eikonoklastes*, in Merritt Y. Hughes, *Complete Prose Works of John Milton* (Yale, 1970), V, pp. 404, 435.

68. Cook, *King Charls*, pp. 25–6.

69. Cook, *King Charls*, p. 37.

70. Cook, *King Charls*, p. 25: '[f]or any man to say [that the King can do no wrong] . . . is blasphemy against the great God of Truth and Love: for onely God cannot erre.'

71. *King Charls Tryal*, p. 31; *contra* Niccolo Machiavelli, *The Prince* eds Quentin Skinner and Russell Price (Cambridge, 1988), Ch. XV: 'the things for which men, and especially rulers, are praised or blamed.'

72. Machiavelli, *Prince*, Ch. XV; Nancy Struever, *Theory as Practice: Ethical Inquiry in the Renaissance* (Chicago, 1991) ; Eugene Garver, 'After Virtù: rhetoric, prudence and moral pluralism in Machiavelli', *HPT*, XVII. 2 (1996) 195–223.

73. *Journal*, 1101–13. A committee consisting of Scot, Marten, Harrison, Lisle, Love, Ireton and Say was established to consider the manner of his death.

74. *King Charls Tryal*, pp. 18, 41.

75. In John Bradshaw's words, 'let God's law, let man's law speak . . . Gen. ix. Numb. xxxv. will tell you what the punishment is': *King Charls Tryal*, pp. 41–2.

76. Cook, *King Charls*, p. 10, citing Rev. 2: 27, 12: 5, 19: 15; and also p. 36, referring to I Kgs. 21.

77. *King Charls Tryal*, pp. 43–4, citing Dan. 3: 6–11.

78. Cook, *King Charls*, p. 5. See also p. 8 for a long exposition of the Samuel text.

79. *King Charls Tryal*, pp. 43–4.

80. Cook, *King Charls*, p. 8; Milton returned to the view that David was as guilty as the heathen kings: *Tenure of kings*, in Martin Dzelzainis (ed.), *Milton: Political Writings* (Cambridge, 1991), p. 12; see also John Canne, *The Golden Rule of Justice advanced*, [16 Feb.] 1649, E543(6), p. 9.

81. Butler, *King Charles's case*, in *Somers Tracts*, V, p. 237.

82. Cook, *King Charls*, p. 9, emphasis added.

83. Cook, *King Charls*, p. 8.

84. *King Charls Tryal*, pp. 5–7.

85. Cook, *King Charls*, p. 10; *A true Narration of the Title, Government, and cause of the Death of the late Charles Stuart, King of England*, published by authority, 5 Feb. 1649, E341(14), and in *Somers Tracts*, V, pp. 248–9.

86. *A true Narration*, pp. 2, 6; *None-such Charles*, pp. 194–5. Among the amazing list of characteristics for which Charles deserved the title 'none-such' was the fact that he walked like a lackey and not like a leader, did not woo like a prince, and never admitted to 'one single conference' with his first mistress (?). Charles was thus damned for being irreligious and damned for being insufficiently virile.

87. Butler, *King Charles's Case truly stated*, in *Somer's Tracts*, V, p. 241.

88. *King Charls Tryal*, pp. 23–4; Cook, *King Charls*, p. 40.

89. *The Humble Advice and earnest Desires of certain well-affected Ministers, Lecturers of Banbury in the County of Oxon, and of Brackley in the County of Northampton*, to Fairfax and the Council of War, 25 Jan. 1649, E540(12), p. 7.

90. I[ohn] M[ilton], *Eikonoklastes, in answer to a book intitled Eikon Basilike*, [6 Oct.] 1649, E578(5), and in Hughes, *Complete Prose Works*, V, p. 410.

91. Another was Colonel Robert Bennet's, *King Charle's trial justified: or Eight objections against the same fully answered and cleared, by Scripture, Law, History and Reason*, 4 Apr. 1649, E554(21).

92. The best edition and elucidation of the text is Martin Dzelzainis (ed.), *Milton: Political Writings* (Cambridge, 1991), pp. 2–48, although it is also transcribed in Hughes, *Complete Prose Works*, III, pp. 189–258.

93. *A shrill Cry*, p. 8.

94. *The Representative of divers well-affected Persons in and about the City of London*, [6 Feb.], 1649, E341(6), p. 8. This was probably written before the king's execution.

95. See Dzelzainis's discussion of these concepts: *Milton: Political Writings*, pp. xii–xiii.

96. J[ohn] M[ilton], *The Tenure of Kings and Magistrates*, [13 Feb.] 1649, E542(12), pp. 17–18; Dzelzainis, *Political Writings* p. xviii.

97. J[ohn] Fidoe, T[homas] Jeans, W[illiam] Shaw, *The Parliament Justified in their late Proceedings against Charles Stuart*, 27 Feb. 1649, E545(14), pp. 8–9.

98. *A True Narration*, p. 8.

99. *GCD*, pp. 384–7; Paul Knell, *A Looking-Glasse for Levellers*, E465(30), a sermon preached by the former chaplain in the king's army, 24 Sep. 1648: 'Nor is it only Carolus, but even Rex that they strike at, going about not onely to kill the Person, but the very office of King' (p. 14); William Bray (ed.), *Diary and Correspondence of John Evelyn* (London, 1854), Evelyn to Sir Richard Browne, 22 Mar. 1649, p. 551.

100. In Scotland, Charles Stuart/Stewart was proclaimed king immediately on receipt of the news of the death of his father: *CJ*, VI, p. 125.

101. I have added the emphasis.

102. Milton, *Tenure*, in Dzelzainis, *Political Writings*, pp. xviii, 8; Cook, *King Charls*, p. 42: 'it is for a Cain to be afraid, that *every man that meets him will slay him!*'.

103. *GCD*, p. 386.

104. Since 1649 a House of Lords was also proven unnecessary, though the act abolishing the Lords significantly left out this part of the trinity: *GCD*, pp. 387–8.

105. *The Kingdomes Grand Quere. What Warrant there is for such Proceeds about the King*, claimed to have been written by 'a Presbyterian Minister', but highly unlikely, 1 Mar. 1649, E345(21), p. 5.

106. John Cook, *Monarchy no Creature of Gods Making*, (London and Waterford) 26 Feb. 1652, E1238(1), pp. 129–30.

107. Cook, *King Charls*, p. 18.

108. Milton, *Eikonoklastes*, in Hughes, *Complete Prose Works*, V, p. 481.

109. Cook, *Monarchy no Creature*, preface, e3; Woodhouse, *Puritanism and Liberty* pp. (65)-(67). Bracketed page numbers are as Woodhouse gives them in his text and refer to his introduction.

110. See also Theophilus P., *Salus Populi desperately Ill of a Languishing Consumption*, [13 Oct.] 1648, E476(18), p. 14.

111. [Marten], *Corrector of the Answerer*, p. 7; Cook, *Monarchy no Creature*, preface, e3.

112. Cook, *Monarchy no Creature*, p. 88.

113. Milton, *Eikonoklastes*, in Hughes, *Complete Prose Works*, V, pp. 462, 481.

114. *A true Narration*, p. 7.

115. Joseph Salmon, *A Rout, A Rout: or some parts of the Armies quarters broken up, by the Day of the Lord Stealing upon them*, [10 Feb.] 1649, E342(5), p. 2. John Lilburne had expressed it as 'scales of blindness' in *Regall Tyrannie*, p. 39.

116. William Cockayne, *The Foundations of Freedome, Vindicated*, answering William Ashurst MP, [7 Feb.] 1649, E341(25), p. 4. Cockayne echoed the banner of Marten's unofficial regiment of 1648, 'a wel-wisher to England's freedomes; but an Opposer of Tyranny and Oppression in any whomsoever', and he was known to and an admirer of Marten, possibly through the connection with Wetton: Leeds, ML MSS 8/82; 65/(1). For these links see the author's forthcoming study of Marten, Chapter 2.

117. Milton, *Tenure*, in Dzelzainis, *Political Writings*, p. 7.

118. Milton, *Tenure*, in Dzelzainis, *Political Writings*, p. 11; the king's title was from 'Flattery, Oppression, Superstition, Ignorance, and the like', Robert Bacon, *The Labyrinth the Kingdom's In*, [7 Feb.] 1649, E541(26), p. 5.

119. 'Verity Victor', *Royal Project*, p. 16; see Chapter 4, p. 111 above.

120. Milton, *Tenure*, in Hughes, *Complete Prose Works* iii p. 204.

121. Marten, *Independency of England*, p. 14.
122. G[eorge] W[ither], *Respublica Anglicana or the Historie of the Parliament in their late Proceedings*, [28 Oct.] 1650, E780(25), p. 42.
123. J[ohn] M[ilton], *Eikonoklastes in Answer to a Book Intit'd Eikon Basilke*, 6 Oct. 1649, in Hughes, *Complete Prose Works*, XXVII, pp. 367–601, p. 454; Hutchinson, *Memoirs*, p. 3; see Chapter 2.
124. [Henry Robinson], *A Short Discourse between Monarchical and Aristocratical Government, Or a sober perswasive of all true hearted Englishmen, to a willing conjunction with the Parliament of England in setting up the Government of a Common-wealth*, [24 Oct.] 1649, E575(31), p. 14. Robinson took as his text I Sam. 8: 6–7. The pamphlet is attributed to Robinson and has not been challenged. For Robinson's career see W. K. Jordan, *Men of Substance* (Chicago, 1942), pp. 38–66.

6

Government New Modelled?

For a government built on such shaky foundations, the child of a purge, a trial and an execution, it was both imperative and difficult to establish its ideological and institutional identity. There was little agreement about what constituted a framework for republican government, either among members of the Rump parliament itself or in its wider constitutency of supporters who, over the course of the government's first months, proferred their views of the way forward. The government and its supporters were, at their own admission, 'an Heterogenial Body, consisting of parts very diverse from one another, setled upon principles inconsistent one with another'.[1] A number of issues which arose in the early months of the Commonwealth forced the Rumpers to tackle the conceptual difficulties of definition: the status of the Rump parliament itself; the possible need for an executive committee to manage day-to-day affairs; the status of the army; the future of the aristocracy; and a possible oath of loyalty to the new form of government. The numerous ideas which were put forward did, however, naturally divide into two approaches. There were those who hoped that the ship of state would not be blown about too wildly and those who expected to explore brave new spiritual or civil worlds.

Royalists sneered that the new republic was an unworkable fiction of the Independents' imagination. After the Restoration, Samuel Butler was free to deride the republicans for having invented fanciful, utopian models for government.[2] Those who tried to aid the government by distributing their own plans for governmental reform, were careful to stress their practicability. Theophilus P. published his recipe for the reform of the electoral system. His prescription hinted at another purge, because Pride's Purge had only moved the malignants and not completely ejected them from the system. In the language of the herbalist whose rhubarb and senna scoured the innards of the human body, Theophilus continued with the metaphor of the body politic. 'I have sent you by her poor servant Theophilus', he declared, 'such

Samples as grow in her own garden; they be no Drugs from Eutopia, or the new Atlantis, they may be of use.'[3] J. Philolaus was equally sceptical of the possibility of a utopia.[4] The urgency of reforming a real state left no time for the abstractions of More and Bacon.

The degree to which the government represented a utopian new model or a statement of continuity was reflected in the way in which it described itself in words and with visual imagery. Its confused self-image was drawn from the various meanings which republicanism had acquired in the seventeenth century. There was the *res publica*, a legitimately constituted government of any form. Contemporary states which governed themselves without a single head of state were sometimes described in Aristotelian terms as republican governments of the few or the many. Finally, there was a concept of humanist 'civic republicanism' which lauded public spirit, moral self-control and virtue. In 1649, the term 'republic' was used only once.[5] The government's initial self-description, a 'republic, without king or house of peers', is a phrase in which the second part acts as a further definition and explanation of the first. Having overturned a government which Charles had described as 'an Hereditary Kingdom for neer these thousand years,'[6] it described momentous change. Occasionally the government employed the term 'Free State', with the connotation that monarchical government had been unfree, and threw the emphasis onto the rhetoric of 1647–8 which had castigated Stuart tyranny.[7] The regime almost always preferred the word 'Commonwealth'. In March 1649, soldiers were sent to Ireland by a 'Commonwealth, without King or House of Lords'.[8] Both the England of Queen Elizabeth and the state of Venice were commonwealths, shifting the emphasis away from past events and towards the practical effects to be expected under this system. The phrase was more easily understood within an English context, held out the prospect of reform of the polity to ensure administration in the public interest, and drew attention away from the specific acts which had ended monarchy. It carried connotations of a unitary state – one in which the allegiance of the citizens and the governance of the rulers was a reciprocal relationship forged for the good of all.

It was argued that it was the very reciprocity of this arrangement which had been lost under the Stuarts. Charles' rule had been self-interested – not in the interest of the common weal. To this extent, the use of 'commonwealth' could be seen as an attempt to capture a mythical but nevertheless potent sense of one nation and shared national glory. The retention of the words 'without king or House of Lords' acted as an additional qualifier of the nature of the administration – almost an afterthought – which made the most of a sense of continuity.

As such, the commonwealthsmen themselves may have encouraged the view at which Henry Marten later complained that 'it was manifested to the World that they understood nothing of a Commonwealth but the name'.[9]

The rhetoric of government was designed to remove the stress which monarchy placed on private spectacles. John Warr believed that 'Kings and Princes have politiques, and Principles of their own, and certain State-maxims, whereby they scorn a loft, and walk in a distinct way of opposition to the Rights and Freedoms of the People; all which you may see in Machiavils Prince', and Ludlow was sure that the people in power after Pride's Purge aimed at least to get away from such self-interest.[10] The Master of Ceremonies, Sir Oliver Fleming, himself continuing in the office which he had fulfilled for the king, sought clarification of the titles by which the worthies of the Commonwealth wished to be addressed, in a confusing mess of person and office:

> I want instructions in the place the commonwealth is pleased to trust me. I desire to know what titles I am to give the Commonwealth and Council of State, in conversing with foreign ministers and strangers of quality . . . It is to be expected that we must wrestle with many difficulties incidental to a new government, now established in a more just and equal way; and that princes, looking upon their common interest, will apprehend the prosperity of the commonwealth may prove an allurement to their people to shake off their yoke . . . It is also feared that other commonwealths will at first make difficulty in giving those titles that this is obliged, in all justice and honour to hold forth to the world as its undoubted right, it being well known that *the kings of England had not these high and great titles given them as particular men, but in relation to the greatness and potency of the commonwealth*, from whence their titles were derived; so that I conceive the title of 'most excellent, most high, most mighty', and such others as hold forth the supreme authority of the nation, should be insisted upon, and *no diminution allowed of honour due either to the commonwealth or to the persons they dignify*.[11]

The Commonwealth needed to use titles in discourse with foreign powers, but if it took on the titles reserved for monarchical governments, it would be accused of being no better than the regime it replaced. The title of 'most mighty' was now defined by the common weal which supported the title, rather than the individual who topped the hierarchy – the office which supported the persons rather than the person who was the office.

In place of the person, the new government hoped to establish an ethos of public mutuality. On 3 January 1649, the House was ordered to discuss 'a Way for the carrying on publick Justice,'[12] and six days later the Commons resolved that 'the Name of any one Single Person shall not be used in the Stile of Commissions under the Great Seal Writs'.[13] The new Seal was designed by Marten and featured the collectivity of the parliament assembled in government, the abstract national symbols of the flags of England and Ireland, and the inscription 'In the First Year of Freedom, by God's Blessing restored, 1648'. This Levellerish statement of a return to fundamental principles was a target which those with high expectations of reform could tilt at.[14] Nevertheless, vestiges of this ethos survived for several years. John March of Gray's Inn wrote as late as May 1651 of the government's 'sweet Harmony of Justice, Honour, and integrity' and its 'noble, and truely generous publick spirit'. It had erected 'one rule in Law, that the publick good and wel-fare is to be preferred before the private'.[15] Even at parish level, local troublemaker, Margaret Lidey of Lyme Regis, who was accused of disturbing the peace of her neighbour, Christina Coxe, found her own identity, even as a troublemaker, defined in terms of and balanced 'agt all people of the Comon wealth of England'.[16]

The visual identity which was formed by ceremonial stressed continuity within a shifting emphasis on public rather than private. Ritualistic days of fasting were continued and were denounced as a continuation of form over substance.[17] In a satirist's version of a thanksgiving day speech to the City, Alderman Aktins is portrayed, gushing to Lord President Bradshaw, 'Oh, how this Scarlet-gown becomes your honor!'[18] Some old images were destroyed. In Portsmouth, Viscount Wimbledon had ordered the soldiers and magistrates to doff their hats towards a bust of Charles, presented by the king on his return from the continent. This was to emphasise that 'any disgrace offered His Majesties figure is as much to himself'. The statue was defaced in the 1640s and taken down in 1649.[19] Cheney Culpeper was optimistic of the possibility of change, but did not seek to minimise the size of the task:

> (yf the royall party be humbled), those whoe are nowe at sterne will be more likely to returne to theire firste purity, or yf not, may yet be more hopefully dealte w^{th}all, then those others whoe beside 500: yeeres prescription, doe soe bedawbe their K[ing] wth their sacred annointinges, & impertinente aplications of Scriptures, as in truthe it is difficulte to conceive, howe the poore Cowntryman, (after havinge beene soe many 100: yeeres conscience bownde towards these sacred & soverayne peeces of Nimrodisme), showlde dare presume to use soe muche of that reason wch God hathe bestowed on them, as but to peepe into the rotten inside of these gaye, maiesticall, sacred holyly annoynted outsides wth wch the K[ing]^s & pristes of these times doe cover their nakednesses.[20]

A republic, being an untried and unknown governmental form in England, required people used to the dazzle of display to cerebrally figure their role in society. While the republican government sought to steer the people gently through momentous change, the royalists created more emotive symbols which possessed immediacy. To add to the crown and the sceptre, the presses churned out images of the martyr king. Even with the final military defeat of the royalist cause at the battle of Worcester, the seed was planted for numerous royal oaks.[21] Monarchy had its 'rights and ceremonies, something that appeals to the eye'.[22]

The nearest that the Commonwealth came to the simple and direct impact of royalist visual imagery was the mace of parliament, the combined national flags of England and Ireland and the new Great Seal, which were mostly for official consumption and did not achieve the popular resonance of their royalist counterparts.[23] In the localities, churches and public buildings which in the past had displayed a wooden painted board bearing the royal coat of arms were ordered to paint them over with the arms of the Commonwealth. But the wheels of revolution ground fearfully slow. It was some thirty months after the proclamation of England as a republic before the corporation of Carlisle paid two shillings 'for washing forth the late Kings Armes in S[t] Cuthbert Church'.[24] It could be argued that the symbols of the republic were established deliberately slowly, to minimise the likelihood that the shock of the new would spark rebellion. The government was also trying to create symbols which connoted representativeness, and the results were designed to be depersonalised in order to emphasise that no power stood above parliament and people.

The attempt to portray the Rump as the representatives of the people was stymied by the legacy of Pride's Purge. The worthies of the Commonwealth consisted of around fifty MPs, which, as one critic who challenged the Rump's authority to try the king reminded them, represented only one eighth part of the full Commons House.[25] There had not been a national ballot since November 1640 and in the intervening years the House had been altered by expulsions, voluntary departures, deaths, recruiter elections and purge. There is no evidence that the Rump did not intend to call fresh elections as soon as it had enshrined the constitutional framework in which they would be set and it did set up a franchise committee. Since Charles Stuart's failure to call free and successive parliaments had been the major plank of the prosecution at his trial, it was imperative for the government to meet this challenge. But the Rump was caught between a rock and a hard place. If it cushioned its power by overseeing the composition of its membership, taking action such as registering the dissenters from the vote of 5 December, it reduced its representativeness. If it called full elections, it might lose the republican momentum. It could lose power altogether.

Leading the interest groups calling for fresh elections was the New Model Army, the instrument of divine vengeance and keeper of the godly conscience, which had won God's battles and established the Rump in power. The tenor of the messages which the House sent to the army, however, was that the soldiers should return to a subservient role, awaiting instructions from men whose history and manners were not as godly as their own.[26] The blood-guilt which had underpinned the regicide had a necessarily limited lifespan: once the object of the guilt was expunged, the role of the avengers was ended. The army had admitted that the Commons was sovereign and should not, except under exceptional circumstances, be coerced, so the parliamentarians had the upper hand so long as the army was unprepared to intervene in civil affairs.[27] Having accepted that those MPs who remained after the purge could legitimately sit in the House, by very virtue of the selection which the purge represented, they could not then gainsay that by withdrawing their support.

The demand that parliament dissolve itself as soon as was conveniently possible was one of the reforms for which the army relied on the Rump. It was also keen to end free quarter and to provide it with pay. However, when the grandees presented their revised Agreement on 20 January 1649,[28] it hit the Speaker's table with a dull thud. The army's messenger, Lieutenant-Colonel Hammond, was told the House would take the Agreement into consideration, 'with what possible Speed the Necessity of the present weighty and urgent Affairs will permit'.[29] By way of amelioration, it declared it expressed good affection towards the army and ordered the grandees' Agreement to be printed. However, the Commons' last statement was damning in its chill dismissal of the army's future usefulness: 'This House doth take notice of your faithful and great Services to the Kingdom, in standing in the Gap, for their Preservation.' Early in December 1648, the MPs now in power had been grateful for the army's support.[30] Now the army had restored the 'authority' of the Commons, the House had no further need of protection, and regarded the soldiers as a petitioning body the same as any other, allowed to offer advice and make requests, but with no automatic right to interfere with the sovereignty of elected representatives.

The army was relegated to a force to keep order, maintain discipline and enforce legislation, which provoked grumbling from radical millennarians, conservative grandees and unpaid cannon-fodder. It strained relations between the parliamentarians and the grandees and between the MPs and the rank and file. With an increasingly fractious soldiery, the leaders of the Commonwealth had great reason to thank certain sympathetic officers and agents who rallied support for the government. Their method was the prayer meeting, which had proved so successful during 1648:

> to that end we have desired Mr Knight (who alwaies attends ye Generall) to receive [and] communicate what the Lord shall putt into y^r hearts to unite to them of ye Lord perswade you to seeke him in the way of his ordering together as you shall thereby bee examples to, soe shall you be as by all those that truly feare ye Lord among you have yor Conversacon wth whom you shall doe well to hold a Christian communion.[31]

The organisers were familiar: William Goffe, who had proposed a prayer meeting during the Putney debates, the republican agents Sexby, Allen and Chillenden, and the radical officers Barkstead and Okey. There were enthusiastic replies from Major-General Lambert and Colonel Robert Lilburne, who were in York at the time of the Day of Humiliation on 30 May 1650, and a less happy response from Thomas Saunders, who was in Oxford.[32]

The prayer meetings served a vital purpose. They united the garrisons with the townspeople, were part of an attempt to win over support for the government, and could be used to test the reactions of both civilians and soldiers to government policies. There were two obvious differences from the prayer meetings of the late 1640s. The army no longer had the spectre of Charles Stuart on which to focus its fears and hostilities: meetings were thus more successful at times when there was an imminent, physical threat to the settlement. Secondly, the army was no longer camped around the capital, each regiment within easy reach of another, but scattered throughout the country. Prayer meetings were therefore arranged by letter. Those which survive reveal the difficulty involved in organising so many disparate regiments and garrisons to pray at the appointed time when letters did not reach their destination until the allotted day had passed.

When the decisions were taken to conquer Scotland and reconquer Ireland, the regiments were disbursed further afield.[33] A prayer meeting response pledged support for the campaign in Scotland[34] but the decision to send troops to Ireland provoked a crisis. Among government supporters were sections pressing for the relief of Ireland, amongst whom were the well-affected of Leicestershire, noted by the House for their 'readiness to the Service of the Publique the last Summer, wherein you did real and acceptable Service to the Commonwealth'.[35] Echoes of 1646, when parliament intended to send the army to Ireland in order to muffle calls for pay and improvements in their conditions, provided the Levellers with a revivalist cause which threatened to split apart those sympathetic to the Rump, although Leveller fears were, on the whole, groundless.[36] William Eyres was among the organisers of a mutiny at Burford, Oxfordshire, when troops on their way to Dublin refused to march any further. Marten's regiment had been withdrawn from Irish service but was causing unrest in the south of England,[37] and soldiers lobbied for Grey of Groby to take over command of the New Model.[38]

A combination of army unrest about military issues and the knowledge that significant sections of the Leveller movement had opposed the regicide gave an opportunity to junior officers, who had been uneasy about Charles' trial, to voice their opinions. They pointed out that the likely reason for governmental instability was its unprecedented action in seizing power. Major Francis White reiterated his belief that the fundamental, 'essentiall' power lay with the people. But the people had covenanted not to harm the person of the king, and his execution had not been in their interests.[39] Captain William Bray (along with William Eyres) had been sufficiently in tune with Leveller thinking in 1647 to lead the soldiers' resistance.[40] At Putney, he had challenged Cromwell's assertion that the soldiers were agents of anarchy.[41] In 1649, however, he claimed that his colonel, Henry Lilburne, had justified the king's assassination when only parliament had the right to bring him to justice: in March he was deprived of his command and imprisoned. His campaign for justice was joined by other soldiers who called themselves 'small beagles' hunting the foxes on the Council of War.[42] The post-regicidal attacks made the distinction between the king's person and his office. The parliament or army may have won the right to assume the powers of kingship but God had not given them sanction to touch the king's person. By doing so, the regicides had acted out private revenge, not public, godly vengeance. Sectarians, who had buoyed up politicians' spirits at the end of 1648 by telling them that royal authority had devolved onto their heads, now warned them that they had taken the only action which deprived them of that authority.[43] Lieutenant-Colonel John Jubbes opposed the conquest of Ireland. He had supported an *Agreement*, but had concluded that there was no specific bar to kingly government within its terms and hoped that the next chosen parliament would approve the young Charles Stuart as the new king.[44]

The need to contain Leveller unrest was liable to create rifts in a government less than six months established. Cromwell was reputed to have said that the Levellers had to be broken, 'or else they will break us [the army or the government?] and make all our work void'.[45] Those former allies of the Levellers, such as Marten and Wildman, who tried to stabilise the Commonwealth, were forced to choose between their former allies and the forces of conservativism.[46] Richard Overton was particularly scathing, accusing Wildman of having sold out to Mammon and Marten of having been bought off when his regiment was incorporated into the New Model, an eventuality which, in fact, does not seem to have materialised.[47] Agitators who expressed support for the Leveller petition of 11 September 1648 made fun of Marten's motto for the Commonwealth. The return to fundamental principles was to the soldiers, 'the first year of the Peoples pretended Freedom but intended slavery, 1649'.[48] Marten's friends, former colleagues and his own troops were part of the Leveller revival: his current colleagues were joining with the grandees to expunge its destabilising influence.

The leadership of the Leveller movement acted as a mouthpiece for those with smaller voice. Once more in prison, Lilburne, Overton and Thomas Prince were more explicit about the reasons why potential supporters had been so quickly alienated.[49] The Commonwealth had seen fit to establish a Council of State, separate from the Commons. A body which went under the name of a Council of State had been mooted in the *Heads of the Proposals*[50] but army grandees envisaged a limited expansion of the personal advice offered by the Privy Council, changing its name to 'state' council. It was designed to meet the objection that a barrier excluded the wisest men from the ear of the monarch. Whereas the Privy Council had been chosen by the king, the Council of State would be made up of 'trusty and able persons' who would check his power and, on occasion, reinforce or check the parliament. It would advise the king while parliament was not in session,[51] control the militia, and would have power over foreign diplomacy which had previously been in the hands of the Privy Council. Declarations of war or peace would be made by parliament.[52]

The proposal for a Council of State in the *Heads* was revised in the second version of the *Agreement of the People*: by late December 1648 the king was no longer to be 'restored to a condition of safety, honour and freedom'.[53] In the *Agreement*,[54] the detailed division of the country into parliamentary constituencies consistently assumed the existence of a Council of State, which was now a body which stood in place of the king, rather than parliament. The constituency structure was the first task of the *Agreement*. The Council of State had only vague definition – it was to be responsible for 'the managing of public affairs':[55] attempts to define its role could be seen as a threat to the Commons. It was held to be 'fundamental to our common right, liberty, and safety',[56] and though the powers envisaged may not have been any more sinister than day-to-day attention to detail, there was no check on the degree of power which the Council could appropriate to itself under the cloak of the 'safety of the people' – a potentially autocratic interpretation of *salus populi*.

After the execution, when the Rump of the Commons was deliberating about the constitutional structure, it was decided that there ought to be a body called a Council of State.[57] On 7 February 1649, Thomas Scot was given charge of a small committee of radical temperament – Scot himself, John Lisle, the Windsor MP, Cornelius Holland,[58] Edmund Ludlow and Luke Robinson, the recruiter MP for Scarborough and dedicated republican – 'to present to this House Instuctions to be given to the Council of Estates; and likewise the Names of such Persons as they conceive fit to be of the Council of Estates, not exceeding the number of Forty; with Power to send for Papers and Writings from Darbey House, or elsewhere'.[59] When the committee reported, on 13 February, the title had become the Council of State and its duties were to maintain the republicanism of the new government by the suppression of any of the Stuart family's interests, to direct the militia, to manage the continuing war against those in open revolt against the Commonwealth, to encourage trade and to manage the presses. It was specifically stated that the Council of State should hold authority from, and be accountable to, parliament. It would continue for one year. There were hints that it was designed to be a temporary expedient and not one which was renewed every year. The letters it addressed to commanders in Ireland indicated that its members found themselves constituted a council by the parliament for the purposes of managing the militia and Irish affairs, but could not say much more 'being but newly entered upon this charge'.[60] It was rather a more accountable version of the Derby House Committee, its primary function the government direction of military campaigns. Despite the careful outline of the Council's duties, councillors once chosen were not sure what to do next.

The following day the House voted on the membership of the Council. It was agreed that 'some of the Officers of the Army shall be of the Council of State', a statement that was made to sound like a generous concession.[61] Fairfax, Skippon and Cromwell were all approved, but Ireton and Harrison were voted down. In the end, only the three highest ranking officers in the New Model were accepted. Only Fairfax was not already an MP.[62] The initial names of members had been nominated by committee, but it is not clear whether its list included Ireton and Harrison, or whether they were proposed from the floor of the House. Since the original intention was that the Council have forty members, the latter would seem likely. The first forty on Scot's list went through with little obstruction. There were republican objections to Philip, Earl of Pembroke, but not to the lords who preceeded him.[63] Once the fortieth name had been agreed, the House began to divide. William, Earl of Salisbury, got past Marten's cavils, though only by twenty-three votes to twenty. Ireton and Harrison were then rejected without a division, and the Council settled at forty-one members. On 15 February, amid some confusion, the House confirmed forty-one members (those already nominated and agreed), but also added committee members Luke Robinson and Cornelius Holland. They set a quorum of only nine – having rejected eleven – and with only nine members, it was referred to as the 'Great Council'. Like the Rump itself, the quorum was, of necessity, embarrassingly low: the House may already have become aware that many of those named would not want to pursue their duties.[64] The Council introduced some notable adaptations which distinguished it from that envisaged in the *Heads*, and aimed to enhance its accountability. In order to demonstrate that power was not going to concentrate in the hands of just one individual, Livesay[65] and Marten blocked an attempt to give the Council a Lord President. It opted instead for a rotating Chair, changing daily. The Chair's role was more to preside than to direct. This might have had some effect had it not proved unworkable so quickly. John Bradshaw was elected to be a permanent Chair, which ensured radical continuity, at least for the first two councils. It did, however, also seem to be a reprise of his role on the High Court of Justice.

Even though a republican committee, with little brief for the New Model, had proposed the Council of State and the councillors had been instructed to bolster the republicanism of the settlement, outside Whitehall it was the army grandees who were held responsible for instigating the new executive. The safety of the government involved policing Leveller and millenarian discontent within the army, and those who were prosecuted by the Council believed it to be a device instituted by the officers for the purpose of stifling free speech. There was some truth in this, especially as the Council's role achieved greater definition. Lilburne, Overton and Prince called for another conference between themselves and sympathetic MPs – the two they trusted were Henry Marten and Alexander Rigby – similar to that which had tried to draw up a second *Agreement*.[66] Their aim was to encourage genuine reform and change, the current constitution being merely 'Notionall, Nominall, Circumstantiall, whilst the reall Burdens, Grievances and Bondages, be continued, even when the monarchy is changed into a

Republike'.[67] They declared that the 'Principles and Maxims of Government which are fundamentally opposite to the Prerogative, and the Kings interest, take their first rise and originall from us', leaving it unclear whether they referred to the people as a whole or the Leveller leadership in particular.[68] The Commons was charged with exceeding their authority by creating law. Although they were in 'good earnest' in instituting a Council of State, no one knew what one was, 'because the Law of England tells me nothing of such a thing'.[69]

The attack on the Commons was hard hitting, but went only as far as the members were seen to be in thrall to the army grandees. The army having purged the Commons, which had failed to refresh its membership with a full election, it was still chosen by the will of 'him, whose head as a Tyrant and Traytor, they have by their wills chopt off (*I mean the King*)'. The army had set up their own 'mock' parliament at Windsor.[70] On the other hand, the Leveller-influenced soldiery declared again that it was not a mercenary force, 'hired to serve the Arbitrarie ends of a Councel of State', and described the day of humiliation which preceded the drawing of lots to choose the soldiers bound for Ireland as 'an Ahab like Fast'.[71] Even then, this was couched in a specific complaint about Colonel John Hewson, considered the grandees' stooge, though his regiment called for Leveller reforms on its way to Ireland.[72] The well-affected of Buckinghamshire complained of lawyers, lords of the manor, impropriators, Committee-men, and army officers – all people who continued to uphold the kingly interest by the mere alteration of titles.[73] But parliamentmen generally escaped the censure. Even a royalist tract, which named the Council tyrants and libertines 'who hate the Scepter, yet would all be Kings' curiously omitted three of the most hardline republican MPs, Cornelius Holland, Henry Marten and Luke Robinson.[74]

The relationship between the Rump parliament and the rump of the Lords also had the effect of reducing the degree to which government was deemed directly representative of and accountable to the people. Two days after the abolition of monarchy, a shorter Act was passed, drawn up by the same committee – except for the omission of Thomas Chaloner – which abolished the upper House. It was a confirmation of a policy which had been foreshadowed by a vote on 18 January, in which the Marten/Grey faction[75] had succeeded, by twenty-five votes to eighteen, in blocking a move which required the Lords' concurrence to the declaration of sovereignty of 4 January. This was followed on 6 February by a statement of intent to abolish the House. The language used about the Lords reflected that which was used about kingship, recycling the clichéd phrase of republican government: as kings were 'unnecessary, burdensome and dangerous', so the Lords, according to the Act, were 'useless and dangerous'.

But they were not unnecessary. There was a reluctance to condemn individual lords, markedly different from the condemnation of king-ship. Individual aristocrats had displayed behaviour which lifted them above that associated with the House as an institution, whereas the individual of the monarch was the institution. Having abolished the House of Lords and declared it a barrier to reform, the Act went as far as it could to enable individual peers, not specifically named as traitors, who were prepared to owe allegiance to the Commonwealth, to play an active part in government: 'Neither such Lords as have demeaned themselves with honour, courage, and fidelity to the Commonwealth, nor their posterities who shall continue so, shall be excluded from the public councils of the nation.'[76] The parliament proved their commit-ment to this principle by naming several lords to the Council of State. They were also allowed to take a seat in the Commons, provided they were chosen in a free election and did not exercise old, customary privileges in order to influence the House.[77]

The principle of allowing lords and commoners to sit in one, elected House had been proposed in the peace terms of 1647, which mooted 'if possible the Lords and Commons sitt together, at least, be declared Joinctly the Supream Judiciature'.[78] The possibility that lords could be elected to the Commons was made during the Putney debates, in an exchange between Ireton and Rainsborough. It was favoured more by the republican, Rainsborough, than the relatively cautious Ireton:

Rainsborough: Itt is offer'd to make them (lords) capable of being chosen.
Ireton: Every Baron by the other exception may bee chosen.
Rainsborough: Is itt nott soe in Scotland?
Ireton: In Scotland every Lord hath his place as Burgesse.
Rainsborough: Why should nott the Lords have the same privilege?
Ireton: I should thinke that [w]as the directest interest to the Kingdome in the world, for that for soe many persons to bee a permanent interest in the House, every two yeares.[79]

Lords Pembroke, Denbigh, Mulgrave and Grey of Warke subsequently lobbied the Army Council to be allowed to be part of the political process, claiming to have registered an interest in the Commonwealth by their actions rather than through their possessions.[80] The Com-monwealth eventually justified the inclusion of individual lords on this basis, provided they did not exercise it adversely by operating a negative voice, by which they could interpose a barrier between the direct representation of the people by the Commons. Lords who had expressed fidelity towards the Commonwealth should be allowed the opportunity of being chosen by the people.[81] When the Commonwealth declared that it served the needs of the poor, the idea that peers could do so was met with merriment: satirists compared the life of Thomas Prince the Leveller cheesemonger with the former earl of Pembroke, Philip Herbert, newly recruited to the Commons for Berkshire, to replace Sir Francis Pile.[82]

The third measure which the Rump introduced to unify sections of its support was equally ill-judged. It devised an oath of loyalty which was to have major ramifications for the way in which both support for and hostility towards the Commonwealth was measured, but which was first to be confined to those at the pinacle of the governmental pyramid, the members of the Council of State. The first meeting of Council was on 17 February. There were fourteen members present; the meeting was well over quorum. The oath, called the Engagement, was offered to all the members, and all except Sir William Masham were willing to subscribe. The other thirteen were from the radical faction among the Rump. Signatories were required to give retrospective approval of the purge of parliament, the trial of Charles Stuart and the verdict of the Court. It was therefore a more hardline statement of regicidal principles than the registration of dissent from the vote of 5 December, which required the signatory only to deny the adequacy of the terms for a treaty. The regicidal aspects – those which harked back to the means by which the Commonwealth had come into being – were sufficient to cause dissent among even the most radical members. Algernon Sidney pointed out the possible loopholes in the oath through which 'knaves' might slip. Grey of Groby chose to interpret this to mean that those who had already taken the oath were knaves. Marten tried to mediate.[83]

Six more councillors signed the Engagement. Then, on 23 February, it was decided to abandon the requirement to take it. Although the Engagement for the Council of State was vacated, it served an important role in the nature of the republican settlement. Its purposes were to incorporate diverse interest groups more closely into the governmental structure. The Rump contained those who had survived Pride's Purge and those who had masterminded it. By naming soldiers such as Fairfax to the Council of State and by asking him to take the same oath of allegiance as those members who had a more parliamentary background, the soldiery were given a say in, and an influence on, the machinery of government.[84] The same was true of former members of the Lords, who were included for the *gravitas* which their status could bestow, because they had expert knowledge and had been faithful servants of the parliamentary cause. The Engagement also had the effect of reaffirming the commitment to *salus populi*, by calling on the councillors to defend both parliament and the 'public liberty and freedom of this nation'.[85] It sought to erect a further layer of representativeness above the Commons and the Council. Like the Great Seal and the arms, the oath – rather than the persons of the Councillors – represented an abstract theory of Commonwealth, though embodied (chiefly) by parliamentarians.

There were several warnings from sections of otherwise sympathetic supporters. The Leveller, William Cockayne, warned that previous attempts to unite the parliamentary forces by swearing an oath had led to their divisions – 'making parties by subscribers and non-subscribers'. Further, it had caused a party – in this case, the Presbyterians – to assume power above the representative.[86] In March, the otherwise loyal party in Leicestershire were worried that 'the gathering *Subscriptions*, in the way you suggest, and which (as we understand) is already practised, may be of *dangerous* consequence, for *dividing* the Kingdome; especially the *godly* and *well affected* therein, who (were) already Generally *ingaged*, by the National *Covenant*, to maintaine the *power and priviledges of Parliament,* in the maintenance of true *Religion*'.[87] John Canne was aware of the potentially divisive nature of an oath, but he singled out the Solemn League and Covenant as an example of a bad oath which could be broken because, in calling for the defence of the king's person, it had opposed the king's 'office and duty'. Rather, he chose to cite the Protestant reformer, David Paraeus, and the Apostle Paul, to counsel that an oath confirmed 'lawfull peace and society between party and party, countrey and countrey, Kingdom and Kingdom'. The oath which Paul had promoted among the Hebrews was a reaffirmation of the covenant of Abraham because, within it, God swore by himself, because he could swear to no greater power. A true oath would end strife because it confirmed the equality of all individuals beneath an authority which they could not seek to overturn.[88]

The Council of State, the Engagement and the inclusion of lords represented a juggling act in which the need for executive control was balanced against the foundation of government, with its starting point that all people, whether part of the government or the governed, should be bound by the same restrictions. This had been the tenor of the declaration of 4 January, in which the people were declared the origin of all just power.[89] The structure which followed the declaration was justified because those inside government could not set themselves up as greater that the people or God, so 'any alteration of Government by them shall . . . tend to the good of the Commonalty, . . . since these Lawes made, must be equally binding to themselves'.[90] The positive, reverse image of the negative anti-monarchical credo – 'unnecessary, burdensome and dangerous' – was that '*no power is intended to be above this Representative*'.[91] The people elected the House. It was not for those elected to then vote in other people or things to symbolise the unity of the nation.

Some pro-government commentators described these adaptations to the statement of 4 January in the terms of traditional Aristotelian debate. Aristotelian theory referred to the three states of monarchy, aristocracy and democracy, which should, in the ideal polity, be equally balanced. When an element claimed powers beyond those of the other two, the result was corruption. Monarchy became tyranny, aristocracy was prone to oligarchy and democracy could corrupt into anarchy or mob rule. Having rather publicly disposed of the person who constituted the monarchical element in the polity of the 1640s, members of the political elite were liable to ask whether power had mutated into an aristocracy or a democracy, or whether the new governors had assumed the mantle of the monarchical element in the triangle. The resort to classical political sources also encouraged some to Latinise government, as the government did itself when dealing with foreign powers, using Latin as a univeral language: '*Parliamentum Reipublicae Angliae*'.[92] Commentators on the government occasionally resorted to the parallel between a council of state and the senate of ancient Rome, with its formula, *senatus populusque Rōmānus* (SPQR).[93] Thus the author of *A True Narration* envisaged the Rump and the Council as a senate because their sovereignty survived that of kings: '[l]et all true Englishmen rejoice and cry "*Vivat Lex, Exercitus, vera eligio, Senatus populusque Angliae*"'.[94]

According to 'N.T.', the lesson to be drawn from Aristotle was that the best form of government was aristocracy with elements of democracy. Therefore, there should be a recognition of the democratical notion that power rested fundamentally in the people, while an aristocratic council of state would exercise power when parliament was not sitting.[95] Three Cambridge students, John Fidoe, Thomas Jeanes and William Shaw, added a fourth type, 'theocracy', to describe the unique form of government given by God to the Jews.[96] In monarchical government sole authority was in the hands of a king, though they disputed whether it had its roots in Adam, Cain or Nimrod. Democratic government was that in which the people had a hand in all that was done. In aristocratic government – the form which existed in Holland – men of 'the greatest parts and trust are singled out for the good of others'.[97] They concluded that the English Commonwealth was also an aristocracy, citing the text most frequently used in its justification: 'that in the multitude of counsellors, there is wisdom.'[98] However, there was a confusion in their minds over the degree to which the new government contained a democratic element. The students accepted *salus populi*, and went on to imply that the people could exercise power over any political decision if they chose to. The Commonwealth must therefore have had a democratic structure or the potentiality for democracy, but the people chose not to exercise their right of constant involvement, instead devolving power to their trusted representatives.

The government, its supporters and indeed its opponents were taking part in two different but complementary debates. On the one hand, there was a war of words between those who wanted radical change and those who prefered as little disruption as possible – Underdown's 'revolutionaries' and 'pragmatists'.[99] Going on at the same time was a debate about the degree to which governments were established on fundamental and immutable principles or were subject to worldly changes of policy or godly design. The government's official statement of March 1649 tried to persuade the political nation that the fundamental laws remained the same, and that their purpose was to secure liberty, property and peace. This end would be achieved by laws implemented by 'the present Government of a Republique, upon some easie alterations of form onely, leaving entire the substance; the name of King being used in them in Form only'. A king had been a superficial accretion, grafted onto and eventually undermining the foundation of freedom.[100] Other commentators questioned what constitued the immutable element. Was it the king's person which never died[101] or was the body of the king killed while his soul lived on?[102] Did kingly sovereignty live on in the persons of the Commonwealth worthies, the army or the godly, or was it political function itself which survived until God saw fit to end all fleshly show?

Those who supported revolutionary change were the most anxious to enshrine immutable principles. The Levellers were concerned to establish the 'foundations of freedom' within an agreement of the people.[103] William Cockayne wanted an agreement which ensured that no power was above the parliament. The parliament itself would be clearly defined, together with provision for biennial meetings. Cockayne and Lilburne castigated their opponent, the MP William Ashurst, who had chosen to voluntarily withdraw at Pride's Purge for believing that government should be made up of men and parliaments which were mutable, since he had 'so fresh a president . . . as no Addresses, Addresses, and no Addresses, Vote out, in, and out again'.[104] It was possible to arrive at the same point by starting from godly principles. The law under the new regime would be godly because it would govern

according to God's law. '[T]he same supream king, Christ Jesus, who as
a mighty monarch ruleth over all Nations', had set up 'one municipall
law, which is that called Morrall; the first and second Tables thereof' and
all magistrates who ruled according to the Decalogue were godly and
therefore just.[105]

For some, it was a matter of pride that the fundamental elements of
English government had not changed with the death of the king. The
world was separable from and operated in a lower sphere from the realm
of the spirit and the actions of the Lord. Politics was not so much
something which was uninteresting to religious figures as something
with which it was unnecessary for them to dirty their hands.[106] Army
chaplain, John Warr, thought 'Anti-monarchicalnes . . . no crime at all,
but a difference in judgement about the Externall Forme of Civill
government'.[107] Warr used the argument about the elemental sinfulness
of mankind to illustrate that changing the external form of government
was not enough to protect rights and property, for 'it is possible for a
Societie to exercise Tyrannie as well as a single Person . . . For Man
being naturally of an aspiring temper.'[108] London congregations warned
their civil governors not to change the government unless they knew
what to put in its place.[109] Another godly commentator agreed that God
had freed England from its burdens, while on the political plane, the
governors continued to rule by the law.[110] Warr was to establish close
links with the Ranters. Joseph Salmon, who was even closer, counselled
men to 'tarry here till God moves higher amongst you'.[111]

For Robert Bacon, kingly power – the term used to describe
sovereignty – had come to rest, through a process of devolution,
with the army. He would not condemn Charles – 'whose person
yet I loved and prayed for' – but called instead for a flowering of Gospel
values, in which the rulers would not be so 'hasty, hot and violent in
condemning the Powers [which] went before you, before your right-
eousnesse, integrity, honesty, ability, impartiality, and bowels of mercy,
pity, and compassion towards the poor and fatherless be justified on all
hands to be of a nature exceeding the pretence of others'.[112] Sectaries in
Norfolk and members of the Northern Association of the army called
on the army and parliament to rule as Christ's officers, while the saints
gathered in their churches to hand power to Christ. This would return
the government to a monarchical form 'as when Christ the Head and
King appears visibly'.[113] The government must 'take to bring in our
spirits unto your selves', a process best achieved by the surprisingly
secular means of reducing taxation and ending free quarter.[114] Although
the Norfolk petition was a piece of proto-Fifth Monarchist literature,
they were not ready to pull down worldly authority. Politicians would

be tolerated and even obeyed until God saw fit to draw their rule to a close. Any action would be subject to the same criticisms which had been levelled at monarchy, because rulers must assume sovereignty if they are to grasp power and authority. If sovereignty was believed to be the sole prerogative of God, the new governors were indeed usurpers. N.T. summed up this fearful warning:

> Unto you, *Oh you righteous Judges . . . of the high Court of Justice*: let me say you have done a good worke, in Avenging the blood of Innocent ones, upon *Charles Stuart . . .* Take heed, Oh take heed; that though you have done Justice, that you do not suffer from God as Murtherers; In my heart I honour you, hence it is that I shall boldly tell you so much, *God certainly will avenge King Charles his blood upon you head, if you did shed it out of a vaine glorious desire to be counted bold, Gallant, or from any particular spleen, or Malice, or ayming at any private or any sinister end.*[115]

The message behind the commentaries of the godly was not so much one of immutability as inertia. This comes as a surprise in view of the apocalyptic language used at the end of 1648. Perhaps the sermons preached to the worthies of the Rump before the execution of the king should have been given greater consideration. In his address, George Cockayne had made specific comments which seemed to point to Charles' trial: 'If God do not lead you to do Justice upon those that have been the great Actors in shedding innocent Blood, never think to gain their love by sparing of them.'[116] The regicides might have asked whether his text from Psalms also applied to themselves: 'I have said, ye are Gods; and all of you are children of the most High: But ye shall dye like men, and fall like one of the Princes. Arise, O God, judg the Earth; for thou shalt inherit all Nations.'[117] The army grandees discussing the future constitution had realised the difficulty and risk associated with governments which ceased to confine their sphere to civil affairs: it chose to 'waive' matters of religious controversy.[118] It did at least mean that for the Rump an even more crucial decision had been delayed: whether the fall of the king had indeed removed the last veil between man and God.

NOTES

1. Cornet Henry Denne, *The Levellers Designe Discovered*, [24 May] 1649, E556(11), p. 8; *Clarke Papers*, I, lix.
2. Samuel Butler, *Characters*, ed. Charles W. Daves (Cleveland, Ohio, 1970), 'A Republican', pp. 55–7.

3. Theophilus P., *Salus Populi dangerously ill*, [13 Dec.] 1648, E476(18), p. 4; J. C. Davis, *Utopia and the Ideal Society* (Cambridge, 1993).

4. J. Philolaus was equally sceptical of the possibility of a utopia: *A Serious Aviso to the Good People of this Nation concerning that sort of men, called Levellers*, 11 May 1649, E555(28), p. 5; *An Enquiry after further Satisfaction*, [29 May] 1649, E556(24), p. 7.

5. This was in the oath of loyalty for members of the Council of State in February 1649 – see below, p. 176. For the changing etymology of the word 'republic', see William R. Everdell, 'From *State* to *Free-State*: the meaning of the word Republic from Jean Bodin to John Adams', *Valley Forge Journal*, 5.3 (1991) 209–49.

6. *King Charls Tryal: A Perfect Narrative of the Whole High Court of Justice*, 27 Jan. 1649, E545(4+5), p. 6.

7. *A Declaration of the Parliament of England, expressing the Grounds of their late Proceedings, and the setling the present Government in the way of a Free State*, 22 March, 1649, E548(12).

8. *CSPD*, 1649–50, pp. 36, 51, 53.

9. Leeds, ML MSS 'Political and miscellaneous', II, p. 24, f.3^v.

10. John Warr, *The Priviledges of the People*, [5 Feb.] 1649, E341(12), p. 1; Ludlow, *Memoirs*, I, p. 211; Ball, *Power of Kings*, p. 4.

11. PRO SP 25/I/62, p. 261, emphasis added. An international republican revolution was advocated by Franciscus Leinsula, *The Kingdomes Divisions Anatomjzed* [*sic*], 1 Mar. 1649, E345(25), p. 2, as part of a worldwide reappearance of Christ.

12. *CJ*, VI, p. 110, as opposed to kingly, private interest.

13. *CJ*, VI, p. 114.

14. Alethophilus Basiluphilus Britannophilus, *Cromwell's recall*, 1 Aug. 1649, E566(22):, 'the first year of our Reigne, 1649'.

15. John March, *Amicus Republicae: The Commonwealths Friend*, 19 May 1651, E1360(1), Epistle to the reader.

16. Dorset Record Office, Court Book and Sessions Book, 1647–70, Lyme Regis, B7/B1/9, n.p.

17. *An Act for setting apart a day of solemn fasting and humiliation, and repealing the monthly fast*, 669.f.14(21); H. R. Trevor Roper, *Religion, the Reformation and Social Change* (Cambridge, 1968).

18. *Hosanna: or a Song of Thanksgiving, sung by the Children of Zion, and set forth in three notable Speeches at Grocers Hall, on the late solemn Day of Thanksgiving*, 7 Jun. 1649, E559(11), p. 2.

19. William G. Gates, *Illustrated History of Portsmouth* (Portsmouth, 1900), pp. 218–20. Wimbledon and Charles were much taken by the continental baroque aesthetic, in which images of royal power were given prominence. Wimbledon chastised the townsfolk for not having their shop signs inset, as was more common abroad, because they obscured the view of the statue. See also Lady Eleanor Douglas/Davies, *Strange and Wonderfull Prophesies by Lady Eleanor Audeley*, [27 Aug.] 1649, E571(28), p. 5.

20. Sheffield, Hartlib MSS 13/262A-B, Culpeper to Hartlib, 15 Aug. 1649; Oxford, Worcester College, Clarke MSS CCLXVII/I f.27^r, 'The Common disease of ye Nation', by J[ohn] R[ushworth], (May 1650).

21. George Wither, *Carmen Eucharisticon*, [29 Aug.] 1649, E572(6): 'We have seen those things despized,/ Which our *Fathers* highly prized,/ And the *whole earth* Idolized'; Nancy Klein Maguire, 'The Theatrical mask/masque of politics: the case of Charles I', *JBS*, 32 (1993) 24–43, pp. 5, 9, 21–2; [Fabian Phillips], *King Charles the First, no Man of Blood*, [25 June] 1649, E531(3) n.p.; D. H[enry] K[ing], *A Deepe Groane Fetch'd at the Funerall of that incomparable and Glorious Monarch*, [16 May] 1649, E555(20), n.p. 1649.

22. William Godwin's *History of the Commonwealth of England*, pp. 501–2, cited in John Morrow, 'Republicanism and public virtue: William Godwin's *History of the Commonwealth of England*', *HJ*, 34.3 (1991) 645–64, p. 656.

23. The work of John Peacock, in studying the fine art of the republic, reveals that the worthies of the Commonwealth incorporated satires of royalism within their portraits, but nevertheless did so by initially appropriating royalist images and poses.

24. Cumbria Record Office, Carlisle, Court Leet books, Ca4/3, 29 Nov. 1651. Portsouth corporation ordered the chamberlain to replace the king's arms with those of the Commonwealth on 7 Oct. 1650; court leet presentments, Richard J. Murrell and Robert East (eds), *Extracts from Records in the Possession of the Municipal Corporation of the Borough of Portsmouth* (Portsmouth, 1884), p. 126.

25. *Six Serious Quaeries concerning the Kings Triall by the New High Court of Justice*, 9 Feb. 1649, 669.f.13(87), broadsheet.

26. *The None-such Charles his Character*, [6 Jan.] 1651, E1345(2), p. 176.

27. Henry Marten made the point retrospectively in 1653: Leeds, ML MSS 'Political and miscellaneous', II, p. 24, f.2.

28. *GCD*, pp. 359–71.

29. *CJ*, VI, p. 122.

30. Eutactus Philodemius, *The Original and End of Civil Power, with some instances, where Generals and Commanders of Armies have been Assistant to the People, to pull down Wicked Rulers, and set up new Government and Governors*, 20 Apr. 1649, [not in Thomason: consulted in the library of Trinity College, Dublin, Gall.3.d.35(1)]. This was written from Gray's Inn.

31. Oxford, Worcester College. Clarke MSS XVIII f.7: a letter from Richard Lawrence, William Goffe and John Pearson to Adjutant Evelyn and Captain Wagstaff at Wallingford, 3 Jul. 1649 and f.13, a letter from Evelyn, Thomas Disury (?) and Richard Wagstaff to Isaac Knight, chaplain of Fairfax's regiment, Wallingford Castle, 8 Jan. 1649(50); XVIII ff.16–17, from the soldiers at headquarters, Somerset House, 4 Feb. 1649(50); for Knight see Anne Laurence, *Parliamentary Army Chaplains, 1646–1651* (Woodbridge, Suffolk, 1990), pp. 141–2.

32. Oxford, Worcester College, Clarke MSS XVIII ff.40–40^v and 48–48^v.

33. Ludlow, *Memoirs*, I, p. 231.

34. Oxford, Worcester College, Clarke MSS XVIII ff.45–46^v, 31 May 1649.

35. *To the Supreme Authority, the Commons of England Assembled in Parliament: The humble Petition of divers well-affected of the County of Leicester, in behalf of themselves and the Nation*, 19 Mar. 1649, 669.f.14(6), broadsheet; see Chapter 3 for the support for republicanism in Leicestershire.

36. Ian Gentles, *The New Model Army in England, Ireland and Scotland, 1645–1653* (Oxford, 1992), pp. 352–3; John Evelyn, *Diary and Correspondence*, ed. William Bray(London, n.d.), p. 556.

37. *Clarke Papers*, II, pp. 212–13. One of the most provocative moves one could imagine the Commonwealth making is an apparent decision to post Marten's regiment to Scotland, though the status of Marten's regiment is unclear: Durham Record Office, D/Sa/E 585 f.5.

38. Norah Carlin, 'The Levellers and the conquest of Ireland in 1649', *HJ*, 30.2 (1987) 269–88; Worden, *Rump Parliament* p. 187; *Mercurius Pragmaticus*, 27 Feb. 5 Mar. 1649, p. 8; 13–20 Mar. 1649, p. 4; Clarke Papers, II, pp. 212–13; *Perfect Occurences*, 13–20 Jul. 1649, p. 1184; *Perfect Diurnal* 16–23 Jul. 1649, p. 9; *Kingdom's faithful Scout* 20–7 Jul. 1649, p. 216; *The Moderate*, 13–20 Mar. 1649, p. 372; *The Resolutions of the Private Souldiery of Col. Scroops Regiment of Horse . . . concerning their present Expedition for the Service of Ireland*, Salisbury, 1 May 1649, 669.f.14(28). The Diggers of St George's Hill in Surrey combined their call to be the real restorers of the liberties lost in 1066 with the injustice of the lots drawn to chose regiments to go to Ireland; [William] Everard, *The Declaration and Standard of the Levellers of England*, 23 Apr. 1649, E551(11); *Clarke Papers*, II, pp. 209–12; Worden, *Rump Parliament*, p. 187.

39. Francis White, *The Copies of severall Letters contrary to the opinion of the present powers, Presented to the Lord Gen. Fairfax and Lieut.Gen. Cromwell*, 2 Mar. 1649, E348(6), pp. 3–4.

40. Gentles, *New Model Army*, pp. 219–26.

41. *Clarke Papers*, I, pp. 411, 419.

42. Oxford, Worcester College, Clarke MSS CXIV f.187, 20 Mar. 1649; CCLXVII/I ff.24–25^v, Windsor Castle, April 1649; William Bray, *An Appeal in the Humble Chain of Justice*, [19 Mar.] 1649, E546(30); *The Moderate*, 13–20 Mar. 1649, E548(2); *CJ*, VI, p. 167; Gentles, *New Model Army*, p. 320.

43. R[obert] Bacon, *The Labyrinth the Kingdom's In*, 7 Feb. 1649, E541(26), p. 46; Salmon, *A Rout*, p. 8; White, *The Copies of Severall Letters*, pp. 3–4; Elizabeth Poole, *An Alarum of War*, 17 May 1649, E555(23+24); *The Souldiers Demand*, (Bristol) 18 May 1649, E555(29), p. 9; William Bray, *Heaven and Earth, Spirit and Blood, demanding reall Commonwealth Justice*, 29 Jun. 1649, E662(9), p. 2.

44. John Jubbes, *An Apology unto the Honorable and other the Honored and worthy Officers of his Excellencies the Lord Generals Army*, 4 May 1649, E552(28), pp. 11, 13; *The Declaration of the Levellers concerning prince Charles*, 17 May 1649, E555(26).

45. Lilburne et al., *The Picture of the Councel of State*, 11 Apr. 1649, E550(14), p. 15. Ludlow was believed to have championed the Levellers. Tuck believes that 'us' refers specifically and solely to the Council of State, though I am not convinced of this point: Richard Tuck, *Philosophy and Government, 1572–1651* (Cambridge, 1993), p. 251; Gentles, *New Model Army*, pp. 320–1.

46. Maurice Ashley, *John Wildman: Plotter and Postmaster* (London, 1947), pp. 69–70.

47. *CJ*, VI, p. 129; [Richard Overton], *Overton's Defyance of the Act of Pardon: or, The Copy of a Letter to the Citizens usually meeting at the Whale-Bone in Lothbury*, 2 Jul. 1649, E562(26), p. 7.

48. Robert Ward, Thomas Watson, Simon Graunt, George Jellies, William Sawyer, *The Hunting of the Foxes from New-Market and Triplow-Heaths to Whitehall, by five small Beagles*, 21 Mar. 1649, E348(7); John Naylier, Richard Ellergood, John Marshall, *The Foxes Craft Discovered*, 2 Apr. 1649, E549(7); Bray, *Heaven and Earth*, p. 2.

49. Evelyn, *Diary and Correspondence*, p. 554.

50. *GCD*, pp. 316–26; Austin Woolrych, *Soldiers and Statesmen: The General Council of the Army and its Debates, 1647–1648* (Oxford, 1987), pp. 163, 246.

51. *GCD*, p. 317.

52. *GCD*, p. 320.

53. *GCD*, p. 321.

54. The 'officers' *Agreement of the People*, *GCD*, pp. 359–71.

55. *GCD*, p. 368.

56. *GCD*, p. 371.

57. *CJ*, VI, p. 133.

58. Cornelius Holland had risen under the auspices of Sir Henry Vane the elder, but in 1649 was part of the Berkshire axis which seems to have hung on the coat-tails of Henry Marten. Daniel Blagrave was another. Underdown, *Pride's Purge*, pp. 51–2, 205, describes them both as careerists, though Holland is also considered to have been a 'dedicated revolutionary'. Ludlow believed him a revolutionary (Ludlow, *Memoirs*, I, pp. 183, 200) and Lilburne to be a friend of the Levellers: *Legal Fundamental Liberties*, p. 32.

59. *CJ*, VI, p. 133; Ludlow, *Memoirs* i p. 223. Ludlow claims that the committee originally decided to nominate thirty-five people, 'best qualified with integrity and abilities sutable to so important a station. Four of them were lords, and the rest commoners.'

60. *CSP Ireland* 1647–60 pp. 786–7, Council of State to Monck and Jones, 27 Feb. 1649.

61. *CJ*, VI, p. 140.
62. Underdown and Tuck debate whether or not the membership of the Council constituted a division between a legislature and executive. I tend to support Tuck's contention that it did not: Underdown, *Pride's Purge*, p. 199; Tuck, *Philosophy and Government*, pp. 249–50.
63. The tellers against the motion on this vote were Livesay and Marten: *CJ*, VI, p. 143.
64. Sarah Barber, 'The Engagement for the Council of State and the establishment of the Commonwealth government', *HR*, 63.150 (1990) 44–57.
65. Worden, *Rump Parliament*, pp. 51–2; Underdown, *Pride's Purge* p. 31; both give Livesay a bad press, creating the impression of a plegmatic man who flailed his prejudices around like a scourge throughout the Commonwealth period. The tenor of this chapter seeks to challenge the idea that opposition to a single person, titles or subscription to a republican oath of loyalty constitutes a negative or vacuous image of republican government.
66. Lilburne, et al., *Picture of the Councel of State*, p. 22. There were also kind words for Ludlow.
67. John Lilburne, William Walwyn, Thomas Prince, Richard Overton, *A Manifestation from Lieutenant Col. John Lilburn*, 14 Apr. 1649, E550(25), p. 3.
68. Lilburne et al., *A Manifestation*, pp. 5, 7.
69. Lilburne et al., *Picture of the Councel of State*, pp. 5, 6.
70. Lilburne et al., *Picture of the Councel of State*, p. 16. The named leaders of the army faction were Fairfax, Cromwell, Ireton, Harrison, Fleetwood, Rich, Ingoldsby, Haselrig, Constable, Fenwick, Walton and Allen.
71. 'A libbell, scatred abrout the Streets the 25 Aprill, 1649', in manuscript in Thomason's hand, 25 Apr. 1649, E551(21); *An Act for setting apart a day of solemn fasting and humiliation, and repealing the montethly fast*, 669.f.14(21) – 3 May was set for the London area and 17 May elsewhere.
72. George Cook, Richard Lebund, R[ichard] Lawrence, Daniel Axtell, Isaac Ewer, J[ohn] Hewson, Peter Stubbes, Thomas Goddard, Peter Wallis, Robert Phaier, Thomas Beecher, William Thogmorton, John Hurdman, *The Humble Petition of the Officers now Engaged for Ireland*, 10 Jul. 1649, E563(13); Gentles, *New Model Army*, p. 319.
73. *A Declaration of the Wel-affected in the County of Buckinghamshire*, 10 May 1649, E555(1), p. 5.
74. *Tyrants Triumphant: or, the High Court of State*, n.d., 669.f.14(67), broadsheet. Robinson and Holland may have been omitted because they were late nominees to the Council, but the omission of Henry Marten, usually the royalists' first target, seems remarkable.
75. Underdown, *Pride's Purge*, p. 221.
76. *GCD*, p. 387.

77. There were three former hereditary peers chosen to sit in the Rump, none very active: William Cecil, earl of Salisbury; Philip Herbert, Earl of Pembroke; and Edward, Lord Howard of Escrick. Of the three, Philip Herbert was the butt of merciless satire, mostly announcing his premature 'death' as a lord.

78. Oxford, Worcester College, Clarke MSS CLI f.69^v.

79. Woodhouse, *Puritanism and Liberty*, p. 116; *Clarke Papers*, I, p. 395.

80. Newsletter from the army, in Mabbott's hand(?); Oxford, Worcester College, Clarke MSS CCLXVII/I f.20^r. n.d. Dec.(?) 1648.

81. *A Declaration of the Parliament of England, expressing the Grounds of their late Proceedings, and the setling the present Government in the way of a Free State*, 22 Mar. 1649, E548(12), p. 22.

82. Pile, the intended recipient of Henry Marten's 'Opinions' in 1648, had died. *The Speech of Philip Herbert, late earl of Pembroke*, 16 Apr. 1649, E551(6), p. 7; *The Manner of the Election of Philip Herbert*, 24 Apr. 1649, E551(16). There were any number of references to Marten's reputation as a libertine and whoremonger, but the particular county link may explain the willingness to tie the two together in *Mercurius Elencticus, The First Part of the Last Wil & Testament of Philip earl of Pembroke*, 11 May 1649, E555(5), n.p: 'they say the Devil's a good Scholar, he hope Harry Martin to answer the Scots paper, and make the Declaration of Non-Addresses to His Majestie'. Pembroke was said to have left his horse, 'Badge' to Marten, since the latter had ridden over 100 mares in his time. Worden, *Rump Parliament*, pp. 27–8 and *passim*.

83. Jonathan Scott, *Algernon Sidney and the English Republic, 1623–1677* (Cambridge, 1988), pp. 93–4.

84. The parliament took an individual vote about whether the soldiery be included in the Council of State on 14 Feb. and decided in the affirmative: *CJ*, VI, p. 140 For a fuller account of the Engagement for the Council of State, see Barber, 'The Engagement'.

85. *GCD*, p. 384.

86. Cockayne, *Foundations of Freedome*, p. 7.

87. Leics. Record Office, Common Hall papers DLXXVII/xiii/149, letter to Lord President Bradshaw, Nov. 1651; *The humble Representation of the Committee, Gentry, Ministry, and other well afected Persons, in the County of Leicester*, 19 Mar. 1649, E345(22), p. 11.

88. John Canne, *The Snare is Broken*, pp. 15–17; Heb. 8: 7–10.

89. John Lilburne, *Legall Fundamentall Liberties*, 8 Jun. 1649, cited in Don M. Wolfe, *Leveller Manifestos of the Puritan Revolution* (London, 1967), p. 415.

90. *A Shrill Cry*, p. 8.

91. *A Shrill Cry*, p. 7. William Cockayne, *The Foundations of Freedome, Vindicated*, E341(25), p. 7.

92. PRO SP 25/I/87, p. 115.

93. *The Resolver Continued, or satisfaction to some Scruples about the putting of the late King to death*, 12 Mar. 1649, E346(17), p. 17.

94. *A True Narration of the Title, Government and Cause of the Death of the late Charles Stuart, King of England*, 5 Feb. 1649, E341(14), p. 8.

95. N.T., *The Resolver continued, or satisfaction to some Scruples about the putting of the late King to Death, In a letter from a Minister of the Gospel to a Friend in London*, written 20 Feb. 1649, published 12 Mar., E346(17), p. 16.

96. J[ohn] Fidoe, T[homas] Jeanes, W[illiam] Shaw, *The Parliaments Justified*, 27 Feb. 1649, E545(14).

97. Fidoe et al., *The Parliaments Justified*, p. 8. Prov.11: 14, 24: 6: they argued that although it was different in other nations, power was instituted by God for the good of the people. This was a commonwealth (*res publica*). Once that ceased, it became a tyranny (*res privata*).

98. Prov. 11: 14, 24: 6. The Authorised Version usually renders wisdom as 'safety'.

99. Underdown, *Pride's Purge*, pp. 173–6.

100. *A Declaration*, 22 Mar. 1649, p. 24; *The execution of the late king justified*, p. 25; Robert Bennett, *King Charle's triall Justified*, p. 3.

101. *The Second Part of the Religious demurrer*, [MS by Thomason 'against Mr Rous'], 6 Jun. 1649, E530(31), p. 7.

102. Salmon, *A Rout*, p. 3.

103. [Lilburne], *Foundations of Freedom*, 15 Dec. 1648, E476(26).

104. Cockayne, *Foundations of Freedome, Vindicated*, pp. 3, 5.

105. *A shrill Cry*, pp. 12–13.

106. Nigel Smith, *Perfection Proclaimed: Language and Literature in English Radical Religion, 1640–1660* (Oxford, 1989), p. 231.

107. John Warr, *The Priviledges of the People*, 5 Feb. 1649, E341(12), p. 10. The obscure Warr was also the author of *The Corruption and Deficientcy of the Lawes*, 11 Jun. 1649, E559(10); Laurence, *Parliamentary Army Chaplains*, pp. 184–5.

108. Warr, *Priviledges*, p. 4.

109. *The Representatives of divers well-affected Persons in and about the City of London*, 6 Feb. 1649, E341(16), p. 8. This was probably written before 30 January.

110. *A shrill Cry*, pp. 13–14.

111. Salmon, *A Rout*, p. 8; Smith, *Perfection Proclaimed*, pp. 230–6 and *passim*.

112. Bacon, *The Labyrinth*, pp. 41.44.

113. *Certain Queries humbly presented in way of Petition, by many Christian People, dispersed abroad throughout the County of Norfolk and City of Norwich*, 19 Feb. 1649, E344(5), pp. 3, 6–8; *A Declaration from the Northern Associated Counties to the Kingdom of England*, 19 Feb. 1649, E544(6), p. 6; Gardiner, *Commonwealth and Protectorate*, I, pp. 29–30.

114. *An holy Defiance to the Gates of Hell. Through the Strength and Counsell of God*, 6 Mar. 1649, E546(5), p. 24.

115. N.T., *The Resolver Continued*, p. 19.

116. George Cockayne, *Flesh Expiring and the Spirit Inspiring in the new Earth*, 29 Nov. 1648, p. 26, using the examples of the King of Syria and Ahab.

117. Cockayne, *Flesh Expiring*, p. 1; Ps. 82:6–8. This is a direct quotation from the Authorised Bible. This text was also glossed by the author of *The Execution of the late King Justified and the Parliament and Army therein Vindicated*, 26 Feb. 1649, E345(7), p. 4 in order to justify the High Court's right to judge Charles like a man.

118. Oxford, Worcester College, Clarke MSS CXI f.149^v (26 Dec. 1648) and f.150.

7

The Engagement of Loyalty

Luke Robinson, recruiter MP for Scarborough and member of the Council of State, was in an optimistic frame of mind in March 1649. Although he was keen to escape the pressures of government in London which were affecting his health and longed to return to Yorkshire to establish himself in his constituency, he confidently informed his provincial supporters that the government was 'serious' about settling army arrears and disbanding the forces, and that stability would mean he would soon be in a position to return to Yorkshire.[1] His optimism was premature and the 'sweet and quiet peace which the Countie with the rest of the nation, hath enjoyed, through the blessing of God upon the Parliaments Councels, and their Armies endeavours' was rocked by the potential invasion of 'a Rapatious forreign Scottish Army, joyned with a Fugitive rabble of unnaturall Englishmen, endeavouring the ruine of their mother Countrey, for the satisfying of thier own unbounded lusts'.[2]

The sections of the population openly hostile to the Commonwealth regime were growing in number as people became disillusioned at a rate faster than the government could appease them. As such, the question of loyalty became paramount. The degree to which individuals were prepared to owe allegiance to the new government had ramifications throughout all levels of society and affected the ability to function of even the most lowly parish official. John Constable of Bury, Lancashire, caught drinking after hours and asked by the constable what the laws were, replied that he no longer knew, the laws 'were new modelised [and] Cromwellysed'.[3] The return to fundamental principles did not, in fact, involve reinstituting an ancient, native model of government which people could recognise as theirs, but instituted a form of government which was outside the English experience. The government tried to argue that it was an organically derived, participative state in which each individual made an informed decision to place him or herself under its protection and guidance, but that necessitated the people's recognition that they would participate and be protected. In order to build loyalty, the government had to repeat the traditional structures of allegiance, but to a revolutionary system which had arisen through political expediences which were difficult to justify.

The government sought to tackle the problem of loyalty by instituting an oath of allegiance. This was, in itself, hardly a new solution. The Commonwealth oath, the Engagement, tried in significant ways to avoid the mistakes of oaths in the past, but by forcing people to make a statement of their loyalty, the government ran the risk that it would encourage people to think through and articulate their objections. A study of the history of the Engagement rehearses the arguments which were advanced both for and against republican government. It also reveals the ways in which the Commonwealthsmen quickly abandoned their intention to be part of a reforming, radical administration and became, because they were obsessed by the need to stabilise government, the authors of a holding operation bent on survival.

It was barely six years since political leaders had taken the 'Solemn League and Covenant for the Reformation of Religion, the Honour and Happiness of the King, and the Peace and Safety of the three Kingdoms of England, Scotland and Ireland', an oath which required the defence of religion and the king.[4] More precisely, it obligated its signatories to promote a Calvinist national church and the person of Charles Stuart. Conceived as a means of unifying the parliamentarian war effort, defining its aims, identifying its targets and crystallising the nature of the religious crusade on which its soldiers were embarked, it was in itself a factional, political tool. Many of the most radical figures, including Marten, who had made no secret of his belief that the king's person was a dispensable part of the constitution and cared little for questions of religious controversy, signed the Covenant. The younger Vane was one of those responsible for it coming about at all.[5] By 1648, however, many considered that they had been coerced into signing an unjust oath. The Independents redefined the aims of the Covenant and presented it as the means by which those most anxious to see a Presbyterian national church and an accommodation with Charles planned to enshrine themselves in power. The Covenant was considered a disastrous policy by the end of the wars. The godly principles which they sought to uphold had trapped subscribers into defending the one man, they now believed, to have been responsible for the bloodshed.

The Covenant had been a long and complex document which echoed the biblical covenants of Abraham and, more particularly,

Moses. Its religious overtones were integral to a definition of its aims. Most oaths, by their nature, involved invoking the name of God as a testament of fidelity; a covenant implied a sacred relationship between the subscribers and the object of their trust. It did less to bind man to man, and more to bind individuals to their God. Mutual love of God and fear of divine retribution provided the persuasive (or coercive) nature of the undertaking.[6] The Covenant was designed to bring about uniformity of 'religion, confession and catechising' throughout the three kingdoms. Having tendered the oath to MPs on 25 September 1643, its authors were successful in 'encouraging' subscriptions from churches, 'groaning under or in danger of the yoke of Anti-christian tyranny'.[7]

The role of the king had been equally unambiguous. Presbyterian parliamentarians felt a heavy burden to emphasise their loyalty to the Crown in order to counter royalist accusations of republicanism. Lex Rex may have been shaped by Scottish Calvinism, which itself had generated resistance theories, but in the middle years of the 1640s, as English parliamentarianism came under the radicalising influence of soldiers, London citizens and Levellers, Presbyterianism retreated into reaction and conservativism. Though there were possibly republican conclusions behind some of the early Scots-Calvinist literature, the authors of the Covenant were far from implementing them. They were fighting to recover the honour and dignity of the regal office – purging it of 'Catholic' excesses – and as soon as this had been achieved, they were anxious to return Charles to his rightful place in London as the way to bolster the traditional social and political hierarchy. The hopes for this policy would come to ossify in the weak frame of the Propositions of Newcastle.

With the history of the Covenant fresh in people's minds, the Commonwealth government tried to impose its Engagement. The clash of the two oaths – two alternative statements of the nature of the compact of government – brought to the surface inherent tensions within the Commonwealth experiment. These had been represented, however incompletely, by the thinking behind regicide and republicanism, and were now reprised in a new guise. The Engagement, as it was designed for members of the Council of State, had called on them to sanction the trial and execution of the king and approve the form of government as a 'republique, without King or Howse of Peers'.[8] The inclusion of the clause which retrospectively approved the regicide immediately lost the support of some who would otherwise endorse republican government. As Lord Denbigh gracefully admitted as he refused the oath:

There is no other power in England but that of the Commons, In whom the liberty and freedome of the people is soe involved as he is resolved to live and dye with them. And that what government they shall set up and appoint he will faithfully serve to the best of his power with his life and fortune. But saith that in that engagement there are some particulars that looke back.[9]

Algernon Sidney was another who would later offer faithful service to the Commonwealth, and whose credentials as a believer in republican government could not be doubted, who absented himself from Westminster over the period of the trial and was hostile to the agenda behind the Engagement for the Council of State.[10] Within the forty-one hand-picked members of the Council of State, nominated by a republican committee and predetermined by adherence to the honest party, their consistent commitment to the war and willingness to serve in a republican administration, there was a majority who would not endorse the three actions which constituted regicide: the purge of parliament, trial and execution of Charles.

The revival of Leveller activity and agitation early in 1649 was also associated with a renewed sense of outrage at the regicide. It so threatened the loyalty of the New Model that a form of the oath of loyalty was extended to the soldiery. On 3 April, the Council of State wrote to Colonel Robert Tothill, whose regiment, destined for Ireland, was marching towards its embarkation point. He was warned that '[s]everal counties by which your regiment marched complain of the great insolencies and disaffection of many of your soldiers, who openly profess to have served the enemy, and say they will do so again when there shall be occasion. Take care that none so affected may be transported.'[11] The means to ensure that ill-affected soldiers did not cross to Ireland was provided by the Engagement. The oath was offered to Tothill who, having subscribed, represented the pinacle of a pyramid, offering the same to his subordinates, until every member of the regiment had been tested. Those who refused were to be disbanded, and so, in the words of the Council, the regiment would be 'purged'. Colonel Michael Jones, already in Dublin, was to be offered the test by Colonel John Reynolds, whose regiment was supposedly on its way to embarkation in Bristol. Those of Jones' soldiers who refused were to be disbanded in Ireland. The test called on soldiers to be faithful to the 'Commonwealth, without King or House of Peers', to obey the orders of the Council of State, to do nothing to prejudice the Commonwealth and to actively discover plots against it.

A flashpoint came in May. The soldiers of Colonel Reynolds' regiment distributed leaflets in Northamptonshire 'tending to the raising of sedition, and the destroying of all authority'. Reynolds was given the task of subduing the mutinous behaviour of the soldiers heading for Bristol, but Gentles' estimate is that two-thirds of his regiment deserted under the influence of Leveller agitation.[12] The Council of State wrote that it 'expected' service from Reynolds which would benefit the Commonwealth and that riotous behaviour and free quartering would give the people 'little taste of their promised liberty'.[13] This did not auger well for Reynolds' ability to apply the test to Jones.

Mutinous soldiers abandoned their regiments against a background of Leveller, anti-government propaganda. The government was particularly outraged by Gilbert Mabbott when he licensed a third *Agreement of the People*, which the Councillors chose to interpret as an attack on the Commonwealth. The government needed counter-propaganda and thus began the search for pamphleteers prepared to write to a government agenda. The Council employed several hack propagandists, of whom John Milton was the most notable and Marchamont Nedham, who edited the semi-official newsbook, *Mercurius Politicus*, the most influential. A test was also to be applied to them. John Hall,[14] who would collaborate with Nedham on *Politicus*, was contracted during May to generate pro-Commonwealth literature. He was to be paid £100 a year, £30 of which was to be advanced, provided he took the test.[15] No wording was specified for this purpose and was probably similar to that offered to the army. Sir Henry Mildmay, meanwhile, reported to the House that Mabbott had breached his loyalty to the republic, should be sacked from his post as licenser and newspapers such as the pro-Leveller *Moderate* should be suppressed.[16]

On 5 September an Act was passed, to come into effect five days later, which introduced a compulsory oath for all those elected to the London council, and the mayors and officers of the boroughs and corporations. This version read:

> You shall swear, That you shall be true and faithfull to the Commonwealth of England, as it is now established without King or House of Lords: You shall well and truly execute the Office of Major within the City of —— and Liberties thereof, according to the best of your skill, knowledge and power. So help you God.[17]

On 11 October 1649, the decision was taken to extend the Engagement to all public employees in the form of a simple statement: 'I do declare and promise, That I will be true and faithful to the Commonwealth of England, as the same is now established, without King or House of Lords.' Subscriptions were to be required from MPs, soldiers, employees and officers of the state, sheriffs, borough employees, the staff and students of Eton, Winchester, Westminster, Oxford and Cambridge, and all clergy who expected to have a benefice and a place on the Assembly of Divines. They had until 1 January 1650 to subscribe.[18]

The September oath was the point at which the controversial nature of the Engagement, which had previously been debated within closed government circles, began to filter out into the localities. It set the sensitivities of officials to the local political balance in competition with their loyalty to central government. At the end of the month, the Council of State wrote to the mayor of Southampton demanding to know why it had not received the town's list of subscriptions, requiring the mayor to return the names of those who had refused.[19] Richard Rose, MP for Lyme Regis, continued to sit in the House during the lifetime of the Rump, and in 1650, he used his Westminster absence from Dorset as an excuse for not swearing in as mayor of the town. In 1655 he was granted a waiver on the cumulative fines that had been levied for his non-subscription, on the grounds that he had not in conscience been able to swear the Engagement for local office holders. When, five years later, the engaging government had been overthrown, the fines were voided.[20]

The government issued a declaration in an attempt to forestall the inevitable controversy, in which it reneged on the importance of the Engagement as a positive indication of commitment to republican government, and declared at the end of September 1649 that it might have been satisfied had the people been prepared to offer passive obedience. It was active resistance to the government from some sections which made the oath necessary. Presbyterians and moderates had united with royalists to 'make the bringing in again of Monarchy into this Commonwealth, to be the onely means of setling it in Freedom'.[21] Paul's letters to the Romans, which had provided a fundamental plank of royalism in that they denounced resistance to civil government, was, now that the government had changed, used to win over Presbyterian doubters. Romans 13 stated, 'Let every soul be subject unto the higher powers. For there is no power but of God: the powers that are ordained of God. Whosoever therefore resisteth the power, resisteth the ordinance of God: and they that resist shall receive to themselves damnation.' It identified the old enemy, 'the bonds of Monarchy and Tyranny', and claimed it as a common foe, promoted by a handful of delinquents who deceived the majority about the truly godly nature of the Commonwealth. The people's 'innocency and well-meaning' was leading them like lambs back to their former bondage. The declaration was an unsuccessful attempt to convince doubters. This was because it retained vestiges of the old republican language within a framework of new pragmatism. It was, in itself, ambiguous. The air was polluted by the faint smell of failure. Swamped beneath a mass of administrative detail, the government chose to blame domestic opposition for their dilatoriness in creating an ideal state. Using republican language, it naively assumed that Presbyterian doubters would agree that monarchy was the common enemy and regard the new government as their liberators.

The choice of 1 January 1650 as the final date for the subscriptions of local office-holders heralded the extension of the Engagement on the following day to all citizens over the age of eighteen.[22] Had universal subscription been achieved, the Engagement would have fulfilled a function similar to that intended by the *Agreement of the People*, in which all those who benefited from a government's protection, including its officers, contracted to place themselves under that government. The *Agreement* and the Engagement were to have been new civil contracts as 'we do now hold ourselves bound, in mutual duty to each other'.[23] The view of the *Agreement*, from the Leveller leadership, which was outlined in Lilburne's *Foundations of Freedom*, was that subscription was a mark of loyalty to the new constitution and a qualification for the franchise.[24] When the *Agreement* was discussed by the Army Council, all references to an oath constituting a voting qualification were lost. The idea of a declaration of loyalty to the fundamental constitution survived and was subsequently incorporated into the Engagement.

The discussion about a universal Engagement had begun two months previously, when a huge committee had been 'appointed to consider of the Way how the Engagement be taken by the whole Nation'.[25] It was almost equally balanced between radicals and conservatives. There was, nevertheless, room for the committee to be manipulated, because the initial quorum was only five and on 20 November it was reduced to just three.[26] It was chaired by Miles Corbet, a signatory of Charles' death warrant and one of the two Norfolk brothers, both MPs, who clung loyally to the fringes of the republican faction.[27] Over Christmas, a report was issued from Council, '(t)hat the Declaration, which was ordered to be prepared for the Satisfying of the People of this Nation concerning the Test, which is now in a good readiness, may be called upon; the Council being of the Opinion, that it will be of very great Use, for the better carrying on of the Taking of the Test.'[28]

Two months after the passage of the Act, few had taken the Engagement and the time limit for subscriptions was extended to 25 March, despite an attempt by Marten and Livesay to prevent it.[29] The additional time was not met by a corresponding rise in enthusiasm. A resolution of 6 September 1650 indicated a shift from the strident language of the early months of 1649: the Lords Commissioners of the Great Seal were now ordered to appoint appropriate people in the localities to offer the oath and to note all those 'who are willing to take the Engagement'. They were to have the same powers as they had had under the Act of 2 January, 'the Time thereby being elapsed'.[30] On 22 October the militia were ordered to tender the oath.[31] Something which was required had become a demonstration of loyalty by those who were willing, and since there was no rush of willing signatories, tendering had an even more gentle aspect. People's inertia and reluctance even to leave their houses to hear the Engagement, and open statements of disloyalty from those from whom it was most expected, blighted the scheme and turned the Engagement into something completely different. A means to unite all of the people turned into a way to distinguish the loyal from the disloyal.

Evidence of the way in which the oath was 'tendered' is provided by the radicals in Somerset. John Preston, the right-hand man of the more famous John Pyne, has left us a scrap of paper neatly penned in his own hand. The sheet is folded in half and was obviously designed to be so, producing a double-sided paper about the size of a post card. On the one side he wrote the simple, two-line version of the Engagement, to be read out to potential takers. On the reverse he set out 'the reasons of urgeing the Engagment'. It enjoined subscriptions because

> divers disaffected persons doe by sundry wayes & meanes oppose and endeavor to undermine this p'sent goverment unlesse care be taken; & anew warre is likely to breake forth: for the preventinge wherof, & allso for the better unitinge of this Nation as well a gainst Invasio[n] from abroad, as the common enemye at home, & to the end that those who receive benefitt and ptection from this p'sent goverment may give assurance of ther liveinge quietly & peaceably under the same, & that they will neither directly nor indirectly continue or practice any thinge to the disturbance therof.[32]

Luke Robinson and Isaac Newton issued a summons that the Engagement would be taken in North Yorkshire on 16 January, at nine in the morning, at the house of Nicholas Conyers in Pickering. The list of subscribers was to be drawn up by the constables, but 'none are expected to appear upon that summons but such as have augmentations from the parliament or derive there [sic] authority from it'.[33]

The question of loyalty implicit within the Engagement asked potential subscribers to assess the degree to which assent implied compromising one's conscience because one still accepted the terms of previous oaths. The drafters of the Engagement were aware of the degree to which they had to gently stroke tender consciences. Some subscribers were persuaded precisely because the oath was expressed in secular terms.[34] There were casual references to God's witness in two versions of the Engagement – that for the Council of State and that of

September 1649 for borough representatives – but secular rhetoric was a point of some discussion among those who were offered it. Secularism was partly a reaction to the most pointed objection to the Engagement: many of those who were being asked to subscribe, if they had held any position of responsibility within their communities, had previously opted into the religiosity of the Solemn League and Covenant. Trying and executing the king had broken the Covenant in a heinous way and it was difficult to see how past statements could be reconciled with loyalty to the Commonwealth. John Preston, for example, was acting in Somerset in the face of submissions from Presbyterian ministers and congregants who argued that 'Ro: 14.21, 23 & 1 Cor: 8.12 cannot but render the Conscience trembling & doubtfull'. Since they believed themselves to be the faithful, asking them to perform any thought or action of self-denial was a sin which would cast them into the midst of the damned.[35]

In the early forms of the oath, the inclusion of God's witness was not an issue which troubled the government. Those members of the Council of State who had previously taken the Covenant admitted, as participants at Putney had done, that an oath which may have been taken in good faith but which subsequently proved unjust did not remain binding.[36] Similarly, those who were employed by the state, in the army or as propagandists had a particular commitment to the republic which overrode previous oaths. It became a problem with the September oath for borough representatives and came to a head with the October Engagement for all community leaders. Taking the Engagement became a precondition of employment and many were therefore faced with the choice of losing their standing within the community or compromising their consciences by taking two contradictory oaths.

Past oaths had been 'specious and subtle' and the House was now considering 'how such Acts and Ordinances, or any part of them, as they finde penal and coercive in matters of Conscience, which have been made use of for Snares, Burdens and Vexations to the truely sincere hearted people of God . . . may be taken away.'[37] It was the religious element built into previous oaths which had proved a trap, for it had bound oath-takers to keep their word to God even when their fellow men had broken theirs. The framers of the Engagement claimed fellow feeling with those anxious at the implications of taking this oath, because they had been in the same dilemma when they swore in 1643 to defend the king, with God's help, and discovered during the course of the wars that the king had been the Almighty's greatest enemy. It also bore comparison with the dilemmas debated at Putney during the winter of 1647. The Commonwealth Engagement, there-fore, was to be a short, simple and straightforward declaration, shorn of references to the government's route to power, the witness of God or a religious settlement. Henry Parker believed it was not possible to compose anything 'more clearly, or succintly'.[38] It would represent an entirely secular statement of an individual's commitment to live in society with his or her fellows.

The Engagement aimed to minimise the degree to which one's conscience was compromised because it did not dictate to the inner self. *The Grand Case of Conscience* argued that a covenant was the most binding form of oath because God was party to it,[39] but the Engage-ment, by comparison, was 'short, and plain without ambiguity'.[40] MP William Heveningham had signed the death warrant, registered early his dissent from the vote of 5 December, was appointed to the Council of State and took the Council's Engagement. Nevertheless, when he had to take the oath for all MPs, he hesitated. A friend, F.G., sought to persuade him to sign because whereas the Covenant had been a 'Long and Dubious papoir', the Engagement called only for subscribers to be 'civelly ffaythfull' and fidelity 'engageth not with Long Captious Amptibibulogious [sic] expressions'.[41] This type of subscriber was prepared to offer support to the government because, in doing so, he acquiesced in the republicans' contention that past oaths had been an attempt to sway the conscience.[42]

The degree to which the consciences of subscribers might be further compromised depended on the degree to which one believed that the Commonwealth government represented a fundamental change or merely a superficial mutation of governmental forms. If governmental form was incidental, how could it compromise the fundamental part of a person's integrity? If republican government represented radical change, it also dictated a radical reassessment of the concept of loyalty. If the change really was only 'notional, nominal and circum-stantial', such soul-searching was rendered unnecessary.[43] John Wallace used the terms 'old' and 'new' theorists to define the two basic approaches taken by those who subscribed. Wallace applied the term 'old theory' to the revolutionary, pro-republican attitude which was dominant in the first few months of 1649. The 'new theories' were those which characterised conservative accommodation with the government later that year.[44] They could also be described as 'repub-lican' and 'non-republican' strategies for subscription. A straightforward dichotomous distinction such as this disguises the complexity and range of views which characterised supporters of the oath, but is still valuable because it discriminates between those theories which emanated from the 'Presbyterian' tradition and those with their roots in less structured radicalism. There were, in fact, five distinguishable responses to the debate on the nature of loyalty to the Commonwealth government. However, despite the seeming variety of views about the Common-wealth, these positions – with the exception of unrepentant royalism – all drew, in different combinations, on ideas which had been used to attack monarchy or to justify the Commonwealth. The non-repub-licans merely approached the questions from a different angle. The way in which apparently opposed groups sprang from similar intellectual roots helps to explain why the Commonwealth was able to maintain its stable if unpopular and ponderous administration.

The most obvious group of potential subscribers were the committed supporters of the Commonwealth whose support was predicated on the government being a republic. Moves were taken to 'purge' mutinous and ill-affected soldiers and the government was therefore able to claim almost unanimous signings from the regiments. The army was one place where the government might have expected to find support. It was encouraged, in the face of what was otherwise a gloomy prospect, by spontaneous 'engagements' from those who did not wait to be asked to demonstrate their loyalty. The soldiers of Colonel Ingoldsby's regiment were moved to write to Westminster because anti-government agents – by which they meant the Levellers – had 'so farre ensnared' them that they had only narrowly averted a fresh outbreak of war.[45] Gentlemen in Lancashire, Yorkshire and Nottinghamshire signed a spontaneous declaration of willingness to assist the Northern Brigade, commanded by Major-General Lambert:

> against the common enemy of this Nation, and that we shall with the hazard of our lives and fortunes, endeavour the preservation of peace of these Counties, against all forreign oy [recte or] domestique enemies, And do further unanimously declare, and enter into protestation, to live and dye with our Representatives assembled in Parl for establishing the peace of the Kingdom, and perfecting of the great and glorious work in hand; and that we do approve of their late Totes [recte Votes] and Declaration for the government of this Kingdom without a supream or legislative power, either by King or Peers.[46]

Whitelocke reported of the official test that 'not one in a thousand did scruple at the signing of it'.[47] Completely unanimous returns followed from the garrison troops in Carlisle, Hull, Scarborough and New-castle,[48] and according to A Perfect Diurnall, twenty-five garrisons and eleven regiments of foot and horse had subscribed by early December.[49]

Some were prepared to accept the Engagement as a genuine, if flawed, attempt to maintain the ethos which had underpinned the

Agreement. John Lilburne won his release from prison, and his acquittal made him as much of a populist hero as any amount of the self-publicity he could generate by his arrests. Along with Thomas Pride, he was subsequently elected to the Common Council of London in December 1649, and as a Councillor, he was offered the Engagement. More surprisingly, he took it. It may have been, as Worden has pointed out, that he had 'his own reasons' for subscribing. Presumably, he had weighed the influence which he could exercise by sniping from the sidelines against the pressure which could be applied from within the administration, and decided that signing a piece of paper was a small price to pay.[50] The public pronouncement with which Lilburne chose to explain his reasons, however, echoed the original republican arguments which the government had been trying to project with the Engagement for the Council of State. He concurred that it was the purpose behind a universally taken oath, such as the Engagement, to establish obligations which went beyond those owed to specific people or institutional mechanisms. The *Agreement of the People* had sought to establish the highest loyalty to 'the people' or 'the security of the people' or 'the people's liberties' and the Engagement was an attempt to do likewise. Lilburne now announced that he was not being asked to swear allegiance to specific members of the hierarchy – the Council of State, the Army Council or parliament – 'because the Members of the 3. said Counsells take it as well as any others, and therefore it is not abstract to themselves that they take the Engagement to be true to; for it is incongruous in reason, for a man to take an Engagement to be true to himself, because it is inherent in him.'[51] The anonymous author of *Conscience Puzzel'd* used a similar argument. The General, Speaker, House of Commons, Lord President, Council of State and Council of War had all taken the oath, he claimed – at the eleventh hour in the case of Fairfax[52] – and one could not take an oath to oneself. The king had never done so.[53] Gerrard Winstanley, despite digging in Surrey, took the Engagement and pronounced it 'well liked [by] the generality of the people'. The nature of the change of polity must have been sufficiently marked for such people to have taken an oath which, had it been introduced by the parliament five years before, would have offered an excellent opportunity to refuse it, martyr themselves on the cause of individual liberties and denounce such an oppressive imposition in the presses.

Conversely, there were those such as Prynne and the cavaliers who were their mirror image, opposing the Engagement precisely because it represented a republican polity. Royalists insisted that 'the King's Person in England never dies, saies the Law', and therefore they continued to owe allegiance to the king, even if they had seen Charles executed, because the person of the king and the office for which he stood could not be separated.[54] The author of *A Copie of a Letter Against the Engagement* could not take the Engagement because to do so would make him 'as very a Common-wealths man by it, if I take it as Mr. Martin, or the greatest Republican of them all.'[55] The survival of the royalist belief that the nature of governmental office could not be distinguished or separated from the persons who fulfilled it implied that for this author swearing loyalty to the form of government was the same as recognising that the fundamental constitution was a republican one.

The vocal and hard line sections of the Presbyterian churches were correctly identified by the Commonwealth government as a centre of opposition, because they had the greatest commitment to the terms of the Covenant. Thomason collected a handbill, 'pasted upon divers Church doores in London', denouncing nine who had been swayed by government reasoning into taking the new oath and were in 'diametricall opposition and directly contrary to the expresse Letter of the Oath of Allegiance, Protestation, and Solemne League and Covenant, which they have sworne with hands lifted up to the most High God; having perjuriously subscribed the late engagement to be true and faithfull to the Common-wealth of England as it is now established without King or Lords.'[56] William Prynne continued to be a noisy, self-publicising, irritating nuisance to the Commonwealth government. The wordsmith railed against the republicanism of the new regime: its fundamental purpose was to extinguish monarchy, the 'first, antientest, universallest, honourablest, freest, best, happiest, safest, peaceablest, durablest Government of all others in the World'.[57] England would not be rendered a 'free Republick' but a miserable place. He kept up his pomposity to declare that royalists were

> premptorily resolved, by the grace and assistance of our Omnipotent God, rather to endure ten thousand sequestrations, Imprisonments, Deaths; then to betray our King, Kingdomes, Parliaments, Lawes, Liberties, religion, all our earthly comforts, wound our Consciences, damn our immortal souls by our submission or subscription to this irreligious, flagitious, pernicious, scandalous, illegall, irrationall, unconscionable, treasonable New Oath and Engagement.[58]

Some were prepared to owe tacit obedience to the new regime but would not make any declaration of support, usually because this conflicted with previous oaths they had taken and would jeopardise their relations with their neighbours. This group recognised the irreconcilability of the Covenant and the Engagement but were nevertheless prepared to owe obedience to the Commonwealth. They were not, however, prepared to compromise their consciences by taking the new oath. Let *The Humble Proposals of Sundry Learned and Pious Divines* stand as representative of this group.[59] The divines accepted the need for government in human society in order to curb the outrageous behaviour of the wicked. They were, however, able to bring four arguments to bear why they could not openly profess their loyalty by signing the Engagement. Subscription would imply 'full and free' acceptance of the present powers. This had been Sir James Harrington's reason for not subscribing to the oath for the Council of State: he could not 'fully' comply.[60] It had sounded more precious when offered then.[61] Secondly, since the government had promoted the idea of the people as the fount of all authority, it should be bound to respect the people's decision not to subscribe. Thirdly, the Engagement implied – presumably through the statement 'as it is now established' – that subscribers must promote whichever government had the 'possible advantage of power', including that which would succeed the present one. Finally, if they were to take the oath, those who could not grasp the complexities of the issue would accuse them of covenant-breaking and the ministry would lose its authority. Nevertheless, they claimed they were law-abiding citizens and did not deserve to be numbered among the infamous until they had wilfully violated the laws and thereby lost the benefit of them.

The converse of this position accounted for the people who were quite prepared to take any oath of loyalty to the Commonwealth since they had no compunction about breaking it. Lilburne may have been perjuring himself when he took the Engagement, but the reasons he gave for doing so constituted a statement of republican principle. The other imprisoned Levellers took the Engagement for the glaringly expedient reason that 'Mr Walwyn, Mr Prince, and Mr Overton, must either lie in Prison till they were starved, or take the new Engagement; and of the two Evils they choose the less; and have set their Hands to the new Engagement, which they promise to keep as faithfully as Bradshaw, Vain, or Prideaux have done the Covenant.'[62]

Finally there was the most well known group, which has generated the greatest literature, the *de factoists*. *De factoists* are defined as those prepared to support a government which they accept is illegal, provided that its current actions were according to law, because all government must be the providential will of God. Evil or illegal governments must be held to be the wages of the people's sin and therefore owned as an integral part (beyond comprehension) of God's overall divine plan.[63] *De factoists* were usually drawn from the ranks of lay-Presbyterians, but there was the occasional royalist who made the same intellectual journey. In comparison with the signatories of *The Humble Proposals*, who had placed the obligation on themselves to live under the laws because the law, currently administered, was of itself just and godly, the *de factoists* placed the responsibility on the governors to abide by law. The justification of their position was two fold. While they agreed that mankind was a social being and that some regulation was therefore necessary, a specific form of the government had not been designated. The desire for government was sanctioned by God's Providence, so it was therefore not for humble man to question or challenge the form of the administration. Provided the governors acted within the law, all rulers were entitled to loyalty. I choose to make the taking of the Engagement a point of difference between the *Humble Proposals* group which was obedient to the *de facto* government and the group usually referred to as the *de factoists* because it highlights the application of the person/office distinction in this new guise. Those who professed to be loyal but would not take the Engagement were faithful to the people in government. *De factoists* professed loyalty to an immutable body of law, implemented by mutable people. Perhaps the most influential *de factoist* treatment of the Engagement, *The lawfulness of obeying the present government*, by Francis Rous, the long-standing MP for Truro, took as its text a citation from the Book of John, 'judge not the appearance, but judge righteous judgment'.[64]

This tension, which surfaced with attempts to justify the Engagement, was the same dilemma which had characterised the way in which the person-centred arguments in support of the regicide ran parallel to and were in tension with, the arguments for republican government. The piece of semi-official pro-Engagement propaganda, *The Grand Case of Conscience concerning the Engagement Stated and Resolved*, was probably written by John Milton. Milton, we have noted, was one of those who was prepared to elide the two definitions of tyranny, tyranny by title and tyranny by practice.[65] This tract presents us with a good example of the two contradictory arguments about monarchy operating in tandem. While the aim of declarations of loyalty was 'humane affairs' and therefore changeable,[66] the king's name was accidental to the Covenant and therefore most 'critical casuists' accepted that if a thing changed its character, the loyalty previously owed to it was nullified.[67] However, having accepted that the obligation behind the Covenant was invalidated once its object had been removed, the Covenant itself remained valid: 'We have not broken at all the Covenant, nor changed it in any speciall condition of it, but only blotted out an unnecessary and destructive name, and inserted a more direct medium, for the preserving of the Covenant.'[68] The Engagement debate employed two (contradictory) arguments about the fundamentality of monarchy. The first maintained that although the form of the government was immaterial, basic loyalty to government itself was immutable. The Engagement, the Covenant and, before that, the Oath of Allegiance bound citizens to different, even incompatible objects, but existed to defend the same fundamental concept of allegiance to government. The second argument held that once the immediate object of loyalty was removed, all obligation was ended. Therefore, though the Covenant had been valid during the king's lifetime, it ceased to be so once the king had been executed.

The government recognised the way in which *de facto* theory would be more successful than full-blown republican rhetoric in winning over sceptics to the government, but also realised that reliance on *de factoists* would water down its ability to promote the Engagement as a form of fundamental law. At the same time as it prepared its positive declaration in favour of universal subscription to the Engagement, it decided to rely on the persuasive skills of John Dury.[69] The irenicist Dury was a prolific pamphleteer and correspondent of Samuel Hartlib's circle of *virtuosi*. He was recommended to produce tracts, which were invariably *de factoist*, a week before the oath was made a universal requirement, which seems to indicate pessimism at quite an early stage of the government's life. Government strategy thus consisted of a dual approach, offering two different types of justification aimed at two different types of audience. Ironically, it was the ability of *de factoists* to find points of contact with both of the contradictory elements within regicidal/republican arguments which accounted for their success.

Reliance on *de facto* theory meant that the balance of reasoning shifted away from establishing a fixed foundation of freedom enshrined in an Engagement, and towards the idea that one was not owing allegiance to a particular form of magistracy or magistrates because forms were mutable, 'because as *Motion* in bodies *natural, Succession* in *Civil*, is the grand Preventive of Corruption'.[70] This point was taken up by the pro-republican poet, George Wither, who was musing about the nature of government during November 1652 and whose thoughts produced *A poem concerning a perpetuall parliament*.[71] Wither's ideal system could be described as perpetual in that it operated under the law, but within that rather limited interpretation of the foundation of government was constant movement through a rolling series of elections in which each representative would sit for just one year. Marchamont Nedham agreed that government through regular popular assemblies would allow the people control in their own interest, rather than in the interest of a faction or individual. There was some debate about the nobility of the individual, although it was far from clear whether popular government was a good thing because every individual or none wanted to be a ruler.[72] The idea that nobility lay within each individual, 'born with Affections to Rule rather than to Obey, there being in every man *a natural Appetite, or desire for Principality*', was taken from Cicero, but classical allusions had already been made in homespun religious terms. It was the point which the sectaries had made in 1649, that all men were of an 'aspiring temper'.[73] This was a theory which relied on equality between individuals: either everyone wanted a share in power, or nobody was interested in power.

What was to republicans a point of principle could be casuistically employed by stressing the importance of the office and not the specific people who exercised it. Republicans had denounced the way in which the person and office of kingship were irreversibly linked by royalists, who insisted that the person of the king never died. Engagers could recognise the absurdity of this position as well as the republicans. The royalist, anti-Engagement tract, *The Second Part of a Religious Demurrer*, was countered by an Engager who had no difficulty in employing the republican *reductio ad absurdum*: '[b]ut to say that the Kings person cannot dye is a matter of Mirth, or if you will of Nonsense; especially to be put into this Oath; for it amounts to this, that I sweare to preserve the Kings person which needs no preservation, because it cannot dye.'[72] The Covenant had been designed to uphold the person of Charles Stuart, but since Charles' person had already been dispatched, the people were freed from covenant obligations. John Dury, referring to the supposedly binding Oath of Allegiance, claimed it did not tie subjects 'to the King & his Heirs, as they were men, to be true and faithful to their personal wils, but only to them & their wils as they had a Legall standing'.[75] The notion that sovereignty or authority passed seamlessly through bodies and institutions was also urged at Hevening-ham, because 'the Staffe is ffallen ffrom the King to the Parliment & ffrom them to the army', as those concerned with religion explained the providentialism of God's decision to distribute power by devolving it through these three fleshly bodies.[76]

De factoists were able to use republican arguments about the person/office distinction in this way because they had low expectations of the morality of political leaders under any system. In a sermon of 1623, Bishop Robert Sanderson had declared, 'we live not in *Republica Platonis*, but in *faece saeculi*'. Thirty years later the state was still impure. He 'did not expect the magistrate of his native Lincolnshire to transform the country into a New Israel; nor, for that matter, did he believe that the Lord would punish England if her rulers were not the virtuous leaders that Moses and Nehemiah had been.'[77] Despite having accommodated himself to the Laudian church which many of the Commonwealth government professed to despise, Sanderson had less trouble than some more obvious supporters in adjusting to the new regime. He was to accept the jurisdiction of a republican government and encouraged others to do likewise because, while accepting God's will and providence to be immutable, the subordinate actors in God's plan acted wickedly on their own account and not on God's.[78]

The second key aspect of winning over sceptics was the degree to which the government could offer safety and stability, because as Heveningham was reminded, 'it is most Just & True to be ffaythfull to the Government that Gives protection'.[79] The passage of time helped, putting distance between the present and the purge and execution of the king, and by 1650 it became clear that the Commonwealth government may have gained power by conquest but could continue to provide firm government at home and a show of strength abroad.[80] Despite unlawful beginnings, it was amply fulfilling the obligation of government to *salus populi*.[81] T. B.'s *The Engagement Vindicated* declared early in January 1650 that the campaign to put an end to the war in Ireland would improve the reputations of the government and the army, keep England at peace and stave off the 'hydra of confusion', though it would necessitate high taxes.[82] Among the reasons given by Robert Spry for support for the governors was their 'valour and bounty fit for a Soldier'.[83] Algernon Sidney had put distance between himself and the early, regicidal actions of the Rump, but his doubts about the Commonwealth were assuaged by victories at Dunbar and Worcester and the conquest of Ireland.[84] He returned to play an active role after 1652.

In June 1650, Marchamont Nedham reported that 'the Quarrell continues no longer between *English* and *English*, but is translated into *Scotch*'.[85] War in Scotland and Ireland necessitated a Council of State, made gestures of loyalty more urgent and slowed the progress of domestic reform. When the defeat of the Scottish army in September 1651 signalled the end of resistance from Scotland and Ireland and the royalists were defeated at Worcester, thus ending the '*Bellum Presbyteriale*', the tone of *Mercurius Politicus* was transformed. There followed a series of editorials with overt references to the wisdom of ancient Greece and Rome, which culminated in fifteen justifications of a '*Free State*, or a Government by the people in *a due and orderly succession of their supreme Assemblies*'.[86] Such a system would highlight the virtue of the kind of government which could, after a slow process, be established by peace makers, praised by Machiavelli: 'Captains in *Free States*, which purchased themselves a fame, in defence of their Liberties.'[87]

There can be no doubt that the government which Nedham described in these editorials was a republican one. The emphasis was on a popular assembly, regular elections and fluidity and devolution of power. However, government also increasingly came to be described in heroic terms, and the rhetoric best suited for that was derived from classical learning. Thomas Hobbes held that it was immersion in and imitation of the classics which had produced republicans, '[f]or who can be a good subject to monarchy, whose principles are taken from the enemies of monarchy, such as were Cicero, Seneca, Cato, and other politicians of Rome, and Aristotle of Athens, who seldom speak of kings but as of wolves and other ravenous beasts?'[88] Even those whose classical scholarship was of the highest calibre harboured fears that godly men who followed the pattern of Rome or Athens would, in replicating a heathen government, repeat the vices of kings. Milton was conscious not to list too many pagan examples in case he undermined his stated aim of proving Charles to have been guilty of subversive heresies,[89] and the godly of Norwich warned that worldly government was like that of 'Heathen Rome and Athens' and 'too many late overtures . . . caused us to fear' that this was the aim of the Commonwealth.[90] It should be noted that both of these examples came in February 1649, right at the birth of the Commonwealth. The enthusiasm to descibe the successes of the Commonwealth in classically inspired rhetoric and the search for models of republican government within ancient sources, which grew apace from about 1652 onwards, inspired an interpretation of the English republican experiment which is known as 'classical republicanism'.[91]

The problem with presenting the Commonwealth government as heroic was that it relied for its force on the notion of men of heroic stature. Only people could be heroes. Therefore, while one side of the argument was stressing how far Commonwealth structures had minimised man's corrupt tendencies, the side which wanted to present the government as protectors tended to stress leadership and virtue. With double irony, the heroic, protective virtue which was supposed to be the characteristic of the patriotic Englishman was being demonstrated outside England. The future of the English Commonwealth – and in the longer term, the fact that the English Commonwealth did not have one – was decided by acts of heroism in Ireland and Scotland. The government which had built itself on the concept of England's liberties found that this ethos only held if the government was able to cut itself off from outside influences. The conquest of Ireland had been a controversial policy as far as the soldiers were concerned and it was rumoured that they were being exiled, but when they returned a year later, the reputation of the army was newly enhanced along with its 'ever-victorious commander with an aura of invincibility, compelling eloquence, profound conviction of the righteousness of his cause and the certainty of its success, and unconquerable resolution'.[92] Even relations between the English Commonwealth and the Dutch can be represented as a change of policy from one which stressed the two nations' shared republicanism to one in which the Dutch rebuffed English overtures of alliance, and the presses geared up to present Holland as the perfidious ally of the king of Scots against which the English state made bellicose noises as a means to puff up the pretensions of a particular faction in government.[93]

On Cromwell's return from Ireland, Andrew Marvell created verse which, although admittedly teasing, celebrated military valour. Literary scholars debate the degree to which the ambiguous tone contained hidden warnings to the General, but there were certainly also elements of encomium.[94] Cromwell was presented as the man whose warlike valour had rescued the Commowealth's shaky beginnings – 'So when they did design/ The capitol's first line,/ A bleeding head where they begun/ Did fright the architects to run'. As his first year's 'rent' to the Commonwealth, Cromwell had presented them with the kingdom of Ireland, and now 'What may not then our isle presume/ While victory his crest does plume?'[95] Nedham warned those within England who still sought to oppose the Commonwealth that 'if Reason, and their Interest as *Englishmen*, will not reduce them, yet let them stoop with Reverence at the name of that victorious Commander, *Cromwel*'.[96] R. Fletcher's 'resolution of a Free State', praised the General's valour in a long verse eulogy: 'Caesar and Cromwell: why, 'tis all but C . . . Crown'd with the spoils of the worlds royaltie: And all the neighb'ring Continents implore/ To be imbrac'd under the British lore'.[97]

The puissance of the administration, the system it represented and the degree to which it could fulfil its side of the contract of protection were most vividly represented by hero-worship of Cromwell. Although the Commonwealth government was restoring the heroic image of English rule which Charles was held to have damaged, praise for its efforts was directed at neither the laws which the soldiers upheld nor the governors who sent the army into the field, but at the commanders of the forces themselves.[98] The language most appropriated to express the awesome success of Cromwell was taken from that of ancient Rome. Cromwell was a Caesar. Marvell's ode likened him to the Emperor Augustus, who had been encouraged by the Stoic philosophers to hold his status above the generality of the Roman Republic.[99] Eulogies on his greatness were Horatian in their expression. The Stuart family were referred to as both the kings of Scotland but also as Tarquins, the last kings of Rome, but not necessarily the last Roman (anti)heroes.[100]

The army returned to centre stage, changing both the rhetoric and the issues of politics. While they had been engaged in combat, the demands which the grandees had made in January 1649 were left unanswered. There had been considerable progress in raising money, but little seemed to have been siphoned towards meeting army arrears.[101] The Rump had failed to fulfil its stated aim of putting an end to its sitting by calling a fresh ballot. The new sense of security which the news of military victories brought did, however, allow the worthies of the Commonwealth the luxury to return, in November 1651, to the issues brought forward by Sir Henry Vane junior's committee for 'the settling of the Succession of future Parliaments, and regulating their elections'. It had been set up on 15 May 1649. Six months later it had decided on the numbers of members to represent each constituency and the principle that those already sitting should keep their places.[102] The committee met weekly and adjourned weekly on thirty-six occasions, and then reminded itself, on 23 October 1650, that its task was 'filling the House with Members'. The following September it prayed for guidance and changed the chair of the committee to the conservative lawyer William Ellis.[103] The House was engaged in measures to secure the recent victory over the royalists at Worcester and tentatively tried to move forward with the issue of elections. That it was still their intention to recruit was hinted at by the vote of 18 September 1651. Almost concurrent with the start of progress towards a bill for a new representative was a decision to make a fair copy of those MPs who had subscribed to the Engagement. This would therefore provide a definitive list of those loyal to the Commonwealth, and possibly, therefore, a means to determine those who would be suitable to stand for re-election.[104] Finally, on 14 November 1651, the House agreed that the time had come to declare a date for the end of its sitting and four days later fixed on 3 November 1654.[105]

The time which these deliberations seemed to be taking and the prospect of the same people continuing in power fuelled frustration in the army that its agenda would not be addressed by the current crop of governors. In January 1653, the army officers joined together to seek God and decided that the ills of the nation amounted to power having continued too long in the same hands.[106] The official presentation of news to the people about the workings of government went eerily quiet. The licensed *Mercurius Politicus* ended its discussion of the errors of previous policy in August 1652,[107] seldom mentioned domestic issues and concentrated almost entirely on foreign policy, particularly on relations between England and the United Provinces. It saw fit to mention the army only once when a group mutinied in Scotland because twelve pence had been stopped from their pay to provide the finance to build up a store.[108] In the official account of government there was little indication of the collapse of relations between army and parliament.

NOTES

1. N. Yorks Record Office, MIC 1320/1221, fragment of a letter, 6 Mar. 1649.
2. MIC 1320/1221, 1498, Robinson's letter from York, 23 Aug. 1651; Lancs. Record Office, Bradshaw MSS, DDF411/unfol. no. 22, 3 Sep. 1650; Gardiner, History, II, p. 12; David Underdown, Pride's Purge: Politics in the Puritan Revolution (London, 1971), p. 36.
3. Lancs. Record Office, QSP 24/27, Manchester, Michaelmas 1649. This was a repeat of the form of dissent which often exploited the period between the demise of one monarch and the coronation of the next, that period being interpreted as one in which there was no law, or all laws made under the previous ruler were voided.
4. GCD, pp. 267–71.
5. Violet A. Rowe, Sir Henry Vane the Younger: A Study in Political and Administrative History (London, 1970), pp. 23–5; J. H. Adamson and H. F. Pollard, Sir Harry Vane: His Life and Times, 1613–1662 (London, 1973), Chapter 9.
6. GCD, p. 268.
7. GCD, p. 271.
8. House of Lords Record Office, MS Commons' Journals, XXXIII ff.732–4.
9. PRO, SP 25/I/3b(2), p. 2.
10. Alan Craig Houston, Algernon Sidney and the Republican Heritage in England and America (Princeton, 1991), pp. 24–5.
11. PRO SP 25/I/94 p. 69.
12. Oxford, Worcester College, Clarke MSS IXXII/unfol.; The Moderate Intelligencer, 2–10 May 1649, E555(3), p. 2034; Ian Gentles, The New Model Army in England, Ireland and Scotland, 1645–1653 (Oxford, 1992), pp. 332–3;.
13. CSPD, 1649–50, p. 94.
14. Possibly the same one who was employed at the Exchequer Office in 1654, cited in Gerald Aylmer, The State's Servants: The Civil Service of the English Republic, 1649–1660 (London, 1973), p. 130, p. 383 n. 3; More likely the co-editor of Mercurius Politicus: Jonathan Scott, Algernon Sidney and the English Republic, 1623–1677 (Cambridge, 1988), pp. 110–11;

DNB, VIII, pp. 955–6; Richard L. Greaves and Robert Zaller (eds), *Biographical Dictionary of British Radicals in the Seventeenth Century* (3 vols) (Harvester, Sussex, 1983), II, pp. 41–2.

15. PRO SP 25/I/62, p. 305; *CSPD*, 1649–50, pp. 125 and 127; Scott, *Algernon Sidney* pp. 110–12.

16. H. N. Brailsford, *The Levellers and the English Revolution* (Nottingham, 1961) Chapter XX; *CSPD* 1649–50, p. 127, item 35 of Council of State business; Jürgen Diethe, '*The Moderate*: Politics and allegiances of a revolutionary newspaper', *HPT*, IV.2 (1983) 247–79.

17. PRO SP 25/I/94 p. 461.

18. *Resolves of Parliament touching the subscribing of an Engagement by or before the first of January next*, 11 Oct. 1649, 669.f.14(82).

19. *CSPD* 1649–50 p. 323, 29 Sep. 1649.

20. Dorset Record Office, DC/LR B7 D1/1, Order Book of Lyme Regis, 1594–1671, pp. 90–1.

21. *A Declaration of the Parliament of England*, 27 Sep. 1649, E575(9), p. 4.

22. Gender is not specified and leaves open the tantalising possibility that women were to be incorporated into the political and legal nation, perhaps at the level of having to take the Engagement before being party to indentures, making a will or registering a birth.

23. This statement from the preamble survived from the first to the second version: *GCD*, pp. 333, 359.

24. [Lilburne], *Foundations of Freedom*, pp. 7–8. The recent history of the war dictated that delinquents be excluded and the discussion of the freedom of the will at Putney led to the specific exclusion of alms-holders and servants.

25. 9 Nov. 1649: *CJ*, VI, p. 321. There were 46 members.

26. 20 Nov. 1649: *CJ*, VI, p. 324.

27. *CJ*, VI, p. 321; Blair Worden, *The Rump Parliament* (Cambridge, 1974), *passim*.

28. *CJ*, VI, p. 337, 15 Dec. 1649.

29. Sir William Armyne and Salisbury were tellers for the negative: Act of 23 Feb. 1650.

30. *CJ*, VI, p. 463.

31. *CJ*, VI, p. 486.

32. Somerset Record Office, Hippesley MSS DD/HI/467.

33. North Yorkshire RO, Northallerton MIC 1320/1125.

34. As Edward Winslow, pious and godly, was later to say of an oath of loyalty to the Protectorate, if any men should be sent to aid the Western design, 'let us have men of such principles, as will neither scruple to give or take an oath . . . I looke upon an oath as an ordinance of God, and as an essential part of government, the very bond of societys; yea so necessary, as without it the magistrate will not be able determine betweene man and man': Winslow to Thurloe, Barbados, 16 Mar. 1654(5), *Thurloe State Papers*, III, p. 251.

35. Somerset Record Office, Hippesley MSS DD/HI/467. Rom. 14: 21, 23: 'It is good neither to eat flesh, nor to drink wine, nor any thing whereby thy brother stumbleth, or is offended, or is made weak . . . And he that doubteth is damned if he eat, because he eateth not of faith: for whatsoever is not faith is sin.' I Cor. 8: 12: 'But when ye sin so against the brethren, and wound their weak conscience, ye sin against Christ.'

36. A. S. P. Woodhouse, *Puritanism and Liberty*, pp. 1–47.

37. *Declaration of the Parliament of England*, p. 12.

38. Henry Parker, *Scotland's Holy War* [17 Jan.] 1651, E622(16), p. 68.

39. [John Milton], *The Grand Case of Conscience concerning the Engagement stated and resolved*, 9 Jan. 1650, E589(10), p. 3. The attribution is made by Anthony Wood.

40. [Milton], *The Grand Case of Conscience stated*, p. 21.

41. Holkham Hall, Norfolk, Heveningham MSS 684.

42. Glenn Burgess, 'Usurpation, obligation and obedience in the thought of the Engagement controversy', *HJ*, 29.3 (1986) 515–36, p. 521.

43. See Chapter 6, n. 67.

44. J. M. Wallace, 'The Engagement controversy 1649–1652: an annotated list of pamphlets', *Bulletin of the New York City Library*, 68 (1964) 384–405.

45. *A full Narrative of All the Proceedings between his Excellency the Lord Fairfax and the mutineers*, [18 May] 1649, E555(27), pp. 12–13; Gentles, *New Model Army*, pp. 330, 347.

46. Nehemiah Reinoldson, *A Declaration from the Northern Counties to the Kingdom of England*, 14 Feb. 1649, E544(6), p. 3.

47. Whitelocke, *Memorials*, II, p. 125.

48. Whitelocke, *Memorials*, II, p. 128.

49. *A perfect Diurnall*, 10–17 Dec. 1649: 'A list of the regiments and garrisons who have sent up their subscriptions to the Engagement to parliament.'

50. Worden, *Rump Parliament* pp. 215, 227 and *passim*; Gardiner, *Commonwealth and Protectorate*, I, pp. 160–9.

51. John Lilburne, *The Engagement vindicated and explained or the reasons upon which Lieut. Col. John Lilburne tooke the Engagement*, 23 Jan. 1650, E590(4), p. 5; Wallace, 'The Engagement controversy'. Wallace has categorised this as an anti-Engagement tract, possibly misreading Thomason's handwriting on the top of the first page in which 'tooke' looks like 'broke'. It was published by a 'well-wisher to the present authority'. Winstanley also took the Engagement, see Gerald Aylmer, '*Englands Spirit unfoulded, or an incouragement to take the Engagement*: a newly discovered pamphlet by Gerrard Winstanley', *P&P*, 40 (1968) 3–15.

52. Towards the end of February 1650: PRO SP 25/I/95 p. 7; *CJ*, VI, p. 369; Sarah Barber, 'The Engagement for the Council of State and the establishment of the Commonwealth Government', *HR*, 63.150 (1990) 44–57, pp. 54–5.

53. *Conscience Puzzel'd about subscribing the new Engagement*, 20 Dec. 1649, E585(7).

54. *The second Part of a religious Demurrer*, 6 Jun. 1649, E530(31).

55. *A Copie of a Letter against the Engagement, as it was sent to a Minister*, 1 Feb. 1651, E622(13), p. 9.

56. '[B]eing Sunday this paper was posted upon divers Church doores in London', 11 Nov. 1649, E579(6).

57. William Prynne, *Summary Reasons against the new Oath and Engagement*, 22 Dec. 1649, E585(9), p. 8.

58. Prynne, *Summary Reasons*, p. 15.

59. *The humble Proposals of sundry learned and pious Divines*, 19 Dec. 1649, E585(6).

60. Whitelocke, *Memorials*, II, pp. 536–7.

61. Barber, 'Engagement', p. 45.

62. Worden, *Rump Parliament*, p. 227; *Truths Victory over Tyranny*, 16 Nov. 1649, E579(12), n.p.

63. Quentin Skinner, 'Conquest and consent: Thomas Hobbes and the Engagement controversy', in G. E. Aylmer (ed.), *The Interregnum: The Quest for a Settlement* (London, 1972), pp. 79–98; Glenn Burgess, 'Usurpation, obligation and obedience in the thought of the Engagement controversy', *HJ* 29.3 (1986) 515–36; Margaret Judson, *From Tradition to Political Reality* (Hamden, Conn., 1980); James M. Wallace, *Destiny his Choice: The Loyalism of Andrew Marvell* (Cambridge, 1980).

64. Francis Rous, *The Lawfulness of obeying the Present Government. Poposed by one that loves all Presbyterian lovers of Truth and Peace*, [25 Apr.] 1649, E551(22), frontispiece, citing John 7:24; Burgess, 'Usurpation', pp. 519–21.

65. Burgess, 'Usurpation', p. 519.

66. [Milton], *The Grand Case of Conscience stated*, [22 Jun.] 1649, E530(45), p. 10.

67. [Milton], *The Grand Case of Conscience stated*, pp. 11, 20.

68. [Milton], *The Grand Case of Conscience stated*, p. 21.

69. *CJ*, VI, p. 337, 15 Dec. 1649.

70. *Mercurius Politicus*, No. 78, 27 Nov.–4 Dec. 1651, p. 1237.

71. George Wither, *The Perpetuall Parliament. being the Result of a Contemplative Vision, revealing a probable means of making this Parliament to be both perpetuall, and acceptable to these Nations*, consulted from the English Poetry Full-Text Database (Chadwick-Healey Ltd); Z. S. Fink, *The Classical Republicans: An Essay in the Recovery of a Pattern of Thought in seventeenth-century England* (Northwestern University Press, 1962; 1st. edn,1945), pp. 48–51.

72. See the tension between reason 2 (20–7 Nov. 1651) and reason 12 (29 Jan. – 5 Feb. 1652), p. 1381.

73. Warr, *Priviledges*, p. 4; see Chapter 6, p. 164.

74. *A Combate between two Seconds*, [2 Jul.] 1649, E563(13), p. 14.

75. J[ohn] D[ury], *Considerations concerning the present Engagement whether it may be lawfully entred into: Yea or No?*, 27 Nov. 1649, E584(12), p. 2.

76. Holkham, Heveningham MSS 684; Robert Bacon, *The Labyrinth the Kingdom's In*, [7 Feb.] 1649, E541(26), pp. 41, 44; see Chapter 6 above.

77. T. H. Breen, *The Character of a Good Ruler: A Study of Puritan Political Ideas in New England, 1630–1730* (New Haven, Conn. 1970).

78. [Robert Sanderson], *A Resolution of Conscience, by a Learned Divine*, 1 Dec. 1649, E584(8), n.p.; Peter G. Lake, 'Serving God and the times: the Calvinist conformity of Robert Sanderson', *JBS*, 27 (1988) 81–116, pp. 82–4.

79. Holkham, Heveningham MSS 684, 'a letter written by a ffrend to W.Heveningham Esq 2 of January 1649', signed F.G.

80. [Francis Osborne], *A Perswasive to a Mutual Compliance*, (Oxford) 18 Feb. 1652, E655(5), p. 4; John Wallace, 'The Engagement controversy: an annotated list of pamphlets', *Bulletin of the New York Public Library*, 68 (1964) 384–405, pp. 388, 405; Perez Zagorin, *A History of Political Thought in the English Revolution* (London, 1954), pp. 62–70, 121–31.

81. Even Sanderson could cite *salus populi* in defence of his position: Lake, 'Serving God', p. 109.

82. T. B., *The Engagement vindicated from all Objections, cavils, scruples, that wilfull Opposers, or doubtful, unresolved Judgements may be cast upon it*, 7 Jan. 1650, E589(3), pp. 10–11.

83. Robert Spry, *Councel of State-Policy or the Rule of Government set forth* (Plymouth), 30 Oct. 1649, received by Thomason 20 Jan. 1650, E1354(1), p. 19.

84. Scott, *Algernon Sidney*, pp. 110–12.

85. *Mercurius Politicus*, No. 67, 11–18 Sep. 1651, p. 1071.

86. *Mercurius Politicus* between no. 67 11–18 Sep. 1651 and No. 91, 26 Feb.–4 Mar. 1652; no. 84, 8–15 Jan. 1652, p. 1333.

87. *Mercurius Politicus*, no. 68, 18–25 Sep. 1651, p. 1077: 'It is a noble saying, though *Machiavel's; Not he that placeth a vertuous government in his own Hands, or Family, but he that establisheth a free and lasting Form, for the peoples constant security, is most to be commended.*' Nedham is thus paving the way for the transition from good laws to good laws implemented by a virtuous person.

88. Thomas Hobbes, *Behemoth: or the Long Parliament*, ed. Ferdinand Tönnies (Chicago, 1990), p. 158, though Hobbes does in fact say that the MPs in the lower house were almost all drawn from the class of men who were educated to a knowledge of the classics (p. 3).

89. J[ohn] M[ilton], *The Tenure of Kings and Magistrates*, [13 Feb.] 1649, E542(12), pp. 7–8.

90. *Certain Quaeres humbly presented in way of Petition* [19 Feb.] 1649, E544(5), p. 3.

91. Fink, *The Classical Republicans*; J. G. A. Pocock, *The Machiavellian Moment: Florentine Political Thought and the Atlantic Republican Tradition*

(Princeton, 1995); Worden, 'Classical republicanism'; Scott, *Algernon Sidney*, pp. 14–17; J. C. Davis, 'Pocock's Harrington; grace, nature and art in the classical republicanism of James Harrington', *HJ*, 24.3 (1981) 683–97.

92. Abbott, *Writings and Speeches*, II, p. 260.

93. There is no room here to go into the details of the Commonwealth's relations with the United Provinces, but it is hard to imagine the recent account of Steven Pincus being bettered: Steven C. A. Pincus, *Protestantism and Patriotism: Ideologies and the Making of English Foreign Policy, 1650–1668* (Cambridge, 1996), pp. 11–79.

94. J. A. Mazzeo, 'Cromwell as Machiavellian Prince in Marvell's Horatian Ode', in his *Renaissance and Seventeenth-century Studies* (New York, 1964); Wallace, *Destiny his Choice*; H. M. Margoliouth (ed.), *The Poems and Letters of Andrew Marvell* (2 vols) (Oxford, 1971); Barbara Everett, 'The shooting of the bears: poetry and politics in Andrew Marvell', in R. L. Brett (ed.), *Andrew Marvell: Essays on the tercentenary of his Death* (Oxford, 1979); Annabel M. Patterson, *Marvell and the Civic Crown* (Princeton, 1978); John C. Coolidge, 'Marvell and Horace', *Modern Philology*, LXIII (1965) 111–120.

95. Andrew Marvell, 'An Horatian ode upon Cromwell's return from Ireland', in Margoliouth, *Andrew Marvell*, I, pp. 87–90.

96. *Mercurius Politicus*, No. 1, 6–13 Jun. 1650, p. 3.

97. R. Fletcher, *Radius Heliconicus: the Resolution of a Free State*, [28 Feb.], 1651, E622(13), p. 9.

98. David Armitage, 'The Cromwellian Protectorate and the language of Empire', *HJ*, 35.3 (1992) 531–55, pp. 531–5.

99. M. Hammond, *The Augustan Principate* (London, 1933); L. R. Taylor, *Divinity of the Roman Emperor* (London, 1931).

100. *Mercurius Politicus*, No. 2, 13–20 Jun. 1650, p. 17. The Tarquins were the last kings of Rome, forced to flee after their overthrow. Nedham extends the Tarquin image to all the surviving Stuarts, No. 14, 5–12 Sep. 1650, p. 211; Milton, *Eikonoklastes*, in Merritt Y. Hughes, *John Milton: Complete Poems and Major Prose* (New York, 1957), p. 810.

101. Sean Kelsey estimates that only one per cent of the army establishment as it stood in 1648 had received recompense for war expenses and arrears: Sean Kelsey, *Inventing a Republic: The Political Culture of the English Commonwealth, 1649–1653* (Manchester, 1997), p. 174; Sarah Barber, 'Irish undercurrents to the politics of April 1653', *HR*, 65.158 (1992) 315–35.

102. 9 Jan. 1650, *CJ*, VI, p. 344.

103. *CJ*, VII, p. 27. Ellis also sat on the committee which attempted to draft law reform as a result of the deliberations of the Hale Commission: Mary Cotterell, 'Interregnum law reform: the Hale Commission of 1652', *EHR*, LXXXIII (1968) 689–704; Alan Cromartie, *Sir Matthew Hale, 1609–1676: Law, Religion and Natural Philosophy* (Cambridge, 1995), pp. 70–3; Worden, *Rump Parliament*, p. 320.

104. *CJ*, VII, p. 19.
105. *CJ*, VII, pp. 35, 37; Ludlow, *Memoirs*, I, p. 334.
106. Oxford, Worcester College, Clarke MSS XXIV f.107; Ludlow, *Memoirs*, I, p. 348.
107. *Mercurius Politicus*, No. 114, 5–12 Aug. 1652.
108. *Mercurius Politicus*, No. 123, 7–14 Oct. 1652.

8

The Active and the Passive Life

The patience which the army grandees had shown towards the parliament's efforts at reform finally ran out on 20 April 1653. Cromwell called his troops into Westminster Hall and forcibly ejected the Rumpers from power. Subsequently, the reasons for Cromwell's actions have been thoroughly investigated. It is now generally thought that he was dissembling when he issued a declaration two days later in defence of his actions. He accused the House of intending to introduce a bill to recruit further members, whereas it is believed that it was in fact about to call fresh elections on conditions which would have minimised the army's future role.[1] However, the committee which had been discussing the new representative had maintained a policy of recruitment from its inception, so complete elections would have represented a late change of strategy.

There was no edition of *Mercurius Politicus* for the week 21 to 28 April and the edition which followed began '[a]ll is quiet in the *Highlands*'.[2] Nedham then printed Cromwell's declaration in full, with the rather throwaway line that it had already been published, but his newspaper claimed to give an overview of news.[3] Although a 'matter of such concernment' could not be 'let slip', coverage of the fall of the Rump parliament was scant. The presses seem effectively to have been shut down.[4] The anger of those whose power depended on the Rump does emerge, but not in print. The outrage of Rumpers has to be gleaned from the scanty manuscript sources which remain. Thomason copied by hand one of the very few defences of the Rump[5] and both he and Henry Marten obtained manuscript copies of a satirical poem about Lenthall's ability to retain his place despite the changing regimes around him.[6] Marten – whose creditors were chipping away at his power, waiting for him to fall – prepared some scathing attacks on Cromwell and the army, some of which were pastiches of the encomiums to the General which appeared around the city.[7] The Commonwealth of 1649 to 1653 had been, according to Marten, 'the best frame of lawes yett extant in ye World'.[8] In his return to first principles, Marten compared the purge of 1648 with the 'invasion' of 1653, quite deliberately choosing terms which referred to change from within the charmed circle of governance which represented English liberties, and something which collapsed a polity from outside. Although he claimed that the army grandees were using the history of their intervention in setting up the Commonwealth as a precedent for another which ended it, there was a fundamental difference between the two, 'the first being to place the power in the people, and so cõstitute and restore a Comonwealth, and this latter to take the power from the people, (even in the instant when it was to bee restored to them) and to place it in the Sword'.[9] He thought better of sending any comments to the press, but in his reflection, his bitterness against Cromwell and the army increased in its daring expression.

Other defences of the laws of 1649 to 1653 come from memoirs written several years after the fall of the government. Ludlow praised the Rump parliamentarians as 'disinterested and impartial' men who after twelve years of 'sovereign power of the three nations' had not kept as much of the spoils of government for themselves as the army managed to do in just the summer of 1653. He also returned to first principles, looking back to 'the time that the Parliament consisted of but one House, and the Government was formed into a Commonwealth'. The system which the House had elected to pass on at its dissolution was a Commonwealth of representatives, with a council of state chosen by and accountable to parliament and which would sit in the intervals between parliaments. To which end, the House was about to put an end to its sitting when the army barged in.[10] Lucy Hutchinson, likewise, found the parliament retrospectively worthy of praise:

> [t]he Parliament had . . . restored the commonwealth to such a happy, rich, and plentiful condition, that it was not so flourishing before the war, and although the taxes that were paid were great, yet the people were rich and able to pay them: they were in a way of paying all the soldiers' arrears, had some hundred thousand pounds in their purses, and were free from enemies in arms within and without, except the Dutch, whom they had beaten and brought to seek peace upon terms honourable to the English: and now it was time to sweeten the people, and deliver them from their burdens.[11]

One of the few printed justifications for the Commonwealth's type of free state was a new edition of Robert Spry's *Council of states-policy*, in which he had discussed a free state in the form of a dialogue between an Oxford scholar and a countryman, reissued as *Rules of Civil Government, drawn from the best examples of Forreign Nations and Commonwealths*. He presented it to the Lord General in July 1653 as a 'word in season'.[12]

The silence of the presses is eloquent testimony to the thoroughness with which both gentry and classical republicanism in the Rump were quashed in April 1653. Many protagonists had not lived to see the edifice fall. Thomas May was not there to record its achievements;[13] Alexander Rigby had succumbed to fever on one of his judicial tours around the country. Other leading figures, such as Marten, were so indebted that they could not summon the power to push their writings to the press. Colonel Hutchinson retired from politics and opted for the life of a country squire:

> Colonel Hutchinson, who thought them (the army) greater usurpers on the people's liberties than the former kings, believed himself wholly disengaged from all ties, but those which God and nature, or rather God by nature obliges every man of honour and honesty in to his country, which is to defend or relieve it from invading tyrants . . . and to suffer patiently that yoke which God submits him to, till the Lord shall take it off; and upon these principles, he seeing that authority, to which he was in duty bound, so seemingly taken quite away, thought he was free to fall in or oppose all things, as prudence should guide him, upon general rules of conscience. These would not permit him in any way to assist any tyrant or invader of the people's rights, nor to rise up against him without a manifest call from God; therefore he stayed at home, and busied himself in his own domestic employments, having a very liberal heart, and a house open to all worthy persons of all parties.[14]

On the other hand, London councillors who were active in complaining that even under kings England had not been completely without a parliament were themselves ejected from office.[15]

The exception was John Wildman, who did publish a response to the dissolution in the form of a positive model to be pursued by those framing a bill for a new representative, 'so long in agitation not yet published'. Wildman's contribution, *A Mite to the Treasury*, is virtually devoid of classical allusion but uses the heightened biblical language of the late 1640s. It is also reminiscent of the first *Agreement of the People*, a simple statement of fundamental principles and measures – the 'briefer, plainer and more equall Rules' – required to enshrine the notion that 'Power is Primarily and Originally in the People'.[16] What was required were the real reforms which would ensure that 'those good words, *Common-wealth, free-state, free People, Iustice, Liberty, Priviledges, Ease, place, safety*' were matched by the things themselves.[17] Among the practical measures he suggested were a committee of grievances, freedom of worship, reform of the law for debt,[18] a reduction in the number of capital crimes, registration of all land claims, provision for wounded soldiers, widows and orphans, and the readmission of the Jews into England. More importantly for the direction of republican thinking were two further suggestions. The former may have been influenced by Machiavelli's assertion that the revolutionary nature of the Roman Republic needed to be protected from mankind's invariably evil tendencies by establishing tribunes of the people.[19] Ten 'Faithfull uninterested, unbiassed & able Persons' should constitute 'Conservators' while the new representative was being elected – the role, in other words, which Ludlow remembered for the Council of State. Specifically, this was not the role of the army. The army would remain, but only until a new parliament could pay it and address its grievances; then it would be disbanded.[20] Secondly, the representative would constitute a perpetual and unbreakable circle, justified because it was regulated by laws and not by men. Each representative body would last two years; each member would sit for just one year, on a 'commission' from the electorate to govern in justice, love and mercy. Should they be considered not to have done so, they would be accountable to their successors in the next representative.[21]

The response to Wildman was provided by the Fifth Monarchist, John Spittlehouse, who pointed out a fundamental change which he believed had taken place with the fall of the Rump. The Commonwealth was not something to be 'conserved' but 'protected', and rather than being the worst people for the task, who better to protect the people than their army? The ejection of the Rump confirmed a role for the army which had been gaining in prestige throughout the life of the parliament: soldiers based in Scotland, claiming to speak for all, confirmed that the Lord had 'made you happy Instruments in purging' and would now own them in dissolving.[22] Cromwell having already gained a reputation as Augustus, and with the gathered churches in a lather of excitement about their imminent spiritual freedom, Spittlehouse presented Cromwell as Moses, leading the godly to a promised land.[23] The propaganda which supported the change of regime made much of the Book of Exodus, including the injunction found in chapter 18, verse 21: 'Thou shalt provide out of all the people able men, such as fear God, men of truth, hating covetousness.' The abstract republican form of words – 'unnecessary, burdensome and dangerous' – was replaced with the rule of good magistrates. The new catchphrase of government would, in various guises through the lifetime of Cromwellianism, be drawn from a list including good conversation, ability, integrity, fear of God, hatred of covetousness, fidelity and honesty.[24] There would be a mixed government of the three elements of monarchy, aristocracy and democracy in which the people's liberties were balanced against the rulers' safety. The deliverer would be joined by seventy elders to bear the burden of government with him. Thus was announced Barebone's nominated assembly, based on the notion of the Hebraic Sanhedrin.[25] It was a government established by men whose objection to the Stuart monarchy had been that good laws had been abused by a bad man. Now godly magistracy had been restored.

The army Council was said to have debated whether government should be in the hands of the few or the many and, at first, decided on the latter, since it would be more in keeping with the wishes of the generality of the soldiers, and settled on men 'fearing God, and of approved fidelity and honesty'.[26] Barebone's was an experiment in representative government and personal regeneration[27] by the godly, but was deemed an abject failure. John Lambert's *Instrument of Government* was instead accepted as a constitution for the Protectorate of Oliver Cromwell.[28] A Protectorate in which 'supreme legislative authority' resided in 'one person, and the people assembled in Parliament' explicitly returned to the situation in 1649, when parliamentarians and grandees had debated whether their revolution was about removing Charles Stuart or the whole issue of single person government. The central statutes of the Commonwealth had referred to the illegality of any single-person rule, not just to rule by a particular house. The Commons' resolution which had declared against the 'Office of a King . . . and to have the Power thereof in any Single Person', reflecting the dichotomy between person and office, must in February 1649 have referred to various branches of royal families.[29] A situation had not yet arisen in English history in which an individual from outside the monarchical lineage had laid claim to executive power. Indeed, the only way to ensure that a claim to rule would be taken seriously was to demonstrate or pretend descent from the customary royal families. In 1649, the statement, 'king or any single person' had expressed a hypothetical situation.

In May 1654 John Milton published *Angli Pro Populo Anglicano Defensio Secunda,* a response to the anonymous of *Regii Sanguinis Clamor ad Coelum adversus Parricidas Anglicanos.*[30] The latter had appeared in 1652, but in the intervening changes of government, Milton had become as critical as Cromwell of the republicans who had once employed him. The perceived failure of the Rump was put down to the individuals who made it up, reinvigorating the debate about the ethical behaviour of magistrates by now comparing the (godly) General and his officers with the Rump politicians where once the comparison had been with the Stuarts. While the Commonwealthsmen had lauded impartial government by a 'frame of laws', the debate now returned to government by people – good or evil. When the General dismissed the parliament he abused several members reluctant to vacate their seats. They were self-serving, had lavished bounty on their friends and been parsimonious towards the army who were the real defenders of liberty.[31] They had made sure that they had received personal recompense for the expense of blood and treasure, emphasising the materialist elements of their personal sacrifice rather than the liberties for which the sacrifice had been made. Some members were drunkards and others were whoremasters.[32] Milton, with his added invective spin, repeated the calumnies:

> Should they have charge of the public purse, which they would soon convert into a private, by their unprincipled peculations? Are they fit to be legislators of a whole people who themselves know not what law, what reason, what right and wrong, what crooked and straight, what licit and illicit means? who think that all power consists in outrage, all dignity in the parade of insolence? who neglect every other consideration for the corrupt gratification of their friendships or the prosecution of their resentments? who disperse their own relations and creatures through the provinces for the sake of levying taxes and confiscating goods – men, for the greater part the most profligate and vile, who buy up for themselves what they pretend to expose for sale, who thence collect an exorbitant mass of wealth, which they fraudulently divert from the public service, who thus spread their pillage through the country and in a moment emerge from penury and rags to a state of splendour and of wealth?[33]

Cromwell had taken centre stage and, according to Milton, was to be praised as a superlative individual who led a group of virtuous men, resembling the heroes of classical Rome and Greece, both mythological and historical.[34] Those 'few' who opposed the Protectorate because they viewed it as a Cromwellian usurpation were incapable of realising that 'supreme power should be vested in the best and wisest of men' and that, among these, the General was a man of 'unrivalled ability and virtue'.

In writing this panegyric for Cromwell, Milton was also shifting the nature of republican discourse. Liberty was no longer expressed through the civil state but was a measure of individual dignity, defined as sobriety and integrity of conduct. Cromwell was fit to be the protector of liberty because he 'first acquired the government of himself', in contrast to the profligacy and licence practised by 'men of loose or debauched principles and corrupt minds' who polluted the republic.[35] There was even a hint within this moral discourse that Cromwell was suitable to be called a king, though Milton went to great lengths to show that Cromwell's personal worth was so elevated as to soar above the debased title.[36] Milton's opponent, Salmacius, had admitted that if a ruler was a bad man, he must automatically be a tyrant. All good men were kings, a proposition with which Milton did not now seem to argue.[37] The personal conduct of Cromwell was thus open for debate as that of Charles had been five years previously. Ironically, for the fastidious and pious General, the spotlight of public scrutiny could more easily pick out the moral debauchery of a single person:

> And though it be of a dangerous import, that they [executive and legislative power] should both rest in the hands of any single person, excluding the Community; yet the consequents are abundantly more pernicious, when they are grasped by many: because a particular person is easily noted for his excesses; so particular offenders find shelter in a Multitude.[38]

Cromwell's ethical behaviour would be accountable to the people in a sense that the electability of representative government had not been. Where once 'in the multitude of counsellors there is safety [wisdom]' meant the safety of the people as a whole, it was now reinterpreted by those disillusioned with the Rump to mean that the safety of the counsellors had been their shield from detection and accountability.

The second sense in which Milton shifted the emphasis of republicanism was in terms of its extent and boundaries. The republicans of 1648 had been almost entirely concerned with English liberties. Carrying their message to Scotland, Ireland and the United Provinces had been a risk which soon generated a seige mentality about their own rightness, surrounded by fickle powers who wore republican masks only when it suited.[39] On the other hand, Cromwell's reputation had been made in the campaigns in Ireland and Scotland and now the English people's patriotic cry was that 'people of this island are transporting (liberty) to other countries' and 'disseminating the blessings of civilisation and freedom among cities, kingdoms, and nations'.[40] This was reflected in the universalised language of classicism with which the defence of the English was reshaped into one in which individual valour contributed to national fame. Sir John Clerk, who looked at the history of the union from the early decades of the eighteenth century, believed that the most significant aspect of Cromwell's rule was that 'he followed the example of the Romans, who gave citizenship to those they defeated and shared all the privileges of the conquerors with the conquered.'[41]

The person/office distinction was deployed to demonstrate that when Cromwell assumed power there had been no change in the fundamental direction of the revolution, because there had never been a design to contend against particular persons or forms of government. Protectorate worthies returned to the defence that they had 'never fought against the King, as King, . . . (but) because he demeaned himself as a tyrant'. It was only in this tyrannical sense that rule by a single person was incompatible with liberty, because the army had not 'entertained any thought of excluding Government by Kings, provided they were *Elective*'.[42] Milton used the person/office distinction to justify his own reputation. In 1646 godly soldiers had claimed they stood apart from others because they were not motivated by money. The new breed apart were intellectuals. Milton had such an inflated regard for book-learning that writing about the republic became more important than acting for it. Feeling himself to be weak of body – the seventeenth-century equivalent of flat feet? – he had resorted to his study during the civil war because fighting was something 'in which any common person would have been of more service than myself'.[43] From the safety of his rooms he 'calmly awaited the issue of the contest, which I trusted to the wise conduct of Providence and to the courage of the people'.[44] Thus he was relieved from having to participate in the momentous decisions which changed the government from kingship to republic, and separated the role of the common soldiery and their political allies who had made the republic a means to recover the expense of English blood and treasure, from more elevated learned men who studied the classical heroes of the ancient world.[45] The exception was Cromwell himself, who combined both martial prowess and personal integrity, though for all that remained a man of action and not a man of letters. Milton was restoring the distinction between the active and passive life, between doing and thinking.

Presumably, study brought wisdom. As such, Milton had not fully resolved the difficulty that those who were wise should govern but that those who governed did not have time to reflect. In *Tenure of Kings and Magistrates*, Milton had praised Aristotle's classic definition of aristocracy as government by the best men, with which rule by an emperor or king was not necessarily incompatible, though the power of the executive was derivative.[46] The failure of the form of government which was ended in April 1653 was attributed to the legislative and executive power being in the same hands. The Protectorate sought to re-establish a Polybian balance in which the three branches of authority operated as checks and balances for each other.[47] Thus for Marchamont Nedham, the Protectorate was the providential culmination of the various 'Turns of Affairs' and 'great Changes and Revolutions' by which the English people had secured their liberties and fully complied with the original ends of the initial 'Controversie' with the king.[48] Under the Protectorate, '[i]f War be, here is the Unitive vertue (but nothing else) of *Monarchy* to counter it; and here is the admirable Counsel of *Aristocracie* to manage it: If Peace be, here is the industry and courage of *Democracie* to improve it.'[49]

The three issues which were enshrined in the 'great Bottom of this present Establishment' were religion, the civil rights and laws of the Nation, and the army.[50] They received their first practical test under article seven of the *Instrument of Government*, which called for triennial meetings of parliament, the first to be summoned on Cromwell's providential day, 3 September 1654.[51] No provision had been made for the registration of voters and the results were thus not as easy to control as the government might have hoped. Edmund Ludlow, always keen to see politics in terms of parties, implied that reactions to the *Instrument* had already become polarised, with an organised campaign by its supporters and a counter campaign by 'well wishers to the public interest . . . judged faithful to the public cause'.[52] Former MPs who did not seek to disguise their contempt for the Protectorate, such as Henry Marten, were able to stand, though Marten was not returned.[53] Others managed to get elected. Signators of the king's death warrant, such as Bradshaw, Scot, Robert Wallop[54] and on appeal Grey of Groby, were returned. John Wildman entered the Commons, returned for Luke Robinson's former seat of Scarborough, though his election was almost immediately overturned as 'a great disturber of the law and peace, one with such guilt upon him'. Herbert Morley played down the role of personal popularity and cited the controlling powers of the wills of the people and the Almighty, 'since without my seeking or solliciton over ruling pvidence hath by y^r free election devolved upon me, I shall not resist a call from heaven but am the more free to enterteine the same.'[55] Four of the godly who had sat in Barebone's parliament were re-elected. The faction opposed to the *Instrument* consisted of barely twelve people, although Ludlow believed that the debates which opened the session provided an opportunity to persuade younger members.[56]

Given a stern talking to by Cromwell, who reminded the obstreperous members of their duty to abide by the *Instrument* which had summoned them, some withdrew from the Chamber.[57] The squeeze was strengthened by the addition of the Recognition, a simple oath which bound members to abide by and not to seek to alter the fundamental system of government in the form of a single person and a parliament.[58] It was subsequently clarified that the Recognition did not apply to the whole *Instrument*, but solely to the clause about single-person government, but Cromwell's insistence on the oath was odd in the light of the tiny handful of republicans elected. It is hard to believe that a dozen people could bring down the Protectorate. The height of their presumption was to throw scurrilous verses out of carriages, which made the suggestion that elected members were Cromwell's team of horses.[59] Cromwell did not see the same threat from the radical sectaries, who started to petition against Cromwell as soon as the *Instrument* was agreed. Thomas Harrison was released from prison and well entertained by Cromwell as soon as the numbers of signatures to the Recognition started to pick up.[60] Ludlow and Marten both suggested that after the elections, people 'had no more of liberty left but the name', and that for all the Commonwealth's faults, its demise left citizens with a straight choice between liberty and tyranny.[61] Marten did not embrace the dynamism of factionalism as Machiavelli had done, but there was little doubt which side he favoured in the 'controversy between Mr. Hobbs and Machiavell conc'ning tiranny and liberty or to weight in an equall balance the inconveniencies which arise from oression in the one, and factions in the other'.[62]

The dissolution of the Rump, the fall of Barebone's and the Protectorate elections of 1654 provoked practical political action rather than intellectual musing. The effect was to throw republican thinking back to the polarisation of the binary division of power. The experience of the Commonwealth had confirmed the inadequacy of mixed government based on a tripartite Polybian balance, and the *Instrument of Government* revived the notion that any element of single-person government was an opportunity for self-aggrandisement. The language of 1648 was applied to Cromwell. On hearing that Cromwell desired to be made king, Colonel Whetham charged him with being Ahab.[63] Power brought out all of an individual's worst characteristics. The ethical behaviour of one person, either good or bad, could sway the people away from their responsibility to participate in the political process and could override fortune.

According to Ludlow, opposition to Cromwell was well developed among the army in Ireland, where sectaries were setting up gathered churches. In England, opposition started to organise itself in the autumn of 1654. John Wildman, excluded from parliament, returned to his contacts in the regiments to draft a petition which recruited signatures by prompting a memory of the heady days of the army radicalism which had culminated with the Remonstrance from St Albans in November 1648. There were undertones of tyrannicide. The negotiations which led to the Remonstrance were those recalled in Lilburne's *Legal Fundamental Liberties*, which described army representatives all for chopping off Charles' head, and the Leveller delegates trying to ensure that the removal of one evil man (Charles) did not result in government by the army.[64] Senior soldiers were now directly made aware of the ringing phrase with which they had reminded parliament of the Vote of No Addresses and called for Charles' trial: '[t]hat principle of the Kings unnaccountableness (was) the grand root of Tyranny, and declared by us, to be begotten by the blasphemous arrogancy of Tyrants, upon their servile paracites.'[65] The Petition presented the *Instrument* as a wholly regressive measure. It returned control of the militia to a single person possessed of a veto and the power to operate with even greater freedom outside parliament's sittings. The army could thus become Cromwell's mercenary standing army, a power beyond that of the Stuart's Commissions of Array which would 'render all the blood and treasure expended in this cause, not only fruitless, but us and our Posterities under an absolute Tyranny and Vassallage'. The effect of the Protectorate was to make void the purpose and result of the 1649 revolution:

> We are hereby enforced to make this humble Address, and to pray your Highness most serious thoughts of that high price of blood and treasure which the Commonwealth had paid for, it's Right and Freedom, which was naturally and morally due unto it before, and of the accompt that must be given to the dreadful God for all the blood we have shed; and that can be deemed no better than Murderers, if the integrity of our hearts in the prosecution of the just ends of the War, do not render us justifiable therein.

Old themes were reiterated in the new circumstances of Cromwell's Protectorate. Representativeness was partially defined as accountability which was undermined by the moral abuse of an office. Pride, and an individual's inability to subsume his or her will to the will of God, encouraged the development of tyrannous powers. The threat of a standing army in Cromwell's hands repeated, in the guise of an individual commoner, one of the chief dangers of Stuart rule in the last years of the 1630s. The *Instrument* had re-established the arguments about the way in which Charles' tyranny developed during the war into questions of the single person's ability to veto the decisions of the representative element of government by means of the negative voice and the personal treaty.[66]

The Protectorate regime was soon on to these rumblings of discontent: Colonel Francis Hacker tipped off Secretary of State, John Thurloe. A copy of the petition was seized in the chambers of Colonel Matthew Alured, where it had been subscribed by himself and Colonels John Okey and Thomas Saunders.[67] The colonels were arrested and although the petition was published, its premature discovery deprives historians of a fuller list of army malcontents. Cromwell retained the loyalty of the vast majority of the military by lenient treatment and the payment of long-awaited arrears. The petition had hinted at tyrannicide, using the equity principle which dictated the same treatment for the same crimes, but the admission that Cromwell was a usurper and a tyrant justified more active plotting. Marten was relatively powerless by

1654 but was still able to stir the most extreme thoughts. He penned but did not publish a mock encomium to Cromwell, in which he charged the General with being able to override the classical mistress, *Fortuna*, because he ignored (or bought[68]) the fickle opinion of the people. Marten mocked the General's 'filling the throne', but since the address was composed in Latin, throne (*solium*) could also be translated as 'tub' or, in the light of potential tyrannicide, more interestingly it could mean 'coffin'.[69] The way in which he framed Alexandrian questions of Cromwell – 'Is this right? Where is he from? What a man? Where is he going? Where does he stop?' – mark Marten out as a collaborator on the most fully formed of the Cromwellian tyrannicide tracts, Edward Sexby's *Killing no Murder*. Sexby asked '[w]ho made thee a prince and a judge over us? If God made thee, make it manifest to us. If the people, where did we meet to do it? Who took our subscriptions? To whom deputed we our authority? And when and where did those deputies make the choice?'[70]

There was active opposition to Cromwell during 1654 and 1655 as politicians and army officers who remained loyal to the notion of a republic plotted the usurper's downfall.[71] This group was led by Wildman, who had taken over the reins of republican figurehead from his bankrupt uncle-in-law, Marten. Edward Sexby continued his loyalty to and trust in both. They were joined by the three colonels Okey, Saunders and Alured and their counterpart in the navy, John Lawson.[72] Grey of Groby was involved to the extent that he lost his place in the army and was imprisoned; Captain George Bishop was also implicated. Ludlow provides the names of Haselrig, Love and Scot, to which we can add his own.[73] In Scotland, opposition was led by Major-General Robert Overton, whose plotting led to his imprisonment.[74] Spittlehouse continued to link Wildman with Lilburne.[75]

The republicans were imprisoned, although some subsequently escaped or were released, but they had been successfully isolated and they were pushed into finding new allies and possibilities for action. Wildman entered negotiations with royalists, both at home and in exile. He also set up his servant, William Parker, in an ale-house in London's Bow Lane which, with undoubted irony, was called Nonsuch House.[76] Here, the republican wits and drunkards could find solace in a glass and discuss unfashionable politics in relative safety. Much of the debate, however, was still triggered by and centred around the practical possibilities for republican action.

During 1656, two political issues provided a framework for republican discussion and action. The first was the proposal to alter the *Instrument* in order to constitute an hereditary Protectorate, an action subsequently instituted by the *Humble Petition and Advice* in May 1657.[77] This provided a fillip for the debate about Cromwell's moral worth, which asked whether his contribution to the struggle throughout the 1640s and 1650s be considered greater than that of his fellows. Was it just to erect him above those others who had risked their lives and livelihoods? Ethically, was he a man of sufficient character to be chief magistrate of the three kingdoms? The conclusion, that Cromwell was an individual head and shoulders above any other, was canvassed in March by the author of *A Copy of a Letter written to an Officer of the Army*.[78] It purported to be part of the commonwealth country ideology which opposed the new courtliness surrounding Cromwell. In fact, it supported the Protector.[79] In particular, it flagged the problem of factionalism. Too many different interest groups were springing up and elective magistracy allowed those in opposition to foment dissension. In particular, the debate about the division of the spoils had not gone away. Every group felt that it had the greatest right to the fruits of the revolution because each considered its own contribution the most prodigious. Since the author regarded all men equally sinful, they would never agree on an equal division: an election would exacerbate the situation by encouraging 'injustice and ingratitude' towards Cromwell.[80] In the early years of the war, every common soldier had been at the same risk as every officer, but now the General was at greatest jeopardy and had hazarded most. In particular, he stood to lose his posterity, and (in an inversion of the slogan of Rainsborough at Putney), 'I would fain demand of any of them that are fathers of children; was not the honour & advancement of their house one great motive to this undertaking.'[81] Other canons of the later 1640s were overturned. There was a return to the theory of state interest with which Ireton had countered the soldier-Levellers' claim to equal entitlement to the franchise. Although the author knew that a minority still believed that 'every person and every family engaged in this Cause, should enjoy an arithmetical proportion of power and advantage with that of their superiors, both in electing and being elected',[82] this form of elective magistracy was deemed to have always historically resulted in the confirmation of an eminent family. The gentry republicans' notion of bipolar balance was deemed to be mistaken. In 1646 the republicans, Marten and Chaloner, had been castigated by the royalists who had used Proverbs 28:2 against them. Now it was redeployed to advance to Protectorate:

> There was a time indeed when Monarchy and Tyrannie, Parlaments and Liberty were thought to be the same, but the experience of our condition under

that long, long, long, Parliament a [*sic*] and that little one since; hath rectifyed our judgements, and brought us to look on that Text as Canonical, and on him as a wise man that said, *For the wickedness of a Land many are the Princes thereof, but by a man of understanding the State thereof is preserved, Prov.* 28.2.[83]

The reply was probably *The Picture of a new COURTIER*, a dialogue between Protectorate politicians who claimed it was justifiable to serve under the *Instrument*, represented by Mr Time-server and the hero, the commonwealthsman, Mr Plain-heart.[84] The author was probably John Streater, who had landed in jail the previous year for setting up a printing press which disseminated anti-Protectorate pamphlets. Released on bail, he did not print a publisher's name or commit his pamphlets to a bookseller or hawker. Instead they were 'cast about the streets'.[85] His surreptitious lobbying aimed at uniting the commonwealthsmen's cause with that of the soldiery and the sectarians, behind a conventional republican crusade to rid England of monarchy 'root and branch'. Republicans should remember the three engagements and four acts which Cromwell was overturning. They had made engagements at Triploe Heath and St Albans, and another to be true and faithful to the commonwealth of England without king or House of Lords. There had been four founding Acts of the commonwealth which defined loyalty without a chief magistrate – 30 January, 17 March, 17 May, 17 July 1649.[86] For every gross act by the old king, there was a worse action by the new one. Cromwell had unjustly imprisoned the commonwealth's friends. In foreign policy, Charles' disasters at the Île de Rhé and La Rochelle were as nothing in comparison to the farcical Hispaniola expedition of the Western Design, in which the English navy had been 'most shamefully beaten by a few Cow-killers'.[87] Streater also returned to the canonical texts of 1648, Belshazzar's feast and the balance metaphor of the set of scales, and employed them in the traditional way against the new monarchy: 'Alas, alas! what will become of my dear Master, when his Kingdome is weighed in the Ballance and found to [*sic*] light?'[88] As if to confirm that the debate was still about a straight choice between the liberty of elected parliaments or the tyranny of a single-person magistrate, William Ball's polarity between *majestas imperii* and *salus populi*, last aired in 1649, was resurrected to respond to Thomas White's *Grounds of Government and Obedience*.[89] Ball's piece continued to argue that people expressed an equitable voluntarism in placing themselves under an authority, and that the fundamental law was the only element to be absolute. When rule relied on people it promoted 'the Bondage of Boundless Government, or rather Governors'.[90]

The calling of a further Protectorate Parliament provided a second issue around which republicans could base (admittedly muted) campaigns. The decision had first to be made whether to participate at all in elections called under the *Instrument of Government*. 'England's Remembrancer' believed that it was a duty to take every opportunity to participate, because the fundamental birthright to exercise a voice was God-given. The providential opportunity to 'gather the people, call a solemn Assembly, go and reason together, for in the multitude of counsellors there is safety' would not entail tacit approval of the Protectorate because God was an immutable aspect of parliaments and could not be taken out.[91] A soldier, who claimed to have been an officer in Ireland since August 1649, was so disillusioned with his commander's politics that he was prepared to resign his commission. The balances in which an individual's morality was weighed and all the people found to be equal meant that any form of monarchy, no matter how limited, turned government into a battle between the interests of mankind on the one hand and the interest of one person on the other. The Protector might be shocked to hear so bold a statement from one so lowly, but 'no man who is too mean to be calumniated, can be too inconsiderable to defend himself'.[92] He agreed with Streater that all changes of government stemmed from the *Instrument of Government*, which had established 'Monarchy bottomed in the sword'. There would be no point in participating in Cromwell's creature parliament. Republican reductionist logic highlighted its absurdity. If it were true that all power originated with the people there could be no power superior to the Commons. Besides, under the economically flourishing Commonwealth, the new balance of landed interest dictated that England would always bottom out as a republic. If the people's sovereignty had been a lie, 'what need they be disturbed in their harvest work, to chuse and send needless Cyphers up to *London*?'[93]

Most republicans tried to stand for election while arguing that they were deliberately being kept away from their own lands so as not to obstruct the election of Cromwellians.[94] If returned – like veterans Sir Arthur Haselrig, Thomas Scot and Thomas Saunders – they were again barred. Excluded members expressed their feelings in a petition to those allowed to take their seats, claiming their participation had confirmed Cromwell's heretical self-assessment that his contribution outweighed all others, having 'assumed an absolute arbitrary soveraignty (as if he came down from the throne of God) . . . as if he were their absolute Lord, and had bought all the people of England for his slaves; doubtlesse if he would pretend only to have conquered England at his own expense.'[95] The most bitter invective from an excluded member expressed in country-party rhetoric the way in which Cromwell's professions of personal ethics had been disabused:

> It was then little thought (for into what heart could it enter?) when we oppos'd our selves agaynst the illegall exorbitancyes of the Court, that a Person of so great austeritie of life, so frequent in bewayling the miseries of his Countrey; so sedulous and vigilant in his Charge; so tender of the Lawes, and Libertyes of the Nation, and so narrowly searching into all the hidden corners of arbitrary and encroaching Policy, should at the last arrogate to himself a jurisdiction farre greater then that which hee contested, or then yet any King of England ever assumed.[96]

The Protectorate was accused of wasting, on 'these late inglorious Enterprizes', the economic wealth which the Commonwealth had amassed, and Cromwell's major-generals were charged with extracting illegal taxation far in excess of the Stuarts.[97] The constant theme was the waste of the effort of the Commonwealth years:

> How much better it had been for us patiently to have borne the yoke of Kingly Government, then after the effusion of so much bloud and the expense of so great Treasure, after all our glorious victories over our Enemies to bear this mans yoke, and that heavier, and more insupportable then eyther wee, or our Fore-fathers ever endured.[98]

The issue was still the 'expense of blood and treasure', with Cromwellians weighing their master's contribution to the cause heavier than any other and the republicans keen to express how much they had personally donated. Ludlow described Sir Henry Vane as a man who committed £4,000 a year towards the defeat of the king and received but £1,000 in return. During the Commonwealth he made no complaint, such was his zeal to the public cause, but after Cromwell's 'defection' he '[b]ore a constant witness against his usurpation'.[99] In May 1656, Vane anonymously published *A Healing Question*.[100] This was Thomason's attribution and the authorities agreed, hounding Vane for the sentiments expressed there. The ferocity of the way in which Vane was pursued may have reflected the Protector's unhappiness at a close friend's betrayal, but Ruth Mayer suggests that Vane having initially given Vane some latitude, the authorities closed in when he tried get elected to parliament, and David Armitage offers the explanation that Vane had overstepped the mark by firmly attaching the sin of Achan to Cromwell himself for his disasterous Caribbean foreign policy.[101]

Unlike the other republican tracts of this year, Vane attached the name of printer Thomas Brewster, but his comments were veiled and elliptical. In the wake of a call for a day of public humiliation, he was sure that unity would prevail because the common enemy, the cause and the personnel pursuing it were unchanging. The 'late interruption' seems to refer to the Protectorate, which established the private interest of families and became, with echoes of the act abolishing monarchy, 'unrighteous, burdensome, and destructive' to the liberty of legal and political authority. The idea that power originally lay with the people had been watered down because the cause was defined only by the morally worthy, who believed that 'the happiness of a People lieth not in having this or that Government, but in the justice and righteousness of those that govern'.[102] Power could be bestowed on one person and/ or a council of state, as long as there was free access to government to prevent the one or the few from taking liberty to themselves.[103] The interruption and decline of access may have referred to the dissolution of the Rump, but of all the republican tracts, this was the least hostile to the notion that single-person government was compatible with a free parliament. It was, in the ethical language of the saints, an elitist aristocratic vision of government in the hands of 'the choicest light and wisedome of the Nation that they are capable to call forth'.[104]

Vane's contribution was the least redolent of gentry republican, country-party sentiment, but does foreshadow the aristocratic, classical republicanism which was more frequently expressed later in the century.[105] James Harrington's *Commonwealth of Oceana*, published in the autumn of 1656, is more complex, and cannot be neatly positioned at the genesis of classical republicanism. It was a response to an invitation to 'show what a commonwealth was', which is borne out by the structure of the work itself. It was an amalgam of past republican notions, not a definitive statement of a working republic.[106] Some notions did not sit easily with others. It attempted to draw together the strands of the republican debate articulated during the Protectorate. Harrington belongs to the school seeking to find a workable English commonwealth between the rival conceptions of Hobbes' Leviathan on the one side and Machiavelli on the other, and not necessarily imitating either. Neither does it fit neatly either a gentry or a classical republican genre.[107]

He employed two fundamental laws as a balance to ensure stable and right government. This was specifically not the Polybian balance of Machiavelli – which Vane also denied[108] – in which the three elements of monarchy, aristocracy and democracy counterbalanced each other. Harrington used the balance of the scales, placing government on one side and the governed on the other, which he described as a 'balance of dominion'.[109] Indeed, rumours of a plan to return to a system of 'three estates' such as had been proposed in the Nineteen Propositions of 1641 may have sparked *Oceana* itself.[110] Harrington's two fundamentals were the Agrarian and the Ballot. Was this not what the soldier had fought for all this while? What had so long been expressed negatively as the expense of blood and treasure could be transformed into a positive statement of rights to property and franchise.[111]

Harrington used the *lex agrariae* of ancient Rome, by which public land had been allotted to the citizens, and in his Agrarian it became a mechanism to ensure that land was proportionate to political influence. The distribution and redistribution of the spoils of war had to take into account the investment of some and the delinquency of others. Unlike Aristotle and Machiavelli, therefore, the true heart of a commonwealth was the gentry. Even Harrington's beloved Venice was not an aristocratic republic but one run by gentlemen. Husbandry was 'the best stuff' and 'tillage, bringing up good soldiery, bringeth up a good commonwealth'.[112] The love of Venice emerged in discussion of the ballot. The mocking speech of the Lord Epimonus de Garrula, that the franchise would allow the foolish a say, make Oceana look foolish and deprive those men who had worked hard for their money, reads like a burlesque parody of Ireton's concern with those of the landed interest at Putney.[113] In fact, the ballot would enable all to be equitably subject to fortune.

It is in the details, not the centre or fundamentals but the circumference or orbs, that Harrington differs from the republicans of the later 1640s. Harrington settled on both a senate and a popular chamber, not to mention the Lord Archon who establishes the framework of laws. There was a hierarchy of representation, in which parishes became hundreds, tribes, galaxies and 'the annual galaxy of every tribe consisting of two knights and seven deputies, whereof the knights constitute the senate, the deputies the prerogative tribe'. The regulations for ensuring this mechanism was workable are labyrinthine.[114] This is more in keeping with the constitutional regulations attached to the *Instrument of Government* or to the second version of the *Agreement of the People*. Both constitutional documents were not a simple statement of the fundamentals, such as Wildman had called for in *A Mite to the Treasury*. These were intricate statements of how a multi-layered system would function.

The comments which other republicans made on *Oceana* are few and far between, leaving it as a mighty symbol of an attempt to integrate strands of republican thinking. We know that Henry Marten was impressed by it, though not altogether in agreement with it, but we do not know why or to what extent. He believed both himself and

Harrington to be a powerless minority taste.[115] What had emerged through Harrington's work, however, was a confirmation that during the living experiment of the Rump parliament and the opposition regroupings of the Protectorate, there had emerged a diverse group of people who sought unity of expression through the Good Old Cause – what Vane called the 'good Party', others the Honest party, the godly party or the commonwealthsmen – but who, individually, revealed the diversity of views as to what constituted the old cause of republican liberty. It was not that no one knew what the Good Old Cause was: everybody knew; and everyone knew different.

NOTES

1. Austin Woolrych, *Commonwealth to Protectorate* (Oxford, 1982); Blair Worden, 'The Bill for a New Representative', *EHR*, LXXXVI (1971); Sarah Barber, 'Irish undercurrents to the politics of April 1653', *HR*, 65.158 (1992) 315–335.
2. *Mercurius Politicus*, No.150, 21–8 Apr. 1653, p. 2381.
3. *Mercurius Politicus*, No. 150, 21–8 Apr. 1653, pp. 2386–2391; *A Declaration of the Lord Generall and his Councel*, 22 Apr. 1653, E692(6) and E693(3).
4. Derek Hirst, 'The politics of literature in the English Revolution', *Seventeenth Century*, V.2 (1990) 133–55, p. 141; Hull Corporation Record Office, L566.
5. 'Ten Queries: by a ffrend of ye new dissolved Parlement', in MS in Thomason's hand, E693(5).
6. 'Lenthalls Lamentation', in MS in Thomason's hand, 10 May 1653, E694(11); Leeds, ML MSS 16/164. Lenthall, however, did not keep his role as Speaker under Barebone's parliament. This honour went to former engager, Francis Rous.
7. Leeds, ML HML26–58/11; 32/unfol.; 28/549; 28/633; 31/1298; 95/26; 'A verse, written under Cromwell's picture and hung in the Exchange', in manuscript by Thomason, E697(17), 29 May, 1653.
8. Leeds, ML MSS 93/40 f.4.
9. Leeds, ML MSS, Political and miscellaneous, II f.40.
10. Ludlow, *Memoirs*, I, pp. 349–51.
11. Lucy Hutchinson, *Memoirs of Colonel Hutchinson* (London, 1965), p. 288. The way in which the army had profited financially to an extent way beyond others was also made by Marten: Leeds, ML MSS 93/40.
12. Robert Spry, *Council of States-policy* (dated Plymouth, 30 Oct. 1649), 20 Jan. 1650; *Rules of Civil Goverment* [sic], *Drawn from the best examples of Forreign Nations, and Commonwealths*, [5 Jul.] 1653, E1484(3); John

Wallace, 'The Engagement controversy: an annotated list of pamphlets', *Bulletin of the New York Public Library*, 68 (1964) 384–405, p. 396.

13. For a close textual interweaving of republican politics and libertinistic lifestyle, see the poem 'Tom May's Death', in H. M. Margoliouth, *Poems and Letters of Andrew Marvell* (2 vols) (Oxford, 1971 edn), I, pp. 90–2. Marvell's authorship is disputed. Susan Wiseman, ' "Adam, the Father of all Flesh", porno–political rhetoric and political theory in and after the English civil war', *Prose Studies: History, Theory, Criticism*, 14.3 (1991), 134–57.

14. Hutchinson, *Memoirs*, p. 304.

15. *To His Excellency Oliver Cromwell . . . the humble representation of severall Aldermen . . . and other citizens of London*, signed by 36 named individuals, 20 May 1653, 669.f.17(8); *The Petition and Representation of several Aldermen and other Citizens of London concerning the Re-sitting of the late Parliament*, 26 May 1653, E698(16).

16. J[ohn] W[ildman], *A Mite to the Treasury, of consideration in the Commonwealth*, [5 May] 1653, E694(5), Epistle to the 'impartial reader'. The response was provided by John Spittlehouse, *A Warning-piece Discharged: or, Certain Intelligence Communicated*, [19 May] 1653, E697(11), who confirmed that he was disputing with Wildman – 'you thinke you have played the *Man*, albeit a *Wilde* one, by saying it is acknowledged by most rationall men, that power is primarily, and originally in the people, as in your Epistle' (p. 21).

17. [Wildman], *A Mite*, p. 6.

18. Wildman's creditors sued for his release during his imprisonment by the Protectorate on the grounds that they could not recover their money while he was not a free man: *CSPD* 1655–6, p. 387.

19. Machiavelli, *Discourses*, Chapter III: 'mediators between the plebeians and the senate' to 'check the insolence of the nobles', from the translation of Peter Bondanella and Mark Musa, *The Portable Machiavelli* (Penguin, 1979) p. 183.

20. [Wildman], *A Mite*, pp. 5 and 16.

21. [Wildman], *A Mite*, pp. 5–6.

22. *Mercurius Politicus*, No. 152, 5–12 May 1653, n.p., pages misnumbered.

23. Spittlehouse, *Warning-piece*, pp. 7–16; *The Army no usurpers, or the late Parliament not Almighty and Everlasting*, [20 May] 1653, E697(13), which used as its text Exod. 7: 4: 'but Pharaoh shall not harken unto you, that I may lay my hand upon Egypt, and bring forth mine armies, and my people the children of Israel, out of the land of Egypt by great judgments.'

24. The summons to appear in Barebone's Parliament: *GCD*, p. 405. In the *Instrument of Government*, this had become 'persons of known integrity, fearing God, and of good conversation': *GCD*, p. 411, clause XVI; Bill for a new constitution presented to the first Protectorate parliament: *GCD*, p. 428 (cap. 6); p. 436 (cap. 31).

25. *The Faithful Post*, No. 92, 15–27 Apr. 1653, pp. 209–10; *The Moderate Publisher of Every daies Intelligence*, No.130, 22–9 Apr. 1653, E211(26), p. 1033; *The Armies Scout Impartially communicating*, No. 114, 23–30 Apr. 1653, E211(27), n.p.

26. Summons to attend 'Barebone's Parliament', 6 Jun. 1653, in *GCD*, p. 405; [Marchamont Nedham], *The True State of the Case of the Commonwealth*, 9 Feb. 1654, E728(5), p. 12.

27. [Nedham], *True State*, p. 13.

28. *GCD*, pp. 405–17, 16 Dec. 1653.

29. *CJ*, VI, p. 133.

30. *Joannis Miltoni Angli pro Populo Anglicano Defensio secunda*, 30 May 1654, E1487(3). The author of *Regii Sanguinis* was in fact Peter du Moulin and it was edited by Alexander More.

31. A charge for which there is considerable evidence, though it is in the nature of a revolution that it needs to be protected by rewarding those who brought it about and employing those on whom it could rely. The equity principle was carefully invoked to reward those who had suffered losses for the cause, see the redistribution of the Earl of Winchester's lands to Sir Thomas Jervois MP: Hants Record Office, 44M69/G2/39; W. R. N. Stephens and F. T. Madge (eds), *Documents Relating to the History of the Cathedral Church of Winchester* (London/Winchester, 1897), pp. 75–84, on lands awarded to Robert Wallop, Henry Mildmay, Nicolas Love, John Lisle and Colonel Norton. Sean Kelsey, *Inventing a Republic: The Political Culture of the English Commonwealth, 1649–1653* (Manchester, 1997), pp. 153–165; Worden, *Rump Parliament*, p. 93.

32. *Declaration by the Lord General and the Council on the Dissolution of the Long Parliament*, cited from *GCD*, p. 401; Whitelocke, *Memorials*, IV, p. 5, who claimed that Cromwell was picking out Henry Marten and Sir Peter Wentworth when he referred to personal moral failings. Ludlow, *Memoirs*, I, pp. 352–3; R. W. Blencowe (ed.), *Sydney Papers: Consisting of a Journal of the Earl of Leicester, and Original Letters of Algernon Sydney* (London, 1825), p. 139.

33. Milton, *Second Defence*, [30 May] 1654, E1487(3), here cited from Merritt Y. Hughes (ed.), *John Milton: Complete Poems and Major Prose Works* (New York, 1957), who uses a translation by Robert Fellowes made in 1806, pp. 817–38, pp. 836–7.

34. For Cromwell as (super)man see Milton, *Second Defence*, in Hughes (ed.), pp. 832 and 834; Zera S. Fink, *The Classical Republicans: an Essay in the Recovery of a Pattern of Thought in Seventeenth-Century England* (Northwestern University Press, 1962), pp. 90–1.

35. Milton, *Second Defence*, pp. 830 and 832. As Secretary for Foreign Tongues under the Commonwealth, Milton, like Cromwell, had presumably to visit Derby House, which after 1652 was owned by Henry Marten. Here, he and his common law wife, Mary Ward, who was partial to wearing scarlet satin, ran the liveried household, which

must have scandalised the godly: Leeds, ML MSS39/25; HMCR 5th report, App. p. 192, cited in J. G. Muddiman, *The King's Journalist 1659–1698* (London, 1923), p. 38; Berks Record Office, D/ELs F18 f.1; Marchamont Nedham, *A True State of the Case of the Commonwealth of England, Scotland, and Ireland*, [8 Feb.] 1654, E728(5), p. 4. This was what the modern idiom would call a party political point by Nedham, who was not lauded for his personal morality.

36. The *Instrument of Government* was said to have originally contained the word king: Ludlow, *Memoirs*, I, p. 370; Burton, *Diary* I, p. 382.

37. Milton, *Second Defence*, p. 822; Salmacius was the author of *Defensio Regia pro Carolo Primo* in November 1649, which had provoked Milton's first defence, *Defensio pro Populo Anglicano*, published on 24 Feb. 1651.

38. [Nedham], *True State*, p.10; an inversion of the republican text 'in the multitude of counsellors there is safety' (Prov: 11: 14, 24: 6).

39. See Steven C. A. Pincus, *Protestantism and Patriotism: Ideologies and the Making of English Foreign Policy, 1650–1668* (Cambridge, 1996), pp. 60–75.

40. *Second Defence*, p. 819.

41. Sir John Clerk, *History of the Union of Scotland and England* (Scottish History Society, Edinburgh, 1993) (translated and edited by Douglas Duncan). Clerk is here referring to the 30 Scottish MPs allowed to sit in Barebone's Parliament, but the comment could equally well apply to the Protectorate.

42. [Nedham], *True State*, p. 5. Nedham also maintained that the army had not breached the Covenant (p. 6).

43. *Second Defence*, p. 819.

44. Ibid. p. 830.

45. Ludlow, *Memoirs*, I, p. 365: 'The perfidious Cromwel having forgot his most solemn professions and former vows, as well as the blood and treasure that had been spent in this contest'.

46. Milton, for example, engaged in a complete U-turn over the part of Augustus. In *Areopagitica* (1644), he had cited Augustus as the worst example of Roman dictatorship, for his use of censorship and the suppression of free speech: Hughes, *Complete Prose Works*, pp. 722–3; *Tenure of Kings and Magistrates*, ibid., p. 755.

47. [Nedham], *True State*, p. 10.

48. [Nedham], *True State*, pp. 1–3.

49. [Nedham], *True State*, p. 51.

50. [Nedham], *True State*, pp. 14, 50.

51. GCD, p. 406; Gardiner, *Commonwealth and Protectorate*, III, pp. 171–8. The date 3 September was that of the battles of Dunbar and Worcester and was to be the day on which Cromwell died.

52. Ludlow, *Memoirs*, I, p. 388.

53. Leeds, ML MSS 78/62; 89/1.

54. These were three identified by Edmund Ludlow, *A Voyce from the Watch Tower*, ed. A. B. Worden (Camden Society, 4th. ser., 1978), p. 241. For

Wallup see Mary Freer Keeler, *The Long Parliament, 1640–1641: A Biographical Study of its Members* (Philadelphia, 1954), p. 378.

55. East Sussex Record Office, Rye 47/149/13 and also 47/149/12 (the news from Rye corporation of his election for the borough). Morley was subsequently also elected for Sussex county and chose that in preference to the borough seat (Rye 47/149/14); Ludlow, *Memoirs*, I, p. 390; Maurice Ashley, *John Wildman: Plotter and Postmaster* (London, 1947), pp. 84–5.

56. Gardiner, *Commonwealth and Protectorate*, III, p. 178; *The perfect list of members returned and approved*, 669.f.19(8); Ludlow, *Memoirs*, I, p. 391.

57. Ludlow, *Memoirs* i p. 392; Abbott, *Writings and Speeches*, III, pp. 435–6.

58. Gardiner, *Commonwealth and Protectorate*, III, p. 194; *CJ*, VII, p. 368; Abbott, *Writings and Speeches*, III, pp. 451–63, 12 Sep. 1654. A proposed bill for the constitutional settlement of the three nations, presented to the first Protectorate parliament, described the person of the Protector as 'by his good conversation . . . shall manifest himself to be a man of ability, truth, courage, fearing God and hating covetousness': *GCD*, p. 428.

59. 'An ellergie written on the unhappy accident wch befell the Lord Protector', BL Stowe MSS 185 f.85, (29 Sep. 1654?), referring to a team of horses presented to Cromwell by Count von Oldenburg, which ran away while Cromwell was driving them in Hyde Park; Charles W. Daves (ed.), *Samuel Butler, 1612–1680: Characters* (London, 1970), pp. 241–2; Charles Firth, *Oliver Cromwell* (London, 1901), pp. 456–7.

60. Ludlow, *Memoirs*, I, p. 380; Gardiner, *Commonwealth and Protectorate*, III, p. 195.

61. Ludlow, *Memoirs*, I, p. 387.

62. Leeds, ML MSS, Political and miscellaneous, II, f.39.

63. Ludlow, *Memoirs*, I, p. 394.

64. [Lilburne], *Legall Fundamentall Liberties*; Gardiner, *Civil War*, IV, pp. 236–42; *Clarke Papers*, II, pp. 54–5.

65. *To his Highness the Lord Protector, &c and our General. The humble Petition of several Colonels of the Army*, 18 Oct. 1654, 669.f.19(21), broadsheet; *A Remonstrance of his Excellency Thomas Lord Fairfax . . . and of the Generall Councell of Officers, Held at St Albans the 16. of November 1648*, p. 48, in which the principle that the king could do no wrong was 'begot by the blasphemous arrogancy of Tyrants upon servile Parasites, and foster'd onely by slavish and ignorant people, and remain in our Law-Books, as Heir-looms onely of the Conquest.'

66. Austin Woolrych, 'The Cromwellian Protectorate: a military dictatorship?', *History*, 74.244 (1990) 207–231.

67. Ashley, *John Wildman*, p. 86; Barbara Taft, 'The Humble Petition of several Colonels of the Army', *Huntington Library Quarterly* XLII (1978) 15–41.

68. Marten was first going to say that Cromwell had bought the people's support, but instead changed it to overriding their opinion – not so much manipulating the election as making it pointless.

69. BL Add MSS 71532 f.16: I owe the point about the translation to Dr David Shotter.

70. [Edward Sexby], *Killing noe Murder, briefly discourst in Three Quaestions*, previously attributed to William Allen and/or Silus Titus, [May] 1657, E501(4).

71. Ashley, *John Wildman*, pp. 85–94.

72. Who sponsored Wildman for the parliamentary seat of his native Scarborough.

73. Ludlow, *Memoirs*, I, p. 357.

74. Ashley, *John Wildman*, p. 88.

75. Spittlehouse, *Warning-piece*, p. 22.

76. Ashley, *John Wildman*, p. 103; Westminster Local Library H438, H440, H441.

77. *GCD*, pp. 447–59.

78. *A Copy of a Letter written to an Officer of the Army by a true Commonwealthsman, and no COURTIER*, [19 Mar.] 1656, E870(5).

79. The author calls elective magistracy 'elective monarchy' but equates it with a republic.

80. *Copy of a Letter*, p. 4.

81. *Copy of a Letter*, p. 8. In 1649, one Mr Norwood sent his argument to Arthur Haselrig that authority rested with the head of each individual family and not with the king: 'Modest proposals to all ingenuous Protestants of the late King's party tending to a swift peaceable and lasting settlement and the security of theire Proprietyes': Leics Record Office, DG21/275(b).

82. *Copy of a Letter*, p. 9.

83. *Copy of a Letter*, p. 36. The author uses the Caesars and various European princes to show that leading families were confirmed in power in elective monarchies/republics, and draws particular attention to the princes of Orange within the United Provinces; Pincus, *Protestantism and Patriotism*, pp. 106–8 and *passim*.

84. J[ohn] S[treater], *The Picture of a New COURTIER drawn in a Conference between Mr Timeserver and Mr Plain-heart. In which a PROTECTOR having been in part unvailed, may see himself discovered*, [18 Apr.] 1656 E875(6).

85. G. E. Aylmer, *The State's Servants: the Civil Service of the English Republic, 1649–1660* (London, 1973), p. 304; *CJ*, VII, p. 754; Henry R. Plomer et al., *Dictionary of the Booksellers and Printers who were at work in England, Scotland and Ireland from 1641 to 1667* (Biographical Society reprint, 1968), p. 173; *DNB*, XIX, pp. 40–1; Richard L. Greaves and Robert Zaller, *Biographical Dictionary of British Radicals in the Seventeenth Century* (3 vols) (Harvester, Sussex, 1983), III, pp. 211–12. Zaller suggests John Spittlehouse as an alternative author and Spittlehouse is named as one of those commonwealthsmen unjustly imprisoned, but in view of Spittlehouse's encomium to Mosaic Cromwell in 1654, Streater is more

plausible. The words are Thomason's. See also *Englands Remembrancer*: 'scatred about ye street'.

86. The execution of Charles I, the abolition of monarchy, the declaration of a commonwealth and the new treason law.

87. Streater, *The Picture*, p. 5; Blair Worden, 'Oliver Cromwell and the sin of Achan', in Derek Beales and Geoffrey Best (eds), *History, Society and the Churches* (Cambridge, 1985), pp. 125–45; for an interpretation of this process in terms of person and principle see David Armitage, 'The Cromwellian Protectorate and the languages of empire', *HJ*, 35.3 (1992) 531–55, p. 543.

88. Streater, *The Picture*, p. 13. This also comments on Ps. 9: 16, Prov. 14: 11 and Job 27: 13–23, which gives a further indication that this was a reply to *A Letter* by commenting on Cromwell's posterity: 'This is the portion of the wicked man with God, and the heritage of the oppressors, which they shall receive from the Almighty. If his children be multiplied, it is for the sword: and his offspring shall not be satisfied with bread . . . Men shall clap their hands at him, and shall hiss him out of his place.'

89. William Ball, *State-maxims or certain dangerous positions destructive to the very nature very natural Right and Liberty of mankind*, [5 Aug.] 1656, E886(6), by G. Dawson for T. Brewster. There are two possible theories to explain the writings of William Ball. There may have been two men of the same name: the MP, William Ball of Barkham, who died in 1648 and was replaced by Henry Nevile, and another writer of similar views who produced works of political theory. Or, William Ball's works may have had a sponsor (Marten?), who kept reissuing them posthumously at appropriate times, while adding an up-to-the-minute gloss to give them contemporary relevance.

90. Ball, *State-maxims*, p. 27; Beverley C. Southgate, *'Covetous of Truth': The Life and Work of Thomas White, 1593–1676* (Dordrecht, 1993), pp. 54–5.

91. *Englands Remembrancer, or, a word in season to all English men about their Elections of the members for the approaching Parliament*, [1 Aug.]1656, E884(5), p. 2.

92. *A Copy of a Letter from an Officer of the Army in Ireland, to his Highness the lord Protector, concerning his changing of the Government*, [8 Jun.] 1656, E881(3), pp. 1 and 4. It claimed to have been written from Waterford on 24 June 1654, but Thomason considered the date 'feigned'.

93. *A Copy of Letter from an Officer of the Army in Ireland*, p. 15. See the same argument applied to the militia in the second civil war in Grey of Groby, *Old English Blood*, p. 2; Chapter 3 above, p. 83.

94. Leeds, ML MSS 78/98, 8 Aug. 1656; ML MSS 99/7; Ludlow, *Memoirs*, II, p. 15.

95. *To all the Worthy Gentlemen who are duely chosen for the Parliament which intended to meet at Westminster the 17 of September 1656*, signed by 98 MPs, which include republicans such as Haselrig, Scot, Morley,

Saunders, and Weaver and newer and quite surprising 'converts' – Anthony Ashley Cooper, Harbottle Grimstone, John Gell – all the excluded MPs, 7 Oct. 1656, E889(8), n.p.; Gardiner, *Commonwealth and Protectorate*, IV, pp. 256–7.

96. *An Appeale from the Court to the Country*, 27 Oct. 1656, E891(3), pp. 4–5.

97. *An Appeale*, p. 2; see also *Picture of a New COURTIER* pp. 15–16. There is no room here to examine in detail the experiment of the major-generals of 1655, which followed the royalist risings of that year, in which the country was divided into regions, each of which had a military overseer.

98. *An Appeale*, p. 6.

99. Ludlow, *Voyce*, p. 314.

100. [Sir Henry Vane Jnr], *A Healing Question*, [12 May] 1656, E879(5); V. A. Rowe, *Sir Henry Vane the Younger* (London, 1970), p. 204.

101. *The Proceeds of the Protector against Sir Henry Vane*, 29 Jul. 1656, E937(2*); 'The character of Sir Henry Vane by Algernon Sidney', Herts Record Office, D/EP F 45, printed in Rowe, *Sir Henry Vane*, pp. 277–83; Ruth E. Mayers, 'Real and practicable, not imaginary and notional: Sir Henry Vane, *A Healing Question*, and the problems of the Protectorate', *Albion*, 28.1 (1996) 37–72; Armitage, 'Languages of empire', pp. 544–5. The sin of Achan was to disobey the Lord in taking from the city of Jericho, which Joshua and the Israelites had conquered, a Babylonish garment and two hundred silver shekels: Josh. 7: 18–26.

102. Vane, *Healing Question* p. 17; Samuel Richardson, *An Apology for the Present Government*, 1654, p. 6; Mayers, 'Real and practicable', pp. 41–50.

103. Vane, *Healing Question*, p. 16.

104. Vane, *Healing Question*, p. 4.

105. John Hughes also notes the differences between Vane and republicans such as Ludlow, but stresses Vane's mystical concerns rather than differences about republicanism: John H. F. Hughes, 'The Commonwealthsmen divided: Edmund Ludlowe, Sir Henry Vane and the Good Old Cause 1653–1659', *The Seventeenth Century*, V.1 (1990) 55–70; Blair Worden, 'The Commonwealth kidney of Algernon Sidney', *JBS*, XXIV.1 (1984) 1–40; Caroline Robbins (ed.), *English Republican Tracts* (London, 1969), pp. 40–2; J. G. A. Pocock, *The Machiavellian Moment: Florentine Political Thought and the Atlantic Republican Tradition* (Princeton, 1995), pp. 39–42; Margaret A. Judson, *The Political Thought of Sir Henry Vane the Younger* (Philadelphia, 1969).

106. James Harrington, *The Commonwealth of Oceana and A System of Politics*, ed. J. G. A. Pocock) (Cambridge, 1992), p. x.; J. G. A. Pocock, *The Political Works of James Harrington* (Cambridge, 1977), p. 859.

107. Gary Remer, 'James Harrington's new deliberative rhetoric: reflection of an anticlassical republicanism', *HPT*, XVI.4 (1995) 532–57, pp. 548–53; Jonathan Scott, ' "The rapture of motion": James Harrington's republicanism', in Nicholas Phillipson and Quentin Skinner (eds),

Political Discourse in Early-Modern Europe (Cambridge, 1993); Paul A. Rahe, *Republics Ancient and Modern: Classical Republicanism and the American Revolution* (Chapel Hill, 1992).

108. Mayers, 'Real and practicable', p. 47.
109. *Contra* Fink, *Classical Republicans*, p. 53.
110. Pocock, *Machiavellian Moment*, pp. 384–5, and Harrington, *Works*, pp. 24–8.
111. Harrington, *Oceana*, pp. 113–14: 'at the institution of Lycurgus, the nobility having estates (as ours here) in the lands of Laconia, upon no other valuable consideration that the commonwealth proposed by him, threw them up to be parcelled by his agrarian. But now, when no man is desired to throw up a farthing of his money or a shovelful of his earth . . . we are disputing whether we should have peace or war. For peace you cannot have without some government, nor any government without the proper balance; wherefore, if you will not fix this which you have, the rest is blood, for without blood you can bring in no other.'
112. Harrington, *Oceana*, pp. 4–5, 105.
113. Harrington, *Oceana*, pp. 114–17. Pocock believes it may be mocking 'the parliamentary funny man of the period', Henry Marten, admittedly preoccupied with his landed rewards from the state during 1656, since he was in the Upper Bench prison for spectacular debts of around £35,000. In view of what Garrula says this would seem most unlikely and while I take the point that the most frequent satire of Marten was that he could often be seen 'in the park, and with ladies', the equation of sexual licence and Marten can be too often made; J. G. A. Pocock, *Works*, pp. 74, 291.
114. Harrington, *Oceana*, p. 118.
115. BL Add MSS 71532 f.15: 'The considerations of Mr Harringtons commonwealth of Oceana reconsidered by H. Marten & made up in a letter to their Author.'

Epilogue
The Good Old Cause

Republican fortunes revived at the end of the decade, highlighting the tension between those who acted and those who thought. When Oliver Cromwell died, in September 1658, much of the traditionalism, restraint and reaction which had crept back into English politics were blown away again.[1] *Mercurius Politicus* reported that his 'most Serene and Renowned Highness' was interred with great ceremony, his effigy wore a 'Royal large robe' and the 'Cap of Regality', and the Protector had all the honours reserved for a king, except to be called one.[2] In accordance with the *Humble Petition and Advice* which gave him the right to nominate his successor, he chose his eldest son, Richard, as Protector. The army approved:

> being resolved to their utmost to maintain the Succession, according to Law: Which . . . speaks them men of Honor, Prudence, and Fidelity, mindful of the merits of their late great Leader, and common Father, and of the grand interest of the *Establishment*, after all our shakings; so it is but answerable to the worth and nobleness of his Son, who in all respects appears the lively image of his Father, the true Inheritor of his Christian Vertues; a person, who by his Piety, Humanity, and other Noble Inclinations, hath obliged the hearts of all.[3]

The army grandees – nicknamed the Wallingford House group after Lambert's London residence in which they met – and the persons which they approved to lead the government were men of such high qualities that the balance of the 'establishment' would remain in equilibrium.

The quiet succession which was the hope and expectation of the editorials of *Mercurius Politicus* was disturbed by an upsurge of political activism and writing, sparked by the leader's death. The most vocal campaigners against the continuation of the Protectorate were the proponents of the Good Old Cause. The 'cause' had a long history. The earliest use of the phrase which this study has uncovered dates back to 1648 when Sir Arthur Haselrig urged common action for the 'ould cause'.[4] Its usage became more common as a description of republican action almost as soon as the Protectorate was established,[5] but the term is more often dismissed as 'a catchy shibboleth . . . used as a point of departure from which historians have ridden off in various directions',[6] or worse, a 'facile catch-phrase', a 'parrot-cry as a substitute for thought', which measured the decline from the principles of 1640s' action and 1650s' thinking.[7]

The Good Old Cause has been described as a platform which brought together a civilian opposition to the Oliverian Protectorate and disillusioned (usually Baptist) army officers, led by Major William Packer, who when asked by Cromwell what he meant by the Good Old Cause could only think of his opposition to a House of Lords.[8] James Cotton has viewed it as a vehicle for a Harringtonian 'party'.[9] Taft's work, and this study, have argued that the cause was not so much a belief in a particular structure of republican government – although in retrospect, the Rump sometimes received high praise – but a demonstration of consistent loyalty to a series of political actions and principles. After fourteen years of political campaigning, beginning with the Speech without Doors and culminating in the revival of republican possibilities in 1658, there were a number of strands which could be spun in order to create some notion of the mantle of mid-century republicanism represented by the cause.

The late-decade republicans could be recognised as a distinct political entity, capable of tight organisation and tactics. A servant of Edward Sexby's, Samuel Dyer, had already come forward in February 1658 to inform on his master's plottings against the Protectorate. The journey which Sexby undertook towards the end of the 1650s in order to rally the personnel of the republican cause traced individuals who were recognisable as those who had been important years earlier. 'Soon after his highness was declared lord protector', Dyer proceeded, 'there were divers meetings between the said Colonel Sexby, major Wildman, Capt. George Bishop, mr. Cockayne a minister[10], and capt. Lawson.' These distributed the petition of the Colonels Saunders, Okey and Alured. Sexby travelled around the country, first to Grey of Groby's house where they had meetings with Wildman and others, and Sexby and Grey's butler carried 5,000 anti-Protectorate declarations into Leicestershire. From Leicestershire they went to the Berkshire home of Wildman's mother-in-law.[11] Letters went back to Leicestershire and Grey assured the group that there would be 5,000 raised in the South-West, where 'lord Grey's Somersetshire friends would not fail him'. Richard Overton and Wildman's servant, Will Parker, were implicated, along with Saunders, and Overton could be found staying with 'col. Witton [that is, William Wetton] in Covent-Garden'.[12]

The personnel had changed little from the gentry republican alliance of the second civil war.

In order to win more general support, this group formed an alliance with the sectaries and the junior officers of the army. The pamphleteering of February 1659 suggested 'that the Republicans found that they would best win back the army's allegiance by enlisting the pens, or at least borrowing the language, of the saints'.[13] The military/civilian alliance was one which needed to be revived. It had formed in the later 1640s and was lost during the 1650s in the debate between godly magistrates and good laws. The republicans, ten years on, did not need to don other mantles to revive republican morale. They needed rather to find campaigning issues which would recover both the political and millenarian urgency of 1648. A study of the questions which pre-occupied the republican members of Richard Cromwell's parliament is depressingly familiar. The first was the power of a single person, because a bill of recognition required confirmation of Richard as Protector.[14] On 9 March, Thomas Scot, long ally of Marten and Chaloner, questioned the right of Irish and Scottish members to sit in the House, and was pulled down for calling the Scots Pharisees and hypocrites.[15] The parliament went over the old ground by debating control of the military and the status of an upper House.[16]

The overt way in which the language of the 1640s reappeared suggests conscious knowledge that a fragmented alliance would easily recognise it. Towards the end of May, the restored Rumpers were reminded that 'we are your Principals, and you our Agents' – perhaps an admission that the Rump parliament had been flawed, but also a direct quotation from Overton's *Remonstrance of Many Thousand Citizens*.[17] Another composite production from May 1659, which upbraided the army for its decline from its former principles, cited the St Albans declaration from November 1648, and without needing to flag the quotation, merely chided the soldiers that they had already declared the tyranny of kings (and single magistrates) 'begotten by the blasphemous arrogance of Tyrants upon their servile parasites'. Furthermore, they had already declared single person magistracy 'dangerous to this righteous cause, a well as uselesse and burdensome'.[18]

The cause of 1658–9 was little changed from that of 1648–9. It may have been naive of the republicans to think that there was sufficient unity behind ten year-old-policies for them to be revived verbatim, expecting to retrieve the mace from where they had left it in April 1653. The fact that the Good Old Cause became associated with the good old parliament was no 'decline'. The republicans did not accept the interruption of their authority and merely expected to resume the reins of power. As far as 1648–style republicanism was concerned, the intervening usurpation of the Protectorate merely confirmed that politics had not changed: the issues illustrated the general principles which constituted the cause.

The republican faction within the parliament of Richard's Protectorate succeeded in wresting control of the militia and the negative voice from the single person. Without these powers, what they left was 'a round O or Cypher', which brought them back to the point in the debate at which Charles Stuart had been removed from the constitutional equation.[19] The intention was once more to replace the single person with a fundamental statement of law, described as 'virgin' principles. It was the nature of the first principles which was still at odds.[20] Harrington condemned a 'wooden agreement of the people' and the 'eminent establishment' proposed by the Fifth Monarchist, John Rogers, who invoked the (first) *Agreement* and the *Case of the Armie* as 'law paramount'.[21] Harrington, like Milton, preferred to separate doers and thinkers. Harrington distinguished the people's representatives who administered the laws from the eminent persons who devised them, as Milton had argued his private calling to frame public policy in the *Second Defence*. Harrington considered himself a private man, such as Plato, Aristotle, Livy and Machiavelli. '[T]here is not a public person . . . that has written in the politics worth a button',[22] but with 'the aid of some political anatomist' England could produce a statement similar to the second *Agreement* of January 1649.[23]

There were some changes of personnel from the alliance of 1648. Grey of Groby and Lilburne died in 1657, and others, such as Marten, Popham and Wentworth, were weighed down with debts. The task of coordinating republican activity had fallen to Wildman, the author of *The Leveller: or the Principles and Maxims concerning Government and Religion*.[24] In February 1659, *The Leveller* stated explicitly three orthodoxies of the republicanism of 1648. Government should be decided by 'laws and not by men';[25] there should be a form of levelling, which consisted of a natural right to equality before the law, made by the people's representatives; and government was both defined and justified by the voluntarism by which all people placed themselves under the law.[26] These were statements which reframed the principles of the first *Agreement of the People* and Wildman's attack on the Protectorate, *A Mite to the Treasury*. Harrington's reply, the *Art of Lawgiving*, attacked the Leveller for this very reason. Harrington was insufficiently trusting of the notion that good laws made good men not to institute a government which transcended a basic statement of first principles.[27] He mistrusted the idea propounded in *The Leveller*, of a parliament of 400. Neither was he keen on the 1640s' principle that government consisted of a self-contained, circular, mutual dependency between people and their representatives – 'both with debate and result'.[28] Harrington preferred a separation of powers, with the representatives merely implementing the laws and a single person 'inventing' them.[29] Vane, with an eye to the God of judgement, maintained the need for a senate because, all men being wilful, the 'great Body, which we call the People' was corruptible.[30]

Reflecting debates of 1649 and 1650, which discussed which elements of monarchy, aristocracy and democracy were possessed by the Commonwealth, there was a revived polemic about whether a state should have several layers of legislative apparatus, including an upper chamber. *The Leveller* thought not, arguing for a senate which would frame the laws on which the deputies would vote.[31] Ludlow agreed, though he advanced a Harringtonian argument against it. The balance of land had altered since the formation of an aristocracy and its clientage relationship with the Commons, so now the Commons' House was sufficient.[32] Nevile and Harrington argued the necessity for a second chamber, because of the 'threefold balance . . . (which) is the cause of the triple way of government', but they did not go as far as a House of Lords .[33] Captain Adam Baynes, a Member of both Oliverian parliaments but increasingly distrustful of Protectorate government, sat on the fence. If it proved possible to erect a second chamber which was in keeping with the more diffuse distribution of land after the fall of monarchy, so be it. If not, then a senate should be set up instead, for '(t)here must be a balance'.[34]

The different nature of land distribution in 1650s' England was the key sense in which the republican debate had moved on. Harrington churlishly believed many to have adopted his idea without due acknowledgement, but it was a positive restatement and rationalisation of the problems thrown up by the end of the wars. It provided a dynamic which enabled all types of republicans to argue that the restoration of a commonwealth was inevitable. At Putney in 1647, the 'Leveller' side of the argument had claimed that power was iniquitous if it rested on a notion of landed interest; other factors were as important. By 1659, despite continuing niggling about whether the soldiers or the civilians had done better,[35] the redistribution of land had gone some way to satisfying the political dilemma of reparation for the 'expense of blood and treasure'. John Wildman and Adam Baynes were just two who emerged wealthy men through the redistribution of lands. Many others – Haselrig, Love, Marten, Lisle, Pyne – augmented already considerable, if in some cases, spent estates.[36]

Along with personally owned statements outlining a way foward which emphasised the differences between republicans, there were attempts at unity and compromise. *The Armies Dutie* appeared in May 1659 in a bid to win over Fleetwood's army faction to the cause. It was signed by six people of speculative identity.[37] Woolrych, for example, is sceptical of all of the attributions except those of John Wildman and Henry Nevile.[38] *The Armies Dutie*, however, is an amalgam rather than a compromise, and the sections of text sit as uneasily together as the putative names of the authors. Who better to remind the army of their return to first principles than Wildman, author of *The Case of the Armie?*[39] The army should 'render an account to the dreadfull God' for their fall from those principles. This was similar to the attack which the Cromwellians had made against men like Wildman, now turned back on themselves, because they had

> so earnestly contended with a prodigall expence of our bloud and estates; and our hearts are wounded to hear our old cause now made a mock and by-word by our enemies, and to see such a black brand of infamy set upon all the Parliaments adherents, as if they had been all the vilest hypocrites, who made pretences of Religion, and faithfulnesse to their Countries Laws and Liberties, to be only a cloak for the blackest wickednesse, as if none of them had ever intended any more, then by force and fraud to fat up themselves upon the bloud and ruines of other families.[40]

There is a marked change of tone on page nine to republican politics lightened with chiding burlesque, forte of Henry Marten. Fleetwood, who was himself rumoured to be angling to be created Protector, was asked whether his father-in-law had felt safer before 1653, walking the streets followed only by a foot-boy, or after 1653, 'invironed with Guards, and enclosed with locks, and bolts without number'.[41] The same question was asked again of Fleetwood, balancing personal safety against political power:

> The onelie meanes of saftie for such as will exercise great power . . . is a mercenarie Armie. And if that consists of some of the same people [as the ruler's councillors], their interest will change as often as they get estates that are of more value then their pay, and then they will be readie to conspire with any of the people to provide libertie and securitie of their estate for their children, and then the power of the Tirants shake, And of how manie slaughters of the Kings of Israel do we read by their own service'.

Any form of single person would be an all-or-nothing ruler, who, by destroying all current propriety, would invest him/herself with all of the land.[42] The year 1648 was described as an earthquake of liberty which subverted principality. If Fleetwood wished to keep the people at peace, they must be 'wholly Free, or wholly Slaves'. Was this a reworking of Marten's absolute tyrant or no king?[43]

The emphasis on landed distribution was a considerable refinement, shifting the focus from the balance of power to a balance of property. Subversion was automatically introduced when the balance became unequal, when 'the beast of force must graze'.[44] The famous passage in I Samuel 8 which described the kingship of Saul was reinterpreted in keeping with the focus on land. Greater emphasis was placed on the manifestations of Saul's power. His tyranny had been described in terms of his redistribution of the fruits of the commonwealth in his own interest. He had altered the model of property by redistributing people to 'ear his ground, and to reap his harvest', and by taking corn, vineyards, olive groves and seed. William the Conqueror was recast in the same manner, to place the stress on the domesday allocation of England's land to the Norman conquerors. After 1648, the process went into reverse and England was 'unnatural soyl for a Monarch'.[45]

It was with the second refinement that the tensions between individual republicans and the need to forge unity between the group were exposed. The authors of *The Armies Dutie* accepted a mixed polity of three orders. If one of the authors was John Wildman, he had travelled a considerable distance between *The Leveller* in February and these arguments recast in May. *The Armies Dutie* accepted a popular assembly which approved or rejected measures proposed by a senate. However, it also proposed a constitutional figurehead of the type which had been so scornfully rejected as a dangerous cipher in 1648. Magistrates, or possibly a magistrate, 'in whom the Title & Honour of the Commonwealth-wealth, may reside in publicke Solemnities and addresses',[46] would allow government to exercise the best of the three elements of democracy, aristocracy and monarchy within a mixed polity.[47] On top of the pyramid would be a statement of fundamental law called an instrument of government.

With hindsight, we are aware that such attempts to draw up a compromise model of a commonwealth which would unite soldiers, officers, sectaries and civilian republicans failed. Nevertheless, the ideas and sentiments expressed in the mid-seventeenth century remained current in revolutionary America,[48] in the romantic republican revival of the late eighteenth century and amongst anti-Victorians like George Standring. Standring edited a newsheet called *The Republican*, which in 1881 campaigned for the republican, Charles Bradlaugh, to be allowed to take the Commons seat to which he had been returned. The illustrative engraving had Bradlaugh standing on one pan of a pair of scales, tipping them up and sending the pan containing the proponents of monarchy into the air, topped by the caption 'weighed, and found wanting'.[49]

It seems fitting, therefore, to conclude with the Good Old Cause. This study does not seek to cover the ground from the recall of the Rump to the Restoration of the monarchy. Its complexity has been unravelled elsewhere and requires a lengthy exegesis for which there is no room. However, to do so would also give the impression that the continuity of the period was represented by a wheel-like revolution from monarchy and back again. There are two (and no doubt many other) continuities: a monarchical and a republican tradition. The Good Old Cause did not collapse because the English failed to demonstrate the advantages of commonwealth or because it was empty rhetoric. The republicans of the mid-seventeenth century ran out of time before they could establish a workable synthesis of binary and tripartite, secular and millenarian, hierarchical and popular. While they tried to decide whether they were the popular representatives of a goodly people or virtuous governors themselves, military and civilian figures around them were busy looking for a leader, which they believed could be fulfilled by the person of Charles II.

NOTES

1. Bodleian Library, Clarendon MSS 59 f.141: 'At whit Hall they are not a little terrified'.
2. *Mercurius Politicus*, No. 432, 2–9 Sep. 1658, and No. 438, 14–21 Oct. 1658.
3. *Mercurius Politicus*, No. 432, 2–9 Sep. 1658.
4. Bodleian Librry, Tanner MSS 57/1 f.85, or more abusively described by William Lawrence in a letter to his brother Isaac, 30 May 1659, in Iona Sinclair (ed.), *The Pyramid and the Urn: The Life in Letters of a Restoration Squire: William Lawrence of Shurdington, 1636–1697* (London, 1994).
5. Barbara Taft, 'That lusty puss, the Good Old Cause', *HPT*, V.3 (1984) 447–68.
6. Taft, Lusty puss', p. 447.
7. A. H. Woolrych, 'The Good Old Cause and the fall of the Protectorate', *CHJ*, XIII.2 (1957) 133–61, pp. 136, 160.
8. Taft, 'Lusty puss', p. 456; David Underdown, 'Cromwell and the officers, February 1658', *EHR*, LXXXIII (1968) 101–7; Burton, *Diary*, III, pp. 165–6.
9. James Cotton, 'The Harringtonian "Party" (1659–1660) and Harrington's political thought', *HPT*, 1.1 (1980) 51–67.

10. I believe that this was William Cockayne the Leveller, not George Cockayne the minister.

11. This is presumably the long-suffering Margaret Dodsworth Lovelace, although the Lovelace pedigree is far from clear. Margaret Dodsworth died at the very end of 1651 (will dated 1 Jan. 1652), and even here it is confusing which member of the Lovelace family was meant by Wildman's mother-in-law. However, it must be remembered that she was Henry Marten's sister-in-law too, although while Wildman and Lucy Lovelace were a love match, Marten and Margaret Lovelace Staunton famously were not. There is a possibility that the house in Berkshire in which they met was one of the Marten properties, probably Longworth Lodge.

12. Bodleian Library, Rawlinson MSS 57, pp. 403, 409, 27 Feb. 1658.

13. Woolrych, 'Good Old Cause', p. 139.

14. H. M. Margoliouth, *Poems and Letters of Andrew Marvell* (2 vols) (Oxford, 1971) II, pp. 307–8, 11 Feb. 1659.

15. Burton, *Diary*, IV pp. 92–139, especially pp. 92–5: Serjeant Wilde – 'I find those gentlemen sometimes cry up things done by the Long Parliament, when they make for their turn, and again reject them when they do not' (p. 131); see also Mr Ross (p. 137).

16. John H. F. Hughes, 'The Commonwealthsmen divided: Edmund Ludlowe, Sir Henry Vane and the Good Old Cause 1653–1659', *The Seventeenth Century*, V.1 (1990) 55–70, p. 59; Burton, *Diary*, IV, pp. 318–56.

17. [H.N.], *An Observation and Comparison between the Idolatrous Israelites and Judges of England*, [25 May], 1659, E983(29); [Richard Overton], *A Remonstrance of Many Thousand Citizens*, [7 Jul.] 1646, E343(11); Woolrych, 'Good Old Cause', p. 158; see above, Chapter 2.

18. H.M., H.N., I.L., I.W., I.I., S.M., *The Armies Dutie, or Faithfull Advice to the Souldiers*, [2 May] 1659, E980(12), p. 6; *A Remonstrance of His Excellency*, 20 Nov. 1648, p. 48; Cotton, 'Harringtonian "Party"', pp. 56–9; see above, Chapter 3.

19. *A Seasonable Word Or, Certain reasons against A Single Person*, [5 May] 1659, E980(17); Woolrych, 'Good Old Cause', p. 153.

20. R. FitzBrian, *The Good Old Cause Dress'd in it's Primitive Lustre*, [16 Feb.] 1659, E968(6).

21. [John Rogers], *The Plain Case of the Common-wealth neer the desperate Gulf of the Common Woe*, [3 May] 1659, E972(5), John Canne, *No King but Jesus. A Seasonable Word to the Parliament-Men*, [10 May] 1659, E983(1). Rogers and Canne were sectaries who re-established communion with civilian radicals at the end of the 1650s. Christopher Feake remained convinced of the godliness of a separate government of the elect, *A Beam of Light*, [2 May] 1659, E980(5); Woolrych, 'Good Old Cause', pp. 141, 155. Harrington, Rogers and Richard Baxter could not agree which of them believed more in an oligarchic state, a debate which

revolved around the individuals' degree of trustworthiness; James Harrington, *The Commonwealth of Oceana and A System of Politics*, ed. J. G. A. Pocock (Cambridge, 1992), pp. 756–60, *A Parallel of the Spirit of the People with the Spirit of Mr Rogers*.

22. Harrington's examination before Lauderdale, Carteret and Walker, reprinted in J. G. A. Pocock (ed.), *The Political Works of James Harrington* (Cambridge, 1977), pp. 856–9, p. 858.

23. J[ames] Harrington, *The Art of Lawgiving in Three Books*, the third, showing a model fitted unto the present state or balance of this nation (London, 1659), 20 Feb., in Pocock (ed.), *Political Works*, pp. 655–704, pp. 656–8.

24. [John Wildman], *The Leveller: or the Principles and Maxims concerning Government and Religion, which are Asserted by those that are commonly called Levellers*, [16 Feb.] 1659, E968(3); Maurice Ashley, *John Wildman: Plotter and Postmaster* (London, 1947), pp. 136–7; Cotton, 'Harringtonian "party",' pp. 51–3; BL Egerton MSS 2543 f.65–66^v, questions to be administered to J.W., and examination of John Wildman, 26 Nov. 1661.

25. It is tempting to suggest a touch of Marten's burlesque in the notion that men should not be fearful that the Levellers wanted to make all estates equal and decide laws by 'telling noses'. Was this a reference to the Cromwells?: *The Leveller*, p. 5.

26. [Wildman], *The Leveller*, pp. 6, 7.

27. He directly calls the outline in *The Leveller* an *Agreement of the People*, p. 16. His reason for mistrusting the people was, admittedly, because they might vote to reintroduce monarchy.

28. James Harrington, *Art of Lawgiving*, in Pocock, *Political Works*, p. 660.

29. [James Harrington], *A Discourse upon this saying*, 21 Jul. 1659, in Pocock, *Political Works* pp. 735–53; *Art of Lawgiving*, in Pocock, *Political Works* p. 657; Cotton, 'Harringtonian" Party",' p. 53.

30. [Henry Vane], *A Needful Corrective or ballance in Popular Government*, Bodleian Library, Oxford; Ludlow, *Memoirs*, II, pp. 75–6; Woolrych, 'Good Old Cause', pp. 153–4; Hughes, 'The Commonwealthsmen divided', p. 62.

31. [Wildman], *The Leveller*, p. 7.

32. Ludlow, *Memoirs*, II, pp. 58–60.

33. James Harrington, *Valerius and Publicola, or the true form of a Popular Commonwealth*, 22 Oct., 1659, [7 Nov.] 1659, E1005(13) and printed in Pocock, *Political Works* pp. 782–806, p. 783; Cotton, 'Harringtonian "party",' pp. 54–5; Burton, *Diary*, III, p. 134, IV, pp. 23–5.

34. Burton, *Diary*, III, pp. 147–8; G. E. Aylmer, *The State's Servants: The Civil Service of the English Republic, 1649–1660* (London, 1973), p. 234; Derek Hirst, 'The fracturing of the Cromwellian alliance: Leeds and Adam Baynes', *EHR*, 108 (1993) 868–94.

35. See Cromwell's criticisms that the Rumpers were too free in distributing land and information about the sale of land to themselves and their

cronies, in his speech justifying the ejection of the Rump, 22 Apr. 1653; *The Armies Dutie*, p. 6.

36. This was Colonel Birch arguing against the upper House: 'Anciently, the Barons by tenure were of great use, but being now melted down, they are not so useful . . . If all laws that had passed since 48, had been inspected, it would have been much for your service': Burton, *Diary*, IV, p. 60; Sean Kelsey, *Inventing a Republic: The Political Culture of the English Commonwealth, 1649–1653* (Manchester, 1997), pp. 174–5.

37. H.M., et al., *The Armies Dutie*, Epistle to the reader.

38. Woolrych, 'Good Old Cause', p. 157; I have no difficulty in making attributions to Henry Marten and the sectarian radical Samuel Moyer. I am less convinced that I.I. is John Jones, or that I.L. is John Lambert. John Lisle might be a tentative suggestion for J.L., but Lisle was one of the republicans keenest to show loyalty to Cromwell.

39. *The Armies Dutie*, p. 5.

40. *The Armies Dutie*, pp. 5–6.

41. The possession of a bodyguard was a trope frequently used in classical rhetoric to denote tyranny: J. R. Dunkle, 'The rhetorical tyrant in Roman historiography: Sallust, Livy, and Tacitus', *The Classical World*, 65 (1991) 12–20, pp. 13, 17.

42. Dunkle, 'The rhetorical tyrant,' p. 16.

43. *Armies Dutie*, p. 16; Marten, *Independency of England*, p. 14, see above, Chapter 1.

44. *The Armies Dutie* p. 17.

45. *The Armies Dutie*, p. 22; Oxford, Bodleian Library, Rawlinson MSS A62 f.401, and another copy Clarendon SP 59 f.145.

46. *The Armies Dutie*, p. 27.

47. *The Armies Dutie*, p. 25.

48. William R. Everdell, *The End of Kings: A History of Republics and Republicans* (New York, 1983); Peter Karsten, *Patriot-Heroes in England and America: Political Symbolism and Changing Values over Three Centuries* (University of Wisconsin, 1978); J. G. A. Pocock, *The Machiavellian Moment: Florentine Political Thought and the Atlantic Republican Tradition* (Princeton, 1995), Jonathan Scott, *Algernon Sidney and the English Republic, 1623–1677* (Cambridge, 1988), introduction.

49. *The Republican*, VII.4, July 1881.

Select Bibliography of Printed Sources

This is a sample of the printed sources – modern printed editions of contemporary sources and secondary works – most frequently cited. No attempt has been made to compile a list of the contemporary printed material cited in this study, or to the manuscript sources. The reader can obtain a full picture of all of the sources consulted by examining the notes at the end of each chapter.

MODERN EDITIONS OF CONTEMPORARY SOURCES

Dzelzainis, Martin, *Milton: Political Writings* (Cambridge, 1991).

Evelyn, John, *Diary and Correspondence* (ed. William Bray, London, n.d.).

Harrington, James, *The Commonwealth of Oceana and A System of Politics*, ed. J. G. A. Pocock (Cambridge, 1992).

Hughes, Merritt Y. (ed.), *John Milton: Complete Poems and Major Prose Works* (New York, 1957).

Hutchinson, Julius (ed.), *Lucy Hutchinson: Memoirs of Colonel Hutchinson* (London, 1908).

Hyde, Edward, earl of Clarendon, *The History of the Rebellion and Civil Wars in England* (6 vols) (ed. W. D. Macray, Oxford, 1888), vol. V, p. 280.

Margoliouth, H. M. *Poems and Letters of Andrew Marvell* (2 vols) (Oxford, 1971).

Maseres, Francis (ed.), *Select Tracts Relating to the Civil Wars in England* (2 vols) (London, 1815).

Robbins, Caroline (ed.), *English Republican Tracts* (London, 1969).

Walker, Clement, *The Compleat History of Independency* (London, 1661).

Wolfe, Don M., *Leveller Manifestos in the Puritan Revolution* (London, 1967).

Wolfe, Don., *The Complete Prose Works of John Milton* (8 vols) (New Haven, Conn., 1953–82).

Woodhouse, A. S. P., *Puritanism and Liberty: being the Army Debates (1647–9) from the Clarke Manuscripts with Supplementary Documents* (London, 1974).

SECONDARY WORKS

Ashcraft, Richard, *Revolutionary Politics and Locke's Two Treatises of Government* (Princeton, 1986).

Ashley, Maurice, *John Wildman: Plotter and Postmaster* (London, 1947).

Ashton, Robert, *Counter-revolution: The Second Civil War and its Origins, 1646–8* (Yale, 1994).

Blitzer, Charles, *Immortal Commonwealth: The Political Thought of James Harrington* (Yale, 1960).

Brailsford, H. N., *The Levellers and the English Revolution* (Nottinghom, 1961).

Burgess, Glenn, *The Politics of the Ancient Constitution: An Introduction to English Political Thought, 1603–1642* (London, 1992).

Fink, Zera, *The Classical Republicans: An Essay in the Recovery of a Pattern of Thought in Seventeenth-Century England* (Northwestern University Press, 1962).

Gentles, Ian, *The New Model Army in England, Ireland and Scotland, 1645–1653* (Oxford, 1992).

Gregg, Pauline, *Free-born John: A Biography of John Lilburne* (London, 1961).

Hill, Christopher, *The Experience of Defeat: Milton and Some Contemporaries* (London, 1984).

Holmes, Clive, *The Eastern Association in the English Civil War* (Cambridge, 1974).

Kelsey, Sean, *Inventing a Republic: The Political Culture of the English Commonwealth, 1649–1653* (Manchester, 1997).

Laurence, Anne, *Parliamentary Army Chaplains, 1642–1651* (Woodbridge, Suffolk, 1990).

Pincus, Steven C. A., *Protestantism and Patriotism: Ideologies and the Making of English Foreign Policy, 1650–1668* (Cambridge, 1996).

Plomer, Henry R. et al., *Dictionary of the Booksellers and Printers who were at work in England, Scotland and Ireland from 1641 to 1667* (Biographical Society reprint, 1968).

Pocock, J. G. A., *The Machiavellian Moment: Florentine Political Thought and the Atlantic Republican Tradition* (Princeton, 1995).

Riley, Patrick, *Will and Political Legitimcay: A critical Exposition of Social Contract Theory in Hobbes, Locke, Rousseau and Kant* (London, 1982).

Rowe, Violet A., *Sir Henry Vane the Younger: A Study of Political and Administrative History* (London, 1970).

Scott, Jonathan, *Algernon Sidney and the English Republic, 1623–1677* (Cambridge, 1988).

Smith, Nigel, *Perfection Proclaimed: Language and Literature in English Radical Religion, 1640–1660* (Oxford, 1989).

Smith, Nigel, *Literature and Revolution in England, 1640–1660* (Yale, 1994).

Stevenson, David, *Revolution and Counter-revolution in Scotland, 1644–1651* (London, 1977).

Tolmie, Murray, *The Triumph of the Saints: The Separate Churches of London, 1616–1649* (Cambridge, 1977).

Underdown, David, *Pride's Purge: Politics in the Puritan Revolution* (London, 1971).

Underdown, David, *Somerset During the Civil War and Interregnum* (Newton Abbot, Devon, 1973).

Woolrych, Austin, *Commonwealth to Protectorate* (Oxford, 1982).

Woolrych, Austin, *Soldiers and Statesmen: The General Council of the Army and its Debates, 1647–1648* (Oxford, 1987).

Worden, Blair, *The Rump Parliament* (Cambridge, 1974).

Index

ED

3|00-10